Happy Vagrancy

Other Books by Sam Pickering

Essay Collections

A Continuing Education
The Right Distance
May Days
Still Life
Let It Ride
Trespassing
The Blue Caterpillar
Living to Prowl
Deprived of Unhappiness
A Little Fling
The Last Book
The Best of Pickering
Indian Summer
Autumn Spring
Journeys
Dreamtime
The Splendour Falls
All My Days Are Saturdays

Travel

Walkabout Year
Waltzing the Magpies
Edinburgh Days
A Tramp's Wallet

Literary Studies

The Moral Tradition in English Fiction, 1785–1850
John Locke and Children's Books in Eighteenth-Century England
Moral Instruction and Fiction for Children, 1749–1820

Teaching

Letters to a Teacher

Memoir

A Comfortable Boy

Sam Pickering

Happy Vagrancy

Essays from an Easy Chair

The University of Tennessee Press / Knoxville

LIBRARY OF CONGRESS CATALOGING-IN-PUBLICATION DATA

Pickering, Sam, 1941-
[Essays. Selections]
Happy vagrancy : essays from an easy chair / Sam Pickering.
    pages cm
ISBN 978-1-62190-186-0 (pbk.)
1. Pickering, Sam, 1941-
2. Nature.
3. Writing.
4. Life.
5. Old age.
I. Title.

AC8.P65 2015
080—dc23   2014042403

Contents

For Harry Johnson,
Dave Sonstroem, and
Tim Weinland—

Running and walking companions, friends, bright talkers and, happily,
better listeners. You have brought me moments of joy and gaiety.
Age becomes quick and green in your presence, and the black dog
of melancholy ceases to whimper. What gifts you have given me!

Introduction

A reviewer once said that my pen was not fashioned from a feather plucked from an angel's wing. Because gaggles of old tales waddled through my paragraphs, he thought I wrote with a goose-quill pen. The critic did not examine my handwriting closely. I use an aviary of pens. On Thanksgiving I write with pens made from turkey feathers. When I want to awaken intellectual sleepers, I scratch out raucous letters with crow-feather pens. Buzzards' wings furnish me with pens to write letters of condolence. For everyday affairs such as paying bills and declining invitations from strangers demanding that I donate books and time to their good causes, I rely on pens crafted from starlings' wings. To school children who interview me for a class assignment, I use pens made from the feathers of robins. Sometimes the provenance of a pen influences my sentences. Whenever I write about culinary affairs, I write with pens cut from the wings of blackbirds. Sometimes while writing about gastronomical matters, the pen overpowers my thought and a dainty pie rises yeasty, stuffed with, among other ingredients, say, strawberries and rhubarb, and two dozen or so blackbirds. If blackbirds are not available at Super Stop and Shop, grackles will do, although substituting them requires the cook to add an extra cup of sugar to the page. In answering enquiries from schoolchildren, robin-feather pens often tempt me to end my letters with a high-flying quatrain from *Tommy Thumb's Pretty Song Book* (1744), "Little Robin red breast, / Sitting on a pole, / Niddle Noddle Went his head. / And Poop went his Hole." Most of the time, however, I follow the good urgings of the gospel song and "keep on the sunny side of life." As a result, the pens I use most often are made from feathers dropped by the bluebirds of happiness.

For three-fourths of each year, I perch comfortably in Connecticut. Every summer when the temperature rises and black flies swarm, I migrate to Canada. In another life perhaps I would not have been such a dependable nester. Maybe I would have been a great rover. Perhaps I would have stalked across Europe like Byron's Childe Harold. No—becoming the wandering outlaw of my or any poet's "dark mind" was too dramatic, and impossible, for a dutiful boy raised in Nashville, Tennessee. Besides, whenever I viewed a ripening rose, I was too frightened to pluck it. Much safer and more appealing to me were the homey daffodils Mother planted along our driveway to obscure the green patch marking the overflow from a neighbor's septic tank. But, golly, I wish I had been at Harold's side in Rome when he imagined seeing the dying gladiator and stood amid the wreck of the Coliseum and watched the moon "climb its topmost arch" and pause as stars twinkled "though the loops of time."

In this book my bohemian hankerings are not poetic. They are pedestrian and local. I wander tamed woods and meadows, the former often lumbered, the latter once pastures. Occasionally I saunter farther afield, but rarely do I stray beyond convention. I am not able to believe the impossible, and although sometimes a hornet gets under my cap, I am impatient with people whose bonnets are homes to hives of bees. I attend a reunion at my undergraduate college, Sewanee, on the Cumberland Plateau. I cruise the Caribbean, and I explore broken land in Nova Scotia. I wanted what I wrote about Canada to be my *Walden*. Of course I failed. Instead of a pond I produced a puddle, broad and lapping at the door of the university library, but muddy, a scruff of cattails around it, the plants sheltering the neglected life of a small place, spotted turtles and dragonflies, tall tales and letter music. Still, unlike celibate Thoreau and fickle Byron, I've long been a homebody, and scattered amid the flotsam of my ponderings are snapshots of a good marriage.

Last Sunday Vicki and I and our three rescue dogs walked the woods behind Horsebarn Hill on the university farm. We followed deer trails and paths familiar from four decades of living in Storrs. Robins scuttled across shadowy corners of damp fields, and a pair of red-bellied woodpeckers flew high through an oak forest, shrieking whenever they shifted trees. Grape vines tangled through scrub, growing opportunistically along the shoulders of an abandoned dirt road. Cords of poison ivy thick and hairy as wrists grasped trunks and climbing into the tops of trees usurped the crowns. Yellow birch lay rotting on the ground. The pulpwood had crumpled soft into compost, leaving behind sleeves of gleaming bark. Last year's leaves still clung to beech saplings. The leaves curled inward like wings, and their veins shined translucent in the light like shafts running through feathers, the color changing, flicking red and orange, khaki and gold. A winter storm had snapped the great cathedral beech beside Kessel Creek. Three generations of undergraduate lovers carved hearts throbbing with initials into the trunk of the tree. "Oh, weep for those, whose shrines are desolate," I murmured when I saw the wreckage, emending a line from Byron's "Hebrew Melodies."

Spring had not come to Storrs. Buds on beeches remained crisp and keen; black racers were not sunning themselves, and in the Beaver Pond the quacking of wood frogs had not soared into a flocking chorus. Vicki and I saw nothing extraordinary, but ambling made me long to escape the tendrils of clever sentences. After the walk we dallied and bought ice cream cones at the university dairy bar. Because both the boys' and girls' basketball teams won national championships, blue and white sprinkles were free. I had a chocolate brownie fudge cone, and Vicki, a "Husky Tracks," this last a blend of vanilla, fudge swirl, and peanut butter. So many sprinkles covered the ice cream that both cones looked like ski slopes, deep ridges of blue and white moguls layering them. This was the first time I ate sprinkles. "What an experience," I said later. "Yes," Vicki replied, "real life dresses everyone in royal purple."

"The besetting sin" of age, Randolph Bourne wrote, "is apathy." I'm not passionate about apathy. Still, I didn't watch a basketball game all season, and the championships failed to excite me. Aside from sprinkles, victory in the tournaments brought me only beer bottles in the front yard, overturned garbage cans, and at the end of the driveway the newspaper holder torn off its pole. I have aged and lost interest in many things. Other things that I once accomplished easily are beyond me. Nowadays if I imprison an escargatoire of snails in a roll-top dish for thirty-three hours then attempt to decipher their tracks, I cannot predict the future with a high degree of accuracy. The ability to believe has also forsaken me. No longer do I think opals sow discord between givers and receivers or that emeralds promote constancy and deepen friendships.

Escaping time is impossible. Kind-hearted people prevent the old from forgetting that they are gray shadows. In February as my friend David and I jogged around the indoor track at the university, a girl rushed over to us. We had never met her, but for three years we had seen her running in the field house at ten o'clock in the morning. Often we waved at her, and she smiled at us. "I spent fall in Florida on an internship," the girl explained. "I'm an accountant, and I wondered if you two would be on the track when I returned to finish school. What I am going to say sounds terrible. But actuarially, the odds were against your both being here. But here you are, and it is so good to see you guys still running."

In *The Recreations of a Country Parson*, Andrew Kennedy Hutchison Boyd described how he composed a sermon. Boyd wrote sitting outside in his garden. He didn't write steadily. One moment his daughter teased him into hopping out of his chair and racing her around the house. Another moment a weed distracted him, and he pushed back from his table, and dashing to the weed, pulled it out of the ground. Next his gardener reported on the condition of his fall plantings. The disruptions did not bother Boyd. "My sermons," he said, "will be the better for all these interruptions." If I appear not to ignore "those things which of necessity occupy the greatest part of an ordinary mortal's thoughts," he elaborated, my preaching "will come home to men's business and bosom." My essays smack of Boyd's unsystematic system of composition. One ordinary event follows another, the results, I hope, reflecting everyday life and striking readers as almost true to their experiences.

In analyzing a typical writing career, Alexander Smith stated, "A man reaches his limits as to thought long before he reaches his limits as to expression." What really happens is that the experienced scribbler discounts thought and pays more attention to story as well as to expression. "Any sense of aggressive and dominating intellectualism," A. C. Benson wrote describing conversation, was "fatal to good talk." "The harsh intellectualist," he continued, "generally ends by beheading most of the company." If one emends Benson's words changing *company* to *readers* and *talk* to *essays*, the statement is applicable to my writing. Rarely does a reader close one of my books feeling morose or beheaded. I have long worked to lift my writing above leaden seriousness. A circus of characters performs on my pages. None are criminals. A few misbehave, but these wear traditional clown's dress and sport old-fashioned cut-purse names like Peg of the Clink, Crack the Crystal, Jenny Go-Lightly, then Bo-Peep and her misdemeanor-prone husband Big Bo-Peep. Much that I write is humorous. I agree with Gerald Gould who declared he knew "no virtue dearer or warmer than silliness, and nothing nearer to heaven than joy." "Fun," Gould elaborated, "is democracy and charity and freedom: it makes all equal and all kind: it bursts the bonds imposed by respectability."

I receive many letters. Often I cite them. Usually I don't describe my correspondents; I merely annotate one or two of their sentences. The essayist Donald Mitchell preferred studying letters to perusing personality. Letters, he wrote, were monitors, comforters, and "the only true heart talkers." In contrast, speech was molded by circumstance and suggested by observation, remark, and the presence of the person to whom one was speaking. The truest thought, Mitchell said, was "modified half through its utterance by a look, a sigh, a smile, or a sneer." What Mitchell neglected to say was that letters themselves sigh and mold recipients. Long ago when I began teaching, I tried to scribble myself into philosophic profundity. I locked a scowl on my face and hardened my capillaries in hopes that a nacreous mist would rise like a halo around my brow. Alas, inevitably a cumulonimbus cloud of humorous and cheerful letters swept into my days, snapping and crackling, making my veins jump kinetically.

For years the postman has delivered many such letters. Recently I received a note from New Haven containing an effervescently silly anecdote. An aging classics professor at Yale, my correspondent recounted, treated his seminar to lunch at a local bistro. The professor fancied himself an oenophile, and after a cuspidor of guttural hemming, he ordered two bottles of hock for the table. "A trifle cheeky and smacking slightly of after-shave, but withal hygienic and cleansing," the professor said addressing his students. Then succumbing to high academic joie de vivre, the old boy giggled into Latin and said, "Hic, haec, hoc." As could be expected the students laughed appreciatively. One or two even snorted. Time passed, however, and the waiter brought the first course to the table without serving the hock. "My good fellow, where are our tall green bottles?" the professor said, showing off his knowledge of German wines and their bottles. "Wine?" the waiter replied. "I didn't think you wanted wine. You declined hoc."

Andrew Boyd thought most people were like yews and apple trees and needed occasional pruning, saying that without clipping people became "unamiable creatures." I've sawed wayward limbs off at stem collars in hopes of making my pages amiable. Because my children are grown and do not live in Storrs, I never bound up from my desk and race one of them around the house. I do, however, leap fences, creep into writers' dairies, and milk their pages for quotations. Many of the quotes are bookish and creamy, pulled from literary Holsteins. "The cruelest lies are often told in silence," Robert Louis Stevenson wrote. "A man may have sat in a room for hours and not opened his teeth, and yet come out of that room a disloyal friend or a vile calumniator." Even richer, more like milk from a Jersey, is G. K. Chesterton's statement, "Unless people are near in soul they had better not be near in neighborhood. The Bible tells us to love our neighbors, and also to love our enemies; probably because they are the same people." A few quotations come churned and rich with lumpy self-help. A good way of starting a conversation with the "lady whom you do not know" sitting next to you at a dinner party is to "ask her whether by any chance she is fond of string." If she looks frightened and says that she doesn't quite understand, Harry Grahame advised, "you might as well give up the job altogether." But if she says, "I simply *adore* string; and pink tape is a thing I positively *worship!* then you will get on swimmingly." By the end of dinner, "you will be talking confidentially on such subjects as the Immortality of the Soul or the Malice of Inanimate Things and all will be well."

Other quotations are misbegotten, stripped from bovines more like steers than cows, "Losing an arm is less costly than losing a leg because if a person loses a leg he loses something to boot." Into quotations that have long been pasteurized, I sometimes drop a phrase of fresh butter. "When it's raining cats and dogs, rats and mice don't fare well." Occasionally a quotation sours before it slaps the bottom of the pail. Actually, vinegary flavor depends upon the mind of the taster. I winced on reading Eden Phillpotts's condemnation of autobiography. "Can anything be more tedious," he asked, "than listening to a man who has done nothing with his life while he tells you how he did it?" Although Phillpotts's statement came too close to the lead of my pencil for intellectual comfort, it should not have bothered me. Paragraphs animate tedium. They also expose writers to interpretive tripping—to readers soaring beyond the page borne aloft by verbs into fogs of eccentric association. No matter the care with which a person writes once he describes living, he loses control of his days. A man of letters takes his life in his hand each time he picks up a pen, Hamilton Wright Mabie declared in *My Study Fire*. "The curse of publicity which attaches itself not only to his work but to himself is as comprehensive as an Arab imprecation; it covers his ancestry and his posterity with impartial malediction."

I know a brass tray of caffeinated Arab curses, but so far none have been applied to me or my pages. In fact, I doubt that anybody east of the Outer Banks has read anything I've written. In any case, though, readers forever scroll through books whitening out the actual and turning authors into fictional beings. "I have always wanted to ask you," a woman said to me last week at a reading, "what it was like growing up next to Colonel Sanders. Do you like fried chicken? It must have been terrible smelling chicken cooking twenty-four hours a day. Did you hear the sizzling? Was it loud?" "I am writing," a letter began last year, "because you are my father, and I plan to come to Connecticut to meet you. I don't want anything from you. I only want to get to know you. I have read all your books, and you are so like me." A brief contraceptive correspondence followed. Happily, thankfully, when the woman was conceived in South Carolina, I was living in London. In fact, I've never been in South Carolina. Even so, one night in the kitchen at dinner, Vicki said, "Are you sure you aren't the woman's father? Be honest now. The truth won't upset me."

Page matters are never entirely accurate. The *I* described on the page as sitting quietly at the kitchen table and listening to Vicki was not the actual person sitting at the table. I didn't mention the pineapple I was eating or the scrap of fat I surreptitiously dropped on the floor for Binky, the smallest of, in Vicki's words, "our packlet." "No man has ever yet succeeded in painting an honest portrait of himself in an autobiography," Thomas Bailey Aldrich wrote. "In spite of his candid purpose he omits necessary touches and adds superfluous ones. At times he cannot help draping his thought, and the least shred of drapery becomes a disguise." Now that I think about the meal, I was probably eating grapefruit not pineapple. Moreover, Binky is old and creaky, and before she got to the fat, Suzy scooped it up. And I wasn't speechless. If I recall inaccurately, I silenced Vicki by interjecting a quip I discovered moldering in the library earlier that day: "Because they invariably worship their creators, self-made men are more religious than other people."

I like getting my pens dirty. I don't destroy the weeds I pluck. Instead, I spread a blend of words and manure around their roots and plant them in essays. I am especially fond of poetry that many people consider goose grass. For the record, let me assure readers that I never transplant smut grass. Recently, I dug up a stanza shakily attributed to Eugene Ware, a journalist popular at the end of the nineteenth century who wrote under the pen name Ironquill. "The lightning bug is brilliant, / But he hasn't any mind; / He stumbles through existence / With his headlight on behind." Also delighting me was a tongue and mind twister I found in a book of literary oddments compiled by Bert Leston Taylor, a celebrated columnist and a major literary figure in Chicago during the early years of the twentieth century. The poem was three stanzas long and began, "A tree toad loved a she toad / That lived up in a tree; / She was a three-toed tree toad / But a two-toed toad was he." The course of hyla love often runs bumpy, and because Mr. Two-Toes could not please her whims, Miss She-Toad "vetoed" him.

Many weeds I dig are as small as Quaker ladies. The quick phrase "Jacks and Jills on the beanstalk," for example, refers to climbers, both social and corporate. Like daisies, advertisements add smiles and color to gritty workaday paragraphs. "For the Heads of Families" declared a headline running bold across the top of an advertisement for Linchard's Hair Balm and Restorer. "Guaranteed," the advertisement testified, "to Strengthen Follicles, Freshen Roots, Kill Nits, Eliminate Senile Warts, and Patch Peeling Scalps." With every mail-order purchase of three bottles of "Berry's Bunion Salve and Toe Oil," an advertisement in the 1922 spring number of *The Arkansas Farmer* promised, S. Octavous Browne, a pharmacist in Jonesville, would include "A Sketch of Noah's Ark, drawn from an actual photograph." Newspapers are also great distractors. Oddities thrive in them like jimson weed atop a dung pile. The flowers of jimson weed look like trumpets and are pink and white although undertakers usually drain the pink out of obituaries. Last December the obituary of Catherine Elizabeth Noni-Cheek appeared in the *Roanoke Bugle*. "Noni died intestate at age four," the obituary stated. "She was unmarried and left no children or partners behind to serve as pallbearers. Noni was a Renaissance girl and subscribed to *Popular Mechanics* and *Dog Fancy*. She will be sorely missed by her family, especially by Poppy and Grandma Gee Gee, by her favorite doll Sadie Hawkins, Chewzer her pet turtle, and by her classmates in the Little Sisters class at Elizabeth Cady Stanton Yoga Center. They won't soon forget her urging them to wear their yellow ribbons."

In a letter mulling the novel *John Inglesant*, J. H. Shorthouse said his reading of the book was that "God prefers culture to fanaticism." Since Shorthouse wrote *Inglesant*, the statement implies an ease in describing or at least a familiarity with God's opinions. I am not on bosomy terms with any of the many Great First Causes, but I, too, prefer culture to fanaticism. My attitude is, to pay myself an earned complement, elitist. Only an essayist comfortable in Zion and who enjoys the company of books could paste together so many seemingly unrelated topics and quotations. Only someone immune to zeal and sacrosanct belief would be pleased by the results. But I am pleased. Life is a curiosity shop, and I think my essays better and truer for their digressions. If everything were straightforward, conversation would cease. Bamboozlers would become extinct. Sleeping pills would disappear, and doctors would prescribe books for insomnia.

Edward Carpenter said that "modern civilized folk" were like "people sitting helplessly in the midst of heaps of paint-cans and brushes." "Are they," he asked, "going to produce anything lovely or worth looking at in their own lives?" "Heaven only knows!" he exclaimed in exasperation, answering his own question. Who cares what such folk produce? The art of living is not art. To live well a person should throw away pruning shears and loosening the inseams of his trousers kick up his legs and start gadding about. If he feels wondrously adventuresome, he ought to become a culinary libertine and dump a bucket of sprinkles over his next ice cream cone. In this book, I splash paint around and, to use Boyd's words, I try to write so that my essays "come home" to the business of living and the heart of feeling. I hope readers find the book amusing and observant. My ideal reader will suspend analysis and "go" with the absence of flow. In any case, no catechism legislates a divine right way of reading. Readings are Protestant and personal, and interpretations are idiosyncratic. "The chicken does not exist only to produce another egg," Chesterton wrote in mulling the latitudinarian possibilities of things. "He may also exist to amuse himself, to praise God, or even to suggest ideas to a French dramatist." Anyway, "there are some books, like some people,"

Edmund Gosse wrote, "of whom we form an indulgent opinion without finding it easy to justify our liking." Certainly the pleasures caused by reading are not always straight-forward. Some are roundabout and result from boredom and disappointment. Fatigue, for example, often makes readers appreciate easy beds and enjoy balmy sleep. How sweet it is to assuage mumbling resentment with a tall glass clinking with ice and beaded with good cheer.

At times, I am more opinionated than indulgent. I blame age. According to the ancient saying, when a person becomes old and can no longer set a bad example, he gives good advice. I rarely misbehaved when I was young. I lived the good example. Now that I am old I think no advice worse than "good advice." Inevitably, good advice preaches accommodation with whatever exists. It celebrates law and precedence and so invigorates pedantry and dogmatism that it sucks life out of people and drains spontaneity. Such advice hampers rather than frees thought and urges common sense when what the world and people need, to quote Lewis Carroll's mock teacher, the mock turtle, is "uncommon nonsense."

Even though I prefer candied opinions, I won't be upset if readers succumb to megrims and send me acetous notes justifying their disliking. The world contains, J. C. Squire wrote at the beginning of the twentieth century, "a great many people who think—or, rather, think they think, or, rather talk as if they thought they thought—that man exists for the two only purposes of producing goods, and more men to eat and wear them." I buy little, and I produce less. For forty-four years I was a teacher, and academic freedom, as Yale's Dean Jones defined it at the beginning of the twentieth century, is the "liberty to say what you think without thinking what you say." In any case, criticism is a tonic injecting quickening spasms into game legs and awakening sleepers, silencing adenoidal snores.

Besides, like a never-ending regimen of gamma goblin shots, a happy marriage fosters immunity to criticism. In the kitchen three Sundays ago while Vicki baked chocolate cupcakes, my mind ran to sentences. When I started describing codicils Eve added to her will after she and Adam moved out of Eden, Vicki interrupted. "Go to your study and be quiet. You're not wanted any more for quite a while," she said, pulling a platter of cupcakes out of the oven. I wanted a cupcake later, so I followed orders, left the kitchen, and spent a peaceful afternoon in my study. Being the literary executor of a gal dead since the beginning of human time is a sobering responsibility. I wanted to do right by the belletristic remains of Cain and Abel and especially of Seth who, as the ancestor of Noah, was the great-grandfather of mankind. Actually Vicki's instructions rise to the elbow and enliven gray hours. Moreover,

I have aged beyond being bothered by what people say to me—well, almost beyond being bothered. Last week as I left the examining room, my cardiologist turned toward me and as an after-thought said, "Sam, nothing I do will make you live longer." "Well, *juglans regia*" or perhaps *pistacia vera*, as one of the First Causes remarked after a mob burned his sanctuary and trampled his image into dust.

"When I was a child, there was no one like my daddy," the narrator of the gospel song "Doing It by the Book" recounted. The girl's family was poor, and her father worked "his fingers to the bone." The father "tried to do the right thing no matter what it took," explaining to his family, "I'm doing it by the book." When a neighbor's house burned down, the father shared home and table with the neighbor's family, letting them stay until they "could make it on their own." "In these troubled times when this old world gets crazy," the narrator said, she returned to memories of sitting on her mother's lap and listening to her father read the Bible. Like him, "I found I can't go wrong when I'm doing it by the book." The part of the book that guided the girl's father was the Sermon on the Mount blessing the merciful, the pure in heart, and the peace-makers, urging people to suspend judgment and not simply to turn the other cheek to evil but to love their enemies as well as their good neighbors.

If everyone lived in the light of the Sermon on the Mount, earth would become heaven and hell an old wives' tale. Unfortunately, the Sermon on the Mount is a minute part of the book. Much of the Bible celebrates bloody insanity. Among the countless brutes are the genocidal maniac Joshua and mad Abraham who heard a voice commanding him to murder his son. Today Abraham would be a Texan. Upon hearing a voice or a choir of voices, he'd settle his boy in the backyard swing, and then after giving the boy a push toward the sky, he'd "bushmaster" him. Probably he'd range beyond the yard and shoot every child in "the whole damned neighborhood." If Abraham were a woman, she'd drown her baby in the bathroom, in the upstairs tub to be nearer to God. Instead of being guided by the Sermon on the Mount, packs of people live according to the rule Jane Collier noted at the end of *An Essay on the Art of Ingeniously Tormenting*, "Remember always to do unto every one, what you would least wish to have done unto yourself."

For a good samaritan like the gospel singer's father, religion was a matter of spirit not doctrine. Laws turned earth into hell and heaven into fable. Zeal for forms and ceremonies, Samuel Clarke wrote in the eighteenth century, hindered "the growth of Christian Charity, and, like the Worm at the Root of Jonah's Gourd" ate "out the vitals of true Religion." John Tillotson agreed. "To be of a kind and obliging disposition, of a tender and compassionate spirit, sensible of the straits and miseries of others, so as to be ready to ease and relive them," he said, was "the happiest spirit and temper in the world." Not even miracles could prove "modern schemes of religion" with their absurd, narrow pieties to be true, John Amory wrote. Notions, he said, not characterized by "the moral fitness of actions" were repugnant to the "wisdom and goodness of the Almighty," emphasizing that true Christianity "bore the visible marks and signatures of benevolence, social happiness, and moral fitness." "How happy the world might be if there were no literature of the Bible," Havelock Ellis wrote, "if Augustine and Aquinas and Calvin and thousands of smaller men had not danced on it so long, stamping every page of it into mire."

Living according to something as immaterial as spirit or breath, however, is extraordinarily difficult. Spirit cannot be netted by words, nor can it be tacked into simple declaratives. For many people, living within curtain walls of rules is easier. For such people, curiosity and compassion seem poisonous seeds dropped from the apple when Adam put it aside to fondle Eve. *Precedence* becomes a killing convenience adopted in order to avoid the harder and more disruptive efforts of thinking and understanding. Attempts at originality are suspect. In soporifically mundane verse, Austin Dobson wrote, "The green trees never aim at blue, / They want no change. And why should you? / (Nothing betrays a poor vitality / Like straining for originality.)" In contrast, Charles Colton attacked pedantry in *Lacon* and, by extension, servility to rules. "Pedantry prides herself on being *wrong* by rules, while common sense is contented to be *right* without them. The former would rather stumble in following the dead than walk upright by the *profane* assistance of the living. She [pedantry] worships the moldering mummies of antiquity, and her will is that they should not be buried but embalmed." "Folly disgusts us less by her ignorance than pedantry by her learning," Colton continued, "since she mistakes the *nonage* of things for their *virility*, and her creed is that *darkness* is increased by the accession of *light*."

The webs of rules—irregular nets, sheet, funnel, and orb, social and educational, with their hubs and bridges, study plans, doctrines, traps and guy lines—are endlessly confusing. "A great deal of the trouble of the world is made," A. C. Benson wrote, "by well-meaning, muddled people, men and women who tamely accept and preach traditions and conventions, and still more by stupid and tyrannical people, who are unsympathetic and unimaginative, and bully those who do not agree with them." Critics have often thought rigorous schooling wrong. "It would be pleasant," E. V. Lucas mused, "to know that here and there was a village schoolmaster who was whimsical and eccentric enough to permit his scholars to know as little as might be about spelling and dogma, and give them instead fascinating lessons on the nature around them." "Under a very careless or eccentric vicar this would be possible," Lucas stated, aware that schoolmasters skated on ice too thin to bear the absence of "dogma" and "pedagogy." Edmund Gosse praised Lucas's own books for their "successful resistance to the instinct for teaching." This resistance "to the desire to instruct" and "to occupy a pulpit" made Lucas stand out from and above other contemporary essayists. "Moral reflections, especially if introduced with a certain polite air of solemnity," Gosse wrote, "are to the British public what carrots are to a donkey; they cannot be resisted." A great majority of readers, Gosse stated, expanding his criticism of dull convention, "like to be quite sure of the tone of what they read; they wish an author to be straightforward; they detest irony and they loathe impishness."

Society needed "well-principled" teachers, Robert South stated in the eighteenth century in his "Discourse on the Education of Youth," "it being seldom found that the pulpit mends what the school has marred." When teachers found spirited youths, South continued, "let them endeavor to govern that spirit, without extinguishing it; for when it comes to be extinguished and broken, and lost, it is not in the power or act of man to recover it; and then, believe it, no knowledge of nouns or pronouns, Syntaxis and Prosodia, can compensate or make amends for such a loss." South was not as tolerant as Lucas. His educational beatitudes did not bless all students. "Stripes and blows," he cautioned, "are the last and basest remedy, and scarce ever to be used, but upon such that carry their brains in their backs; and have souls so dull and stupid, as to serve for little else but to keep their bodies from putrefaction." Words may not capture the genial spirits, but like those in South's colorful remarks, they are adequate to imprecations, their venomous intensity, alas, mesmerizing and seducing, making readers comfortable with base remedies.

In the prologue to *In Memoriam*, Tennyson noted, "Our little systems have their day; / They have their day and cease to be." Although stripes and blows have vanished from school houses, parts of speech still parade like boulevardiers through handbooks. "Language," James Russell Lowell warned in *The Bigelow Papers*, "is the soil of thought." "There is death in the dictionary; and where language is too strictly limited by convention, the ground for expression to grow is limited also." The Universal Schoolmaster, Lowell said, attempted to make people talk like books. He did "his best to enslave the minds and memories of his victims" to what he esteemed "the best models of English composition," that is, to writers whose style was so correct that it lacked "blood-warmth." "No language that has faded into diction," Lowell stated, could "bring forth a sound and lusty book." "There are people in this world," Agnes Repplier wrote lightly but seriously, "who always insist upon others remodeling their diet on a purely hygienic basis; who entreat us to avoid sweets or acids, or tea or coffee, or whatever we chance to particularly like." Such people, she continued, tell us "that cress and dandelions will purify our blood" and that celery "is an excellent febrifuge." It is in the same benevolent but intrusive spirit that "kind-hearted critics are good enough to warn us against the books we love, and to prescribe for us the books we ought to read. With robust assurance they offer to give our tutelage their own personal supervision." The zeal of such people, Repplier said, "carried them beyond the limits of discretion." She added that she was indisposed to consider advice "thrust upon" her like "paregoric or a porous plaster."

Dogma and rules other than grammatical continue to monitor classrooms and subdue the lusty and the lively, as doing it by the educational book implies molding more than assisting or directing. Structure and tradition so hampered originality, Holbrook Jackson mulled, that it sometimes seemed that only people outside of or on the margins of society were capable of real accomplishment. "There is something to be said," he wrote, "for the idea that all great endeavor is the result of the abandon which often expresses itself in the rake and the vagabond." One talent was necessary to live a good life, Randolph Bourne stated, "the ability to steer clear of the forces that warp and "conventionalize." The unwary person, he warned, will soon find himself "chained a prisoner for life." Family, church, business, society, and state all offered inducements to forgo choice and conform to "their pattern and type." Pretending to be friends and guides, family and institutions eventually become masters and tyrants. They forced a person "to perpetuate old errors, to keep alive dying customs, to breathe new life into vicious prejudices," and to take a stand "against the saving new." History, Robert Lynd wrote, could be read as the story of a rearguard action "fought during several thousand years by dogma against curiosity." "The dogmatists offer to provide us with all the facts a reasonable man can desire," Lynd continued. "If we persist in believing that there is a world of facts yet undiscovered and that it is our duty to set out in quest of it, in the eyes of the dogmatists we are scorned as heretics and charlatans." To protect himself from convention, Robert Southey declared, "I intend to be a hedge-hog and roll myself up in my own prickles:

all I regret is that I am not a porcupine, and endowed with the property of shooting them to annoy the beasts who come near enough to annoy me."

Times in this "old world" are always troubled, as the narrator of the gospel song put it. Although living according to the Sermon on the Mount appears impossible in almost any society, nevertheless, some people are able to cut the straps cinching them to weighty commandments. Often they do so with talk, their appeals maundering and charming—attracting, rather than coiling and hypnotizing like South's words. For his part, A. G. Gardiner kept a semblance of freedom from rule and expectation by celebrating his untidiness. Because of messiness, the untidy saw life differently and sometimes paradoxically clearer than the neat. "We are rather like cats whose perceptions become more acute the darker it gets." Freed from the compulsion to organize, the untidy were often happier than other people. They escaped conventional expectation and occasionally experienced sudden joy. "Consider the joy of finding things you don't hope to find," Gardiner wrote addressing his reader. "You, sir, sitting at your spotless desk, with your ordered and labelled shelves about you and your files and your letter-racks, and your card indexes and your cross references, and your this, that, and the other—what do you know of the delights of which I speak? You do not know the shock of sudden discovery. . . . No star swims into your ken out of the void. You cannot be said to find things at all, for you never lose them, and things must be lost before they can truly be found. The father of the Prodigal had to lose his son before he could experience the joy that has become an immortal legend of the world. It is we who lose things, not you, sir, who never find them, who know the Feast of the Fatted Calf."

Conformity so strips away the angular and the controversial that people run the danger of popularity. When the crowd applauds him, an old statement warns, a man ought to ask what harm he has done. "A yielding temper, when not carefully watched and curbed, is one of the most dangerous faults," Joseph Neal warned. "It is apt to carry its owner into a thousand difficulties, and, too frequently, to hurry him into vices, if not, into crimes." "There are few kinds of extravagance more ruinous than that of indulging a desire for being excessively good-natured," Neal continued. "A man of circumscribed means may, with comparative safety, keep horses and dogs, drink Champagne and Burgundy, bet upon races and cock-fights; he may even gratify a taste for being very genteel—for these things may subside into moderation; but being very good-natured, in the popular acception of the phrase, is like the juvenile amusement of sliding down Market Street hill on a sled. The further one goes, the greater the velocity; and if the momentum be not skilfully checked, we are likely to land in the water."

In my case, doing by the book means being done by books. I have spent years in the inner wards of libraries, walls of books confining and rising so high above me that I rarely considered darting through barbicans and splashing across moats. I have been, in Robert Southey's words, a relic-monger. "Far be it from me to despise the relic-mongers of literature or to condemn them," Southey wrote in *The Doctor*, "except when they bring to light things which ought to have remained with the dead; like the Dumfries craniologists, who, when the grave of Burns was opened to receive the corpse of his wife, took that opportunity of abstracting the poet's skull that they might make a cast of it." I have dug through cairns of bookshelves searching for ingots of golden paragraphs, glittering bracelets, chains, silver sentences spinning like rings, amulets, spearheads, and brooches. Doctrines of unity and coherence matter little to me. For me, the treasures I unearth or de-page are sufficient unto themselves. Put another way, they are inlays that appeal to me more than the essays in which I insert them.

Reading is an opiate and isn't priapic. If it doesn't shape a conformist, it gelds, making a person socially "safe," that is, quiescent. The number of monsters in the Bible outnumbers that of Good Samaritans: not just Abraham and Joshua, but legions of others; Jael, for example, who gave Siscera milk then lulled him to sleep, after which she drove a tent nail into his temple; Jephtha, who burned his daughter as tribute to a demon he thought the Lord; the adulterous satyr David, who sent Uriah to die in battle so he could enjoy the favors of Bathsheba; and Jehu, who ordered Jezebel's servants to throw her from a window. Afterward he trampled her corpse under the feet of his horse and allowed stray dogs to eat her body, leaving only her skull, feet, and the palms of her hands to be buried.

Conformity fosters and reflects indifference. But whenever I, like the singer's father, ponder doing it by the Sermon on the Mount and damning horrific biblical tales, books do in my intentions. I shovel up a relic. Immediately my fervor cools, and the "saving new" slips from thought as I mull fitting the artifact into an essay. I behave almost like the wise man described by Andrew Kennedy Hutchison Boyd in *Lessons of Middle Age*. When the wise man discovered that most of mankind differed with him on some matter, he sighed wearily and turned silently away, burying his contrary opinion deep in a pocket of his trousers. Recently, while biblical brutality was cooking my thoughts into words, I excavated a mood-leavening story. Two bakers owned shops across the street from one another. The men were rivals and competed for customers. One morning the older baker addressed the younger. "You are going to marry the widow, aren't you?" the baker asked. "What?" the younger baker replied, puzzled by the question, "What do you mean?" "My meaning is clear, unlike your intentions. I mean are you going to marry the widow? You owe her that," the older baker said. "Marry what widow?" the other baker said, almost shouting. "Why, the widow of the man who bought the dozen biscuits from you last week," the older baker said, turning away and walking into his shop, thus ending the conversation.

In advertising a book that contained a sketch of my writing life, a publisher labeled me a provocateur. To my discredit, laughter is the only reaction I have ever provoked. No reader has ever closed one of my books determined to reform and to do the right thing no matter what the cost. In a radio interview a month ago, I said that domesticated dogs were better behaved than house-trained humans. Afterward, two people called the show and said they were "offended." Of course, the truth of the assertion is obvious to all except the bible-blinded. Dogs don't carry guns or knives. They don't buy pornography or play ice hockey. They don't rob collection plates or dip snuff. Euthanasia does not upset them, and they'd rather chew grass than drink ipecac. They are just as happy riding in a Buick as in a Bentley. Coldwater Creek and L. L. Bean do not send them catalogues. They have been inoculated against rabid patriotism and don't froth at the mouth when they watch the evening news. They sense that the supply of puppies is regular; as a result, they think speculating about a better, dogless earth wastes barking hours. They don't worship gods. In fact, most dogs have never heard of Belial or Dagon, Isis, Chronos, Odin, Tarves or Huitzilopochtli. They don't cheat in college, graduate with honors, go to work on Wall Street, and then vote Republican. Moreover, they don't sell self-help books to the woe-be-gone in hospitals or write people suffering from dementia, telling them they have inherited vast fortunes in Nigeria. Although they lap ice cream off the kitchen floor occasionally, they do not drink alcohol. Certainly some mongrels munch yard droppings, but they never, never get "shit-faced."

My remarks are casual, not studied, and upset readers who think irrelevancy disheartening and irresponsible. Such people rarely sympathize with the *flaneur*, who has mastered the difficult art of doing nothing or of seeming to do nothing. Moreover, to quote Oliver Herford, I'm a "Quoter." Like the moon, I am "a second-hand dealer in Light." Recently, I have slipped into the chorus of people all nattering on key about university teaching. Some schools have practically called a moratorium on hiring tenure-track faculty, replacing retiring teachers with part-timers or adjuncts whom they pay comparatively little. To earn decent livings, adjuncts teach several courses a semester, usually at different colleges, the number of courses often six or seven. Schools, I said to my friend David one morning as we jogged, are suffering from "adjunctivitis." David is an ardent grammarian and a real scholar. That night he found *adjunctivitis* in *Gray's Anatomy* and sent me the definition. "Adjunctivitis. An academic disease," he wrote, "the most noticeable symptom of which is shortsightedness. Adjunctivitis occurs when foreign bodies are, like warts and fungi, attached to an organism without being fully incorporated into it. The amalgam thus produced causes irritation and swelling. Because the host organism provides little sustenance, the foreign bodies must spread themselves thin to survive. They soon suffer unsustainable stress while the host organism undergoes disintegration and eventual necrosis." For their part, university teachers themselves suffer from "lecturenomia," an influenza transmitted by words and caught by listening. The most noticeable symptom is a frequent attendance at lectures. When full-blown, lecturenomia causes doziness and leads to the conviction that chatter is an adequate substitute for discipline and rigorous study.

Not all the matters David and I talk about are bookishly academic. During one long, humid run, we discussed the merits and demerits of imaginary and real mistresses. Of course, the conversation was platonic. No teacher can match the hands-on experience enjoyed by politicians, dentists, vestrymen, and bull riders. We concluded, however, that ridding one's self of a bone and blood mistress was easier than jettisoning an imaginary mistress. "A few tears, some scratches, and a box of Benjamins," as a prominent postmodern novelist put it, "and a fellow can scamper up the back fence, howl, and set out tom-catting again." Moreover, a real mistress does not undermine character like an imaginary mistress. Weakness of the flesh makes actual immoral cavorting short-lived. In contrast, stamina does not affect the duration of fanciful doings, making it impossible for a man whose mistress is imaginary to escape the shackles of naughty thought. Moreover, barky, creaky limbs limit the activities in which one can indulge with a real person, while in imagination anything is scandalously possible. A fellow's imaginary paramour can turn herself into a man even against the wishes of her lover.

Imaginary mistresses are also notoriously sneaky and can change appearances at a whim. They can have butchy red hair at breakfast and serpentine brown hair at lunch. They can be midgets or giants, walking candy canes or fat, saucy munchables. They are unmanageable distractions and appear any time, any place. They cavort behind the communion rail at church. They leap out of platters of sweet potato fries at Mooyah Burger, sometimes wearing robes of red ketchup, other times "nekkid." While escape from an imaginary mistress is impossible, breaking from a real mistress often reforms a person's character, leading, for a moment at least, to humility, repentance, friendship with Jesus, and miraculously, perhaps, even to invigorated domesticity. Moreover, imaginary mistresses ultimately behave like wives. After long associations, they grow frustrated. They get tired of living in the shadows and expect diamond necklaces. Reputation comes to mean little to them, and they throw take-out into the garbage and insist on dining in public at three-star eateries. In the middle of the night they wake their lovers and demand to go on cruises. They nag and quarrel and threaten to prorogue sexual congress, this last not a powerful threat as it often brings sighs of relief to the lips of elderly imaginary philanderers, even making some so thankful they double their yearly donation to World Wildlife.

Finally the physical activities in which a man indulges with a real mistress are salubrious. They are particularly good for male parts. "Especially the prostate," my friend Sallie said after I described David's and my ponderings. Sallie is a specialist in bankruptcy and a partner in Hartford's most prestigious law firm. She has three children and a good marriage. Rarely does Sallie speak without knowing her subject intimately. After graduating from Yale Law, Sallie clerked for and became the mistress of an aging judge in northern Virginia. "He was a real dear, a sweetheart," she said, "but he was slipping. He worried so much about his prostate that he was garbling his legal opinions and committing endless comma blunders. I just had to help him. It was the Christian thing to do. Once we became intimate, his writing improved and he was almost appointed to the appellate court. Before I returned to Connecticut, Mary, his wife, thanked me for brightening her days and extending the judge's career." "The judge died six months before I married Fred," Sallie continued, "but as a wedding present Mary sent me the family silver service. She and the judge didn't have children, and when my first son was born, I named him after the judge."

I do not provoke. I only observe. Because I am tidy and have a yielding temper and because I rarely wander beyond library wards, my thoughts run to the bookish—conventional stories that, because they have beginnings and endings, don't resemble life. Since his thirty-eighth birthday, David has kept track of the miles he has covered. Three weeks ago, after a seven mile run, he reached 84,999 miles. We arranged to meet early the next morning and spiff through the eighty-five thousandth mile and then five other miles. Unfortunately, flu infected our plans. For six days David did not run. "Suppose David died," I said to Vicki, "that would be hard knocks on him one mile short of 85k but what a story for me. I could lean on it for years." While David was in bed, I gathered the papers Vicki will need when I die: my wills living and personal, lists of useful names and telephone numbers, directions for cremation and for avoiding a memorial service, titles to the cars, retirement papers from the state of Connecticut, tax schedules, Social Security and Medicare instructions, financial statements from Regions Bank, Bank of America, Liberty Bank, ING, Great American, TIAA-CREF, and The Hartford, on and on until I filled a wooden tray. "Wouldn't it be astonishing if I died tonight or tomorrow?" I said to Vicki that afternoon as she sat on the kitchen floor trimming the dogs' nails. "Now that would be a son of a bitch of a story." "That's not a nice thing to say, and you should use polite English," Vicki answered. "Polite," I snorted then quoted H. G. Wells, "Polite conversation always appears to me to be as a wicked perversion of the blessed gift of speech which, I take it, was given to us to season our lives rather than to make them insipid."

For the record, neither I nor David died, non-events, particularly in David's case, that disappointed me slightly. Anyway, David and I are now clipping along and piling miles atop the eighty-five thousand. Living by the book is more complex than paying lip service to the Sermon on the Mount. It means living amid books and seeing life as a bookish affair. Last Sunday night I dreamed Vicki was killed in a car wreck. Monday morning I hid the keys to our cars and refused to let Vicki drive. According to ancient Chaldean belief, dreams accurately predicted the next twenty-four hours of a sleeper's life. Monday night Vicki chugged through my early morning hours on a tractor. The tractor was old and rusty and did not have a roll bar. Vicki handled it like a farmer, however. When I awoke on Tuesday, I knew driving was no longer dangerous, so before Vicki got out of bed I hung the car keys back on the rack in the kitchen. "We are doing it by some book or other even if I write the pages," I said, "The world may be crazy but we are sane."

Often a relic resembles a hilt collar broken from a sword, a fragment that unlike a blade doesn't slice but that awakens imagination or evokes a mood. In *Three of Them* Arthur Conan Doyle described one day in the lives of three small children, Dimples, Laddie, and Baby. The oldest and most active, Dimples, discovered a wasps' nest and stirred it up, after which the wasps "stirred him up." To occupy the children, Daddy handed them an illustrated history of the ancient world. The Hanging Gardens of Babylon were green and lush. In Egypt an overseer directed a team of six slaves. Dimples thought a Neolithic grave containing a skeleton surrounded by funeral pots was the belly of a "Jumbo" containing a man he had eaten. Laddie disagreed, saying that Jumbos only ate buns. And so, Doyle wrote, the children "guessed and prattled" as they turned the pages, "now arguing about the cave-painting of a prehistoric savage, now the picture-writing of an Indian, now some strange dado taken from a Yucatan temple buried in the primeval forest." As the children looked at the book, "Daddy leaned back and smoked and watched and listened in the gathering gloom of evening, while the firelight came and went on the eager features of the children."

The children "were the very last buds at the end of the newest branches of the great tree of life. And here in this book they were gazing at the work of those old, old flowers which had withered so long ago," Doyle wrote. "They too would work and they would pass, and there would come yet others, as far from us as we from Babylon, who would stare and guess and laugh when they saw the pictures of our little ships and airplanes and rude appliances for outwitting Nature. It was all working and working—and to what end! The life-urge was terrific and relentless and it pushed them always on. Monkey men crouching in a cave at one end—pure spirit, perhaps, at the other. There was more in Daddy's mind than he could tell the children as he looked at the three heads clustered over the old book before the fire." "Clustered over the old book in 1919 while the embers of their neighbors' houses smoldered and glowed," I said to Vicki, lifting my voice and raising *old book* into capital letters.

Solitude

"Man does not live for himself alone. He lives for the good of others as well as himself," Samuel Smiles wrote in *Duty*. "Everyone has his duties to perform—the richest, as well as the poorest. To some life is pleasure, to others suffering. But the best do not live for self-employment, or even fame. Their strongest motive power is hopeful useful work in every good cause." Smiles believed the busy world shaped character. "Men," Smiles continued, "are social beings more than intellectual creatures. The best part of human cultivation is derived from social contact, self-respect, mutual toleration, and self-sacrifice for the good of others." Smiles's plea for activism appeals more to the optimistic young than to the aged. Over time optimism becomes a costume one doffs in order to slip unnoticed through and out of conversations. Quick curiosity, a synonym for hope, ebbs. As muscles shrink into cords of cellulite, most people shed duties and commitments. They conclude that "hopeful useful work" rarely benefits others, society, or themselves. Resignedly they observe that bread cast upon waters breaks into crumbs and vanishes. A few people continue their "good works" and struggle to perform small duties faithfully. The ways of the world are harsh, however. In their "twilight years," such people are often neglected, or worse, ridiculed. "All people die alone, but especially the good," an ancient maxim states bleakly.

As people age and lose hearing, the noise of the world swells into a crescendo and paradoxically becomes deafening. The clamor of buying and selling, the shrill warnings of street-corner Cassandras, the jabber of lickspittles, Riches thundering "Look at me," the earnest hawking of peddlers pan-handling religion and education, the fall-out from "bads" detonated by do-gooders, and then less noxious but more irritating than psoriasis the warped music that never buckles the turn-table: in doctors' offices, in restaurants, in bookstores and cafes, from radio and television, from the telephone while one waits for a human being to respond to his "important" call—anywhere, everywhere, endlessly. "Some of the music is remarkably complex," my friend Josh said, adding, "What a pity it is damnably nauseating." The racket is so great and annoying that people retire into themselves seeking restorative silence. As a result, community vanishes from lives. In *The Freedom of the Fields*, Charles Conrad Abbott, the naturalist, described the attractions of solitude. Isolation did not narrow but instead expanded his life and nurtured creativity. "In what men call solitude I have all my friends about me; when in man's presence, all too often, I am literally alone. I fancy that all work of value or even of idle interest to the world is done in secret. We can praise or blame, admire or detest a crowded street; but what we wish others to know must come to us and be recorded when the crowded street is a mere matter of memory." Abbott explained that he grew up "a savage," a boy who disliked company. Visitors meant "unreasonable restraint," "spotless clothing," and "clean hands," things detested by small boys "of average health and spirits." Being alone, he continued, "is a positive pleasure." Smiles's good useful work pruned life into unnatural topiary. "The plain, modest, and compact flower of misanthropy has been too long neglected," Abbott declared. "Plant it where it will be most often seen, and let its blossoms influence our lives to a greater symmetry."

"I prefer an oak-tree to a temple; grass to a brick pavement; wild flowers beneath a blue sky to exotic orchids under glass. I would walk where I do not risk being jostled, and, if I see fit to swing my arms, leap a ditch, or climb a tree—I want no gaping crowd, when I do so, to hedge me in," Abbott elaborated in *Outings at Odd Times*. "If I prefer my neighbor's dog to my neighbor, why not?" he asked, adding, "Have not most people far too many friends?" Abbott believed that urban societies with their privets and beliefs, boxwoods and behaviors clipped into acceptable patterns treated spontaneity and the natural as weeds, as undesirable and as troublesome as crab grass. *Ecclesiastes* warned people against breaking hedges, predicting that they would be bitten by serpents. Abbott ignored the high-walled, straight alleys formed by hedges and spent much of his life alone, wandering, as he phrased it in the titles of his books, wastelands under clear skies and cloudy and exploring treetops and taking notes at night, the compulsion to write the only serpent that bit him.

Abbot celebrated solitude more vigorously than many contemporary writers. Often such writers wistfully admired solitude from afar but reached it only in advanced age. After struggling for decades in London, George Gissing's Henry Ryecroft spent the remnant of his ragged life in a cottage near Exeter. "Every morning when I awake, I thank heaven for silence. This is my orison," Ryecroft recounted. "I remember the London days when sleep was broken by clash and clang, by roar and shriek, and when my first sense on returning to consciousness was hatred of the life about me. Noises of wood and metal, clattering of wheels, banging of implements, jangling of bells—all such things are bad enough, but worse still is the clamorous human voice. Nothing on earth is more irritating to me than a bellow or scream of idiot mirth, nothing more hateful than a shout or yell of brutal anger. Were it possible, I would never again hear the utterance of a human tongue, save from those few who are dear to me. Here, wake at what hour I may, early or late, I lie amid gracious stillness." Often solitude appeared as an earthly paradise, frequently longed for but never achieved. In "Dream Pedlary," Thomas Beddoes wrote lyrically and other worldly:

> If there were dreams to sell,
> What would you buy?
> Some cost a passing bell,
> Some a light sigh,
> That shakes from Life's fresh crown
> Only a rose leaf down.
> If there were dreams to sell,
> Merry and sad to tell,
> And the crier rang the bell,
> 'What would you buy?

> A cottage lone and still
> With bowers nigh,
> Shadowy, my woes to still
> Until I die:
> Such pearl from Life's fresh crown
> Fain would I shake me down:
> Were dreams to have at will,
> This would best heal my ill,
> This would I buy.

In "The Gospel of Nature," John Burroughs observed that as he aged he was inclined to reduce his "baggage" and lop off "superfluities." "I become more and more in love with simple things and simple folk," he wrote. As a person grows older, much baggage becomes too heavy for heart or mind to lift. Words seem carts too frail to support emotion or complex thought. "Every year I feel less inclined than I once was to get upon subjects of the deepest interest," F. W. Robertson wrote explaining his reluctance to talk about the death of his young son William. "Every year I feel that utterance profanes feeling, and makes it commonplace. He is gone,—with all his fresh, bright, marvelous flow of happiness. What is there more to be said than is contained in those dreadful words,—He is gone?" Last fall the only daughter of a friend died. The man was a widower, and he and his daughter were very close. My friend taught English at the University of Indiana and was famously literate. Students said he managed classes like a conductor leading a symphony. Words never eluded him until, like Robertson, he wrote about the death of his daughter. "I miss my girl terribly. She always called me 'Poppy,'" my friend began before stopping suddenly ending with an ellipsis. "Every day I find myself wanting to send her an e-mail. I want to telephone and remind her of things that happened in Scotland where she was born or in New Jersey or Indiana or Aruba where I took her on her eighteenth birthday—but she's not there—or anywhere. . . ."

Older solitaries do not build castles in the air and starve themselves feeding on the fabulous. They abandon the superfluities of place and expectation. Only strong constitutions support vice. As their muscles wane, the old wax virtuous. They wear soft shoes and baggy trousers. Their blood thins, and solitaries drift into tepid coves sheltered from blustery moral concern. Should strangers appear carrying tablets brazen with personal decalogues, solitaries do quick bunks, finding roosts where they can snooze until the visitors shuffle off searching for people not immune to salvation. Solitaries retire on what they owe. They forsake the open road, and their imaginations hunker down in lowlands. There they build cottages. By their front doors they plant lilies of the field. They don't furnish their dwellings with "truths." They bar thuggish honesty from the threshold and appoint rooms with kindly fictions, most snug and humorous.

They don't read biographies lauding the celebrated and influential. Instead they peruse collections of feathery anecdotes, books that make spirits soar. In W. Pett Ridge's *I Like to Remember*, a book popular with people my age, a crowd gathered around a colorfully zealous street preacher and blocked a thoroughfare in South London. When a constable asked the preacher to move away from the street, the man refused, forcing the constable to arrest him and take him to the court of the local magistrate. The magistrate intended to deal lightly with the preacher. He only wanted to bind him over so he would keep the peace and keep out of the road. Doing so required a surety from one of the man's acquaintances. "Have you a friend?" the magistrate asked. "The Almighty is my friend," the preacher replied. "Yes, yes," the magistrate answered, but "the point is, can you give us the name of a friend living nearby?" "The Almighty is everywhere," the preacher said. "I know that," the magistrate replied patiently, "but I am afraid we shall have to think of someone of more settled habits."

Also found on the bedside tables of solitaries, and never in the libraries of movers and shakers, is W. W. Jacobs's *Salthaven*. An "elderly mariner," Captain

Trimblett boarded at a cottage in Tranquil Vale. Mrs. Chinnery, sister of the Captain's friend Peter, managed the house. Mrs. Chinnery was a stickler for order and schedule. Recently Peter had been late for tea. "For years," Mrs. Chinnery said, "you could have set the clock by him," adding that Peter had been late several days in a row including "yesterday." After clearing his throat and mustering a land lubber's courage, the good Captain tried to explain his friend's tardiness, saying, "He saw a man nearly run over." "Yes: but how long would that take him?" Mrs. Chinnery retorted. "If the man *had* been run over, I could have understood it."

Aging solitaries avoid books that bellow and swell pot-bellied as if spaces between the lines were infested with hairworms. They prefer pundigrions to paradoxes. When Balaam's donkey slipped on pavement and bruised a large metacarpal, Balaam accused the highway department of being lax and not filling potholes. Observers disagreed and said the accident was the ass's phalt. The donkey tried to argue with the bystanders, but they couldn't understand him because he spoke he-bray-ic. In any case the injury was e-femoral, and the next day Balaam was back on the donkey. Memoirs of ruffians and the emotionally disemboweled do not appear on the bookshelves of solitaries. They'd rather read the autobiography of a wren that flies in her sleep than that of a "wide-awake" politician. Best-seller lists strike them as beneath the notice of the light-minded, and they agree with Maurice Baring's criticism in *Punch and Judy*. "Modern literature is like a display of fireworks. The rockets shoot up into the sky, and after they have burst in a splutter of many-colored fires drop onto the ground, mere charred sticks, and attract no further attention." When solitaries read, they often re-read. Forbearance and familiar, kindly pages lead them on to "The End." Fervor and idea masked as originality disturb tranquility, and they prefer patched, tweedy book jackets and smudged, annotated pages to the company of brisk strangers.

"My experience of truth is that it is granular and not solid; a kind of dust or powder," E. V. Lucas wrote in *Cloud and Silver*. "Every one of us has some grains of it; but some have more than others, and some esteem the material more highly than others." Rarely are the "some" who value truth found among the elderly. The aging know that lie-ability enriches life. What appeals to solitaries my age are the doings of fictional characters, not the bloviated machinations of actual people, Charles Farrar Browne's showman from Baldinsville, Indiana, Artemus Ward being an appealing example. When Ward interviewed the Prince of Wales, he didn't bow and flatter. As a result, the Prince liked him, and the interview was memorable. We "sot" and "tawked" about matters and things, Ward reported, until by and by "I axed him how he liked bein a Prince as fur as he'd got." Also appealing to solitaries are eccentrics, especially gentle but firm characters more fictional than real, people who are themselves aged. One of E. V. Lucas's favorites was a professor "who objected on principle to make himself uncomfortable by dressing for dinner." The professor disarmed criticism and propitiated hostesses by assuring them that upstairs in his room "was an excellent dress suit for which he had paid a high price." "If it would be any satisfaction to the company," he said, "his secretary would bring it down and display it."

My compatriots do not attach three-car garages to their cottages. Their kitchen cabinets are not rosewood. The cottages lack wine cellars, home theaters, and koi ponds. None are gun-worshippers. Occasionally one goes off on a toot and returns with a cuckoo clock. In Oregon, their pantry doors frequently open into pig pens, making disposing of and stirring marijuana into slops convenient. Home-grown marijuana is a fine tenderizer. Sold under the label "Food for Tuning Out," Oregon hams are famously tender and are popular with yam-eating vegetarians who shop at Wal-Mart. Outside back doors are small organic gardens. Wired to fences surrounding them are signs advertising produce. Near Eugene a once-splenetic poet now aged into contentment describes his wares lyrically. While one sign reads, "No vegetable can ketchup with my tomatoes," another states, "Lettuce, Pray?" after which follow the words "Yes, amen" and a list of lettuces available, among others romaine, red leaf, arugula, mizuna, and butterhead. Sometimes the man sells "Sheep Dip;" this not an insecticide but a tasty mélange of feta and ricotta cheeses, brandy, onions, pine nuts, and dill. Until three "wellness coaches" recruited him for their weight management team, he also sold a carotid artichoke and spinach dip thick with cholesterol dams, their girders mastications of sour and cream cheese.

Despite inhabiting fictions and tending fictional gardens, elderly solitaries are generally clear and near sighted. Only apprehensive youth bracing for failure reads the last lines of Frost's "The Road Not Taken" as an apologia for courageous individualism—"Two roads diverged in a wood, and I— / I took the one less traveled by, / And that has made all the difference." People my age recognize that the speaker is creating an assuaging autumnal fantasy. The narrator sighs resignedly as he imagines having led a life less conventional. In truth he knows that all travelers tread the same path and experience much the same life no matter the number of times their roads divide. Solitaries understand that to live is to be forgotten. In his memoir of the naturalist Grant Allen, Edward Clodd observed, "Man has short memory of his fellows. A line or two of record is the most that the multitude of those who, 'having served their generation, fell on sleep,' may reckon upon, if they care to reckon at all."

"It takes a silence without and stillness within to overhear the heavenly messages," Oliver St. John Gogarty said in *Intimations*. "The practical mind must be diverted and the ears and eyes thrown out of focus on mundane affairs before we can catch the far-off converse of the Immortals, for they are neither seen nor heard by earthly organs, but perceived only by that within us which is like to them." Numinous chatter is short-hand for inspiration, not an affliction to which the old are susceptible. Completely escaping the mundane is impossible, alas, even for rigorous solitaries, like Abbott, over the hills and far away roaming "Upland and Meadow." No matter my efforts I cannot break from the noisy world. At least once a fortnight the telephone rings and disturbs my sleep. I sit up, reach across the bedside table, and lift the receiver. "Hello," I say, but no voice acknowledges me because the phone rang only in dream. Even worse, when I delete a message on my computer, the machine makes a pinging sound. Now the ping sometimes interrupts my sleep. Moreover, a computer screen flashes through my sight when I hear the ping. At first the screen is bright, almost yellow, but as the sound dies, the screen turns black, and I wake.

Solitaries while days away in their snuggeries, hours ambling past like tatterdemalions rarely Windsor-knotted up to haste. Unless they own a telephone like mine, solitaries sleep soundly at night, not ridden by resentments but "visited by troops of stars." Idleness, Charles Morgan declared in *Reflections in a Mirror*, "is a means of dissolving the clouds with which experience darkens originality. Who has forgotten the idle hours of his childhood before the routine of school engulfed him?" Memory, Baring wrote, "is the greatest of artists," "with careless skill" choosing sights and sounds worth recalling. Memory often begets melancholy. A cool breeze from a far country chills the narrator in *A Shropshire Lad*, awakening wistful sadness. What, the narrator asks, are the blue hills, spires, and farms that he envisions? Eventually he answers his own question, saying, "That is the land of lost content, / I see it shining plain / The happy highways where I went / And cannot come again."

Frequently the melancholy mood is pleasurable, not sad, transporting the solitary from the clang of crowded streets to a quieter, often simpler place and time. Artistic memory shapes place and time, however, making them similar to but not replicas of actual spires and days, hills and years. Nevertheless, if remembrances sink a person leaden toward black depression, he can stir saffron in his tea and his spirits will rise and float, the pharmacology ancient but familiar to solitaries. More often than melancholy, though, memory evokes delicious what-if thoughts. Nature is a cunning nurse, A. G. Gardiner wrote. "She gives us lollipops all the way; and when the lollipop of hope and the lollipop of achievement are done, she gently inserts in our toothless gums the lollipop of remembrance. And with that pleasant vanity we are soothed to sleep." What if I had kissed those girls? What if I had taught in West Africa? What if I had not thought obscurity freeing and admirable? What if I had invested my savings in a terrapin farm? Amid such mulling, *if* often is replaced by *will* or *should*. Anyone who weeps at my funeral, I instructed Vicki, should be asked to decamp and will be expunged from the list of my beneficiaries. In "Dirge," Leigh Hunt put end matters best, "A little sod, a few sad flowers, / A tear for long departed hours, / Is all that feeling hearts request, / To hush their weary thoughts to rest."

According to an old aphorism, for every ten people killed by hard work, idleness kills a hundred, not a testimonial congenial to solitaries or conducive to originality. In describing Dreamthorp, an imaginary village, Alexander Smith wrote, "An idle life I live in this place, as the world counts it; but then I have the satisfaction of differing from the world as to the meaning of idleness. A windmill twirling its arms all day is admirable only where there is corn to grind." Smith didn't grind corn. He ground meditation into the meal of essays. For elderly solitaries, *use*, even grinding out words, is a hedging, imprisoning word. Better it is to copy Abbott; forgo the useful and allow the mind to saunter, all the while imagining swinging one's arms, leaping ditches, and climbing trees.

Busy utilitarians are so serious they often seem hidebound and adolescent, practically incapable of changing their opinions. G. K. Chesterton did not admire seriousness. "I think it irreligious. Or, if you prefer the phrase, it is the fashion of all false religions," he explained. "The man who takes everything seriously is the man who makes an idol of everything: he bows down to wood and stone until his limbs are rooted as the roots of the tree or his head as fallen as the stone sunken by the roadside." Solitaries know that snow melts and permanence is an illusion. They realize that most reforms don't better; they only change. They recognize that lies spring from the ashes of truths. They second John Bright's statement that the only virtue of war is that it teaches people geography. They lament the disappearance of brave and sensible cowards and regret that the word *hero* has become an etiolated commonplace. Solitaries think talents are snares and fear the tyranny of possessions. In the presence of others, they hide their intelligence and display their ignorance. If forced to handle stinging nettles, they wear gloves. Self-manufacture appalls them, and they prefer listening to talking.

Debate about evolution bores them, and without a qualm they accept the theory that the father of monkeykind was a man. They eschew the society of the athletic and never spoil conversations by mentioning ball-and-chain sporting matters. They suspect that women's teeth decay because their lips are sweet. Many solitaries are widowers, and late at night they recall the old mill where they once sat with Nellie Dean.

Solitaries understand that if a person copies the busy bee his thighs will turn yellow and people will think him an imbecile. Storms do not affect their vacations because they always visit Nowhere. If a bear buys the cottage next door, solitaries shave their heads. They are aware that the appearance of a bird with a white breast outside a sickroom means the patient inside will die. Solitaries know that the gaps between law and justice, between virtue and generosity, and between the truths of fact and those of feeling are more cavernous that the gulf separating Dives from Lazarus. A few solitaries are dreamers, but never are they diviners, weather-mongers, or traders in corn-plasters. For that matter, no solitary attaches a grandfather's wisdom tooth to his watch fob. Rarely do solitaries lament losing things they never had. If forced to take bulls by the horns, solitaries choose young, small bulls. Even though they never let reason corrupt their lives, solitaries are sensible and do their bests to avoid the fronts of boars, the backs of mules, and all sides of politicians. Whim, not belief, determines their actions, and they are more playful than serious. Amos and Andy are the only Old Testament prophets whose advice they heed. They recognize that any jackass can talk sense while only the talented can talk micacious nonsense. They know that surroundings determine style and that poems composed in gardens beneath the dip and glide of swallows are happier than those written under trees where flocks of starlings roost. The sound of distant thunder lulls them to sleep while the shrill fluting of tree frogs snaps their thoughts into dance. They avoid wearers of sad gray coats and agree with Josh Billings that men live to ripe old age by keeping green. For heaviness of being, they prescribe tablets of light verse. At Storrs Drugs pharmacists often dole out Carolyn Wells's limericks. Among the most effective and effervescent is, "There was a young fellow named Tait, / Who dined with his girl at 8: 08; / But I'd hate to relate / What that fellow named Tait / And his tête-à-tête ate at 8:08."

For my part my heart takes an aortal bounce when I warble verse like "'Tis Sweet to Roam." "'Tis sweet to roam when the morning's light / Resounds across the deep; / And the crystal song of the woodbine bright / Hushes the rocks to sleep, / And the blood-red moon in the blaze of noon / Is bathed in a crumbling dew, / And the wolf rings out with a glittering shout, / To-whit, to-whit, to-whoo!" After I recite light verse, I don't hear heavenly messages, but I notice greening doings inside and outside my cottage window. Yesterday I ordered a "Corded Telephone for Seniors," the first phone I've ever ordered and one that I hope will not ring in the middle of the night. Last week I noticed a safety pin attached to the top of my friend David's right sock. David does not remove the pin even when he runs. When a pair of socks becomes soiled, he clips them together using the pin and tosses them into the washing machine. "I haven't lost a sock in twenty years," he says. Four days ago a box truck was parked outside the university gymnasium. The box was white; scrolling down the side in strident red letters was "Life Fitness." The back of the truck was open, and a Gothopotamus was unloading exercise machines, his Dunlop rolling over his belt and flopping down on the tailgate.

Two weeks ago Vicki celebrated her sixty-first birthday. Snow was heavy and prevented us from driving to dinner, so we walked to the university food court and bought a "mixed greens" salad and two slices of pepperoni pizza. We brought the food home. Vicki poured herself a glass of Spanish red wine, Flavium Premium; I opened a bottle of Shock Top Belgian white beer, and we ate birthday dinner in the television room. For dessert we watched an episode of "Midsomer Murders," an appealingly frivolous British crime drama, creamy with village life and glazed with eccentric characters. The next morning we raked snow off the roofs of the study and garage then shoveled the drive. Aside from the roaring of snow plows prowling state highways, the day was quiet. "I think I heard a wolf shout," I said leaning on my shovel. "Was it calling to-whit, to-whit, to-whoo?" Vicki asked. "Yes, my orison—cheep happiness, as the sparrow said as he sang in the apple tree," I answered then recited a song from the old musical *The Maid of the Mountains*, "Sing hey! Sing ho! / There's no time like the present! / Sing ho! Sing hey! / There's no time like today."

And that is enough about solitude; I'm going into the bedroom, shut the door, and take a nap. Vicki says that one of her fictional characters Hank Nuffertort may come to see me. I want to be alone, and if Hank raps on the door, I'll pretend not to hear him. Hank is a sausage maker. His most popular sausage is made from horse meat, guaranteed, he claims, "to corral nightmares and break them to trace and crupper fork so you can harness your dreams and drive them to church looking just as respectable as the parson." Rarely are university teachers eccentric. Outside the invisible walls of academic conformity, however, lurks a carnival. After my nap, I am going to think about Cyriak Pepper, a local man who died recently.

Pepper farmed two hundred hilly acres eleven miles from Storrs. He owned a flock of pedigreed Blue Texel sheep, supposedly the best Texels in the United States. What interested Pepper more than aristocratic ruminants and the destruction of which contributed to his death was topiary. For years he clipped and trained yews into startling shapes. At one time he was ringmaster of a circus composed of miniature animals, an elephant, two camels, and a tiger, among others. On holidays teachers in the Eastford and Ashford elementary schools made sardine sandwiches for students and took their classes to Pepper's farm. After looking at the circus, the children petted lambs and fed the crusts of their sandwiches to ewes, sardines being the only meat eaten by Texels, a liking probably picked up while the breed evolved near the North Sea on Holland's West Frisian Islands. Pepper always gave the children soft drinks and all-day suckers. He was gentle and so kind that one little girl dubbed him "an angel in sheep's clothing," a phrase that clung to him tight as a fleece.

Eventually, Pepper became bored and chopped the circus down. To replace the circus, Pepper fashioned a biblical panorama. He clipped Adam and Eve into life, turning them into farmers, dressing Adam in overalls and Eve in a loose cotton shift, putting a shovel in Adam's hand and a frying pan in Eve's. Among many other scenes, he sheared a single yew into a clump of bulrushes surrounding the wicker basket into which Yocheved placed her baby Moses. Pepper's best carving was Satan the serpent. Satan was twenty feet long and stretched through five or six yew bushes. Pepper lovingly embroidered his creation, giving the snake arms and wings. He was particularly proud of the apple he "placed" in Satan's left hand. To prevent deer from eating his creations, Pepper wrapped fencing around the panorama. In December, unfortunately, a storm toppled a huge oak. The tree smashed the fence, and before Pepper could rewire it, deer reduced Adam and Eve to naked twigs, felled the Tower of Babel, flattened the Great Pyramid, gnawed the kernels off Ruth's ear of alien corn transforming it into a sterile cob, and shrank Satan to a garter snake, rendering him earthbound by chewing his legs away and nibbling the wings off his back. Even worse, a buck ate the apple out of Satan's hand. Pepper was old. He couldn't bear the damage, and he died shortly after the storm, telling his niece, "I could stand anything but losing the apple. It was a Devonshire Quarrenden sweet as a strawberry. Nowadays you don't see those in Connecticut." Oh, well, goodness me—writers are odd because, as the saying puts it, tales spring out of their heads. In any case, according to H. G. Wells, "to stop writing is the secret of writing an essay." "The essay that the public loves dies young."

Two Kinds

"All things considered, there are only two kinds of men in the world," Kipling wrote, "those that stay at home and those that do not. The second are the most interesting." Taking travel seriously is difficult. No matter the distance a person travels, he will never be quit of himself. On returning home, he will discover old habits clinging to him like a backpack. I'd rather hear no-necked announcers on sports television give a card-by-bid running account of a game of bridge than listen to a well-traveled raconteur describe an interesting life. Such lives are always suspect and relentlessly ordinary. Whenever a man states that he has led "a mighty adventurous life," Heywood Hale Broun scoffed, "We usually set him down as a former king of the Coney island carnival or a recently returned delegate from an Elks' convention in Kansas City."

"Most of us desire to live vividly and variously," Walter de la Mare wrote seriously and analytically. We pine for the curious and the bizarre, but "we return to find our peace in the familiar and the near." "Merely to be alive," de la Mare stated, "is adventure enough in a world like this, so erratic and disjointed; so lovely and so odd and mysterious and profound." During his youth Leslie Stephen was a pioneering mountaineer and a legendary adventurer. Two years before his death, he descended to recollection's flatter lands and wrote an essay celebrating walking. He said his days were bound together by "pedestrian enthusiasm," explaining, "if I turn over the intellectual album which memory is always compiling, I find that the most distinct pictures which it contains are those of old walks." "Among recreations," walking, he elaborated, was "what ploughing and fishing are among industrial labors." Because walking was "primitive and simple," it brought people into contact "with mother earth and unsophisticated nature." Moreover, walking required "no elaborate apparatus and no extraneous excitement." Walking was favorable, he said, "to the equable and abundant flow of tranquil and half-conscious meditation," suitable to the man "who desires not absolutely to suppress his intellect but to turn it out to play for a season."

"Quotations are often a bore," Henry Nevinson said, "but in thinking of books they come flooding the mind." In high school I memorized Tennyson's "Ulysses." At the time I thought the poem a golden call to life. I did not dream of smiting sounding furrows or sailing beyond the sunset. Nevertheless,

I dreamed. I thought Ulysses heroic. Now I think him damnably selfish shucking duty and fleeing responsibility, particularly for Penelope, his "aged wife" who, if she resembled the wives and husbands of countless friends, was slipping into dementia. Tennyson's Ulysses was not a man of deeds but a creature of those lesser, flimsy things—words. On Sunday I received an e-mail from an old friend in Illinois who has nursed his wife for a decade. My correspondent was eighty-two. Instead of decamping, justifying his actions by wrapping rhythm and fine sound around selfishness, declaiming that he wanted to seek a newer world and sail beyond the baths of the western stars, my friend remained at home. He mastered heartbreak and the self and devoted his days to his "aged wife." Sally, he wrote, "no longer understands language. Two summers ago while sitting on the patio having breakfast, I pointed to the sky, the grass, the garage, my hand, and asked her what each was called. She couldn't say, but when I asked, 'Where's the sky, where's your hand, where's the garage?' she pointed at them. She knew language but couldn't command it. Now she no longer recognizes things when I say them. If I say 'Put your shoes on' or 'Go downstairs,' she looks at me without comprehension. But she still says 'I love you' and 'Thank you,' just about the only sentences she can say, to everybody who speaks to her, no matter what they say. And I mean everybody: a waiter, a clerk in a store, people in church, a stranger walking her dog—every person she meets. Those two sentences and her radiant smile have made her the most popular person in our church. People coming down the aisle to go to communion never greet friends sitting in the pews, but they often say something to Sally and pat her, and me, on the back."

The attitudes and thoughts of youth differ greatly from those of age. "We are creatures of fleeting circumstance and the difference between old and young," Eden Phillpotts wrote in *From the Angle of 88*, "is that, while my generation retains memory of bygone, gracious additions to life, when liberty allowed them to delight us and the old paths were good to tread, the young have never trodden those paths and know of no other road than the dusty highway under their feet. They travel forward, these lawful heirs of the future, and find it promising enough to waken courage and keep hope high; but the legacies of the past do not win their gratitude and they set small value on much that we still believe to be precious." As a youth I was too far down the highway exuberantly kicking up dust and seeing mirages to read or listen to a Phillpotts. Now I am old and rarely wander from traditional paths. I think manners more important than ideas, and small habit rules my days like a tyrant. I am what programmatic idealists call a "hetero-patriarchal caucasoid."

But I am not yet eighty-eight, and even today when successfully retrieving a fallen object from the floor is cause for silent huzzahs, Phillpotts's statement seems stuffy. More to my liking is a paragraph written by Ronald Knox. In *Memoirs for the Future* Knox sparred with critics who celebrated the past at the expense of the future. "We do ill," he wrote, "if we fail in veneration for the future—rather, we do impiously, for we begat it, and it is of our blood. The man, the nation that can sneer at unborn loves and unborn enthusiasms is, as if a father should kick his son downstairs, unnatural."

As a boy I did not consider myself a lawful heir of the future. Aside from happy vagrancy I dreamed about matters less legal. I recited Gerald Gould's "Wander-Thirst," the last two lines of which I still recall, "And come I may, but go I must, and if men ask you why / You may put the blame on the stars and the sun and the white road and the sky." I read biographies of explorers, listened to lies about the Civil War, and knew anthologies of neglected verse. I specialized in the romantic, this stanza, for example, from "The Death Feud. An Arab War Song": "Terrible he rode alone, / With his Yemen sword for aid; / Ornament it carried none, / But the notches on the blade." Mungo Park, Captain Cook, Charles Waterton, and *Hammond's Complete World Atlas* were my companions. I saw the golden domes of Samarkand and visited Zenobia's Palmyra. I knew that geography did not matter when two strong men stood face to face despite coming from opposite ends of the earth. I was an only child and had wonderful, loving parents. I did not mind losing my life, but I didn't want to destroy their happiness, so I resisted imagining myself Richard Burton traveling to Mecca disguised as an Afghan physician. Eventually I got to Bukhara, but I wasn't dressed as a dervish like Arminius Vambéry. Still, even now romantic thoughts sometimes disturb my sleep, especially after I've eaten a platter of wild onions at dinner. On these bilious occasions just before dawn when the night turns sapphire, I imagine accompanying Peter III of Aragon when he climbed Canigou in the Pyrenees eight hundred years ago. Pete was left-handed, and I stood on his right side when he threw a rock into the lake at the top of the mountain. The splash awakened a dragon that burst from the water and raged across the sky, his breath dark as a storm, sparks sizzling through it like stars.

"At twenty," James Russell Lowell wrote in *Fireside Travels*, "the eye is sufficiently delighted with merely seeing; new things are pleasant because they are not old; and we take everything heartily and naturally in the right way, for even mishaps are like knives, that either serve us or cut us, as we grasp them by the blade or the handle. After thirty, we carry along our scales, with lawful weights stamped by experience, and our own chemical tests acquired by study, with which to ponder and assay all arts, institutions, and manners, and to ascertain either their absolute worth or their merely relative value to ourselves." At twenty I had not travelled far from my fireside. A decade later, I had wandered but at an eddying pace like the stream that wound through Margaret Barber's prose and years. "Running water has a charm all its own," she wrote in *The Roadmender*; "it proffers companionship of which one never tires; it adapts itself to moods; it is the guardian of secrets; it has cool draughts for the thirsty soul as well as for the drooping flowers." Occasionally a story narrows the passage of life, and for a wrist of time, words gather and splash rapidly and seductively. Recently I read about and almost hankered for a death similar to that of W. P. Ker. Ker was a distinguished British academic. He was a fellow of All Souls for more than forty years and the first holder of the Quain Chair of English at University College London. He died in 1923 at sixty-seven. He had just reached the summit of Pizzo Bianco in the Pennine Alps. He collapsed after gazing at the surrounding mountains and saying, "I thought this was the most beautiful spot in the world; now I know it is."

For me Ruskin's, and indeed Ker's, "Mountain Glory" is morning glory. I've never climbed a tall mountain, but I have planted morning glories. Ker's last words are romantic. Moreover, being surrounded by a halo of mountains disappearing topless into clouds is certainly more appealing than drifting into night in a hospice, monitors flashing beside one's head and drips channeling liquid into one's arms, catheters draining it out. Still, to people my age thoughts of morning glories are more congenial than last words that unfurl like battle flags. Unlike the picturesque, morning glories grow in poor soil, giving the dry and the aged hope that they, too, can still bloom and create. The runners of morning glories weave green hearts through trellises and over backyard fences, then burst into crescendos of blossoms shaping small sublimes. Sight of the blooms elevates the spirits, not just on a single occasion after an exhausting heart-throbbing hike but throughout an ordinary summer. When I look out the kitchen window and see the flowers, my mood lifts. No longer does the breakfast of granola and vitamins, bananas and mysterious pills that I eat every day appear unutterably dreary.

A. C. Benson once wrote that the best stories in the world were "but one story in reality—the story of an escape." How to escape, Benson said, was "the only thing" that interested all people at all times. The mind, he said, instinctively disliked stasis. "An existence in which there was nothing to escape from, nothing more to hope for, to learn, to desire" would be "unendurable." If broadly considered, every moment is an escape from the previous moment. From that perspective, life is a journey without pauses or way-stations, and people are always escaping. Stripping away the differences between two things makes the things the same, however, reducing Kipling's two types of men, the one who travels and the one who stays at home, to the same person. Correspondingly, an empty bathtub and one overflowing with fire ants are both tubs. The difference becomes screamingly apparent, however, when a person hops into the latter tub. Benson's view of story is reductive. Rather than labeling all stories escapes and damning the comparatively stationary, perhaps one should acknowledge that the quiet immobility of the homebound is often more interesting than the frenetic shifting of the traveler.

Many youthful hankerings for adventure smack of playground euphoria, loud and distasteful with the squeal of slide and swing set. "We flung our hats, our 'sheep skins' we flaunted in air; our college days were ended!" the Hook brothers announced in 1876 at the start of *Through Dust and Foam: or Travels, Sight-seeing, and Adventure by Land and Sea in the Far West and Far East.* "Many a time we had sat over our Latin and Greek as the rattling cars went galloping westward over the prairies, and thought, ere our lesson was finished, that train would be out among the scampering buffalo of the plains. We longed to be there, too." The beginnings of many nineteenth-century travel books are so poetic they seem not only swollen and proud but also emotionally gangrenous. In *Around the World on Sixty Dollars*, Robert Meredith wrote, "Life is a sea shore along which we walk and look with longing eyes far away where sky and billows meet, wondering what there is in the great beyond; what blessings lie in wait for those who sail away beyond the horizon." "There is a longing in every human breast," he continued, "to break the bonds of the little circle where earth and sky meet and look into the great beyond."

Despite hymnology like that of Meredith, Charles Whibley thought adventure had leached from "modern travel," stating that the unexpected no longer happened. Traveling, Charles Brooks wrote in 1915, had fallen "to the yellow leaf." Once a long while ago, when life was frequently compared to a journey, Brooks stated, "Wise men rejoiced to question old men because like travelers, they knew the sloughs and roughness of the road." By Brooks's time the figure of speech had atrophied. Brooks said that his contemporaries did not think of their lives as arduous, testing and teaching journeys rich with sunrises, hot noons, and cool evenings. Instead they discussed life and movement in terms of railway time tables. "We leave and arrive at places," he wrote, "but we no longer travel." "Wise men have ceased to question travelers, except to inquire of the arrival of trains and of the comfort of hotels."

Today most travel, even a trip made for the page, is tourism or holiday-making. For Holbrook Jackson, where or when a person went and what he did on arriving were insignificant. The only thing that mattered was not excitement or adventure but change, "the break from the monotony of routine." After their breaks, many people, I suspect, embrace routine with gusto. "What more charming spectacle is to be found than that of a group of sunburnt, bare-legged children making mud pies upon the beach?" Harry Graham wrote in describing a seaside holiday. "How delightful it is to see the little ones enjoying themselves so innocently! Paterfamilias is sleeping gracefully in the center of the castle which his darlings have erected around him, while every now and then baby fills his ears with sand, or little Horace cunningly excavates a channel up which the incoming tide may be directed into his unsuspecting parent's new brown boots."

For Edwin Muir, in contrast, inactivity and routine were boons to thought. The great danger that confronted people who renounced leisure, he wrote, was that they would "become shallow." "Extreme *busyness*," Robert Louis Stevenson said, "is a sign of deficient vitality; and a faculty for idleness implies a catholic appetite and a strong sense of personality." "To sit still with dignity and composure is as difficult as to move with ease and grace," Joseph Clay Neal wrote. "Good listeners," he said, "are rarities. When they die, they should have monuments loftier far than that of Cheops." Rarely do travelers learn to distance themselves from the stir of immediate thoughts and feelings. Charles Colton thought the intellectual benefits of travel were suspect. He believed knowledge acquired by travel was bought too dearly. "The traveler," he argued, "may be said to fetch knowledge, as the merchant the wares, to be enjoyed and applied by those who stay at home." "A man may sit by his own fireside, be conversant with many domestic arts and general sciences, and yet have very correct ideas of the manners and customs of other nations. While on the contrary, he that has spent his whole life in traveling," Colton continued, and who "has made his legs his compasses, rather than his judgment, may live and die a thorough novice in the most important concerns of life." A man, he stressed, "may have been round the world, and over the world, without having been in the world, and die an ignoramus." No matter the appeal of travel, Charles Dudley Warner noted, "the better part of the life of man is in and by the imagination."

The uneventful life is endlessly eventful. In January an old woman cried tellingly in my presence. Her daughter and son were moving her into a smaller apartment, one more convenient and safer than the flat in which she now lived. "They love me and have my best interests at heart," she wept, "but moving will force me to abandon many of my possessions. I have had some things since before I was married. They are my memories, and I can't bear to lose them." "Last week my father had eight biopsies on his prostate, and my mother is blind and has begun to suffer from vertigo. They live in Florida, and I don't know how I can cope with their problems. It is just too much," a middle-aged woman lamented in the Mansfield Library. That night I started reading *The Life of John Buncle, Esq.* published in 1756. Lachrymose octogenarian doings in Connecticut and Florida paled when compared to the denouement of Buncle's courtship of Miss Harriot Noel. "When I thought myself within a fortnight of being married to Miss NOEL and thereby made completely happy in every respect as it was possible for a mortal man to be," Buncle recounted, "the smallpox step'd in, and in seven days time, reduced the finest human frame in the universe to the most hideous and offensive block. The most amiable of human creatures mortified all over, and became a spectacle of the most hideous and appalling." The sight broke the hearts of Buncle and of Miss Noel's father. For her part Miss Harriot died within a month at age twenty-four, sinking the "paradise" Buncle "had in view" into "everlasting night."

As a person ages, "memento mori" become "memento risibles." On Tuesday my friend Josh returned from seeing a graduate school roommate. The man taught American history at Ohio University. What started as a visit for old time's sake became a visit for end time. While Josh and his roommate were walking across the campus to Brown House, home of the Contemporary History Institute, the man had a heart attack, collapsed, and died. Josh tried to save him with cardiopulmonary resuscitation but failed. What Josh did accomplish was neatening the scene. The man fell on a sidewalk. The force of the fall broke open the man's backpack and scattered its contents. Most of the contents were conventional, and Josh pushed them back in the bag: a history textbook entitled *Creating America*, the Owner's Manual for the new 2013 Hyundai sedan, and the latest issue of the *Economist*, on the front of which appeared a Russian tank, a bare-chested gunner looming above the turret hatch. Also in the backpack was a selection of candy: a box of Necco chocolate wafers, two Milky Ways, a Baby Ruth, and an O, Henry! Josh gathered the candy and dropped it into the back pack, all except the O, Henry! bar. "I couldn't resist the caramel. I was a bundle of nerves, and I thought the sugar might settle me," Josh said, "so I ate the O, Henry!" Josh also scooped up and into a zippered pocket on the side of the bag stuffed a handful of ballpoint pens, a packet of Kleenex, his friend's reading glasses, and a plastic pill container filled with statins used to treat high cholesterol.

People whom we assume we know are always more various than we think. Josh's friend was a lifelong Democrat who loathed all things and all people

Republican. "Or so I thought," Josh reported, "until I discovered Ronald Reagan's autobiography, *An American Life*, among the books." Not only were the pages well-thumbed, but Reagan had signed the copy. Clara, the man's wife, was a fiery socialist. In order to have a say about local matters, she registered in Ohio as a Democrat and later had been elected to the town council. "Because seeing the book would have upset Clara," Josh said, "I stole it when nobody was looking. Later I dropped it into a recycle bin on campus." Josh also filched another book, a paperback copy of *The Perfumed Garden*, the famous Arab sex manual translated into English by Richard Burton in the nineteenth century. "I always thought Clara repressed," Josh said shaking his head, "but after finding the *Garden* I don't know what to think. If I weren't married, I'd be tempted to console her two weeks from now when she's no longer wearing black."

Neither Clara nor her husband was the retiring person Josh remembered. Clearly his friend had read and re-read the *Garden*, marking pages with check marks and underlining phrases, even highlighting sentences with a yellow Sharpie. "I couldn't let a stranger, even worse, a student, find the book. My roommate was a beloved teacher and a respected scholar. If people learned that he carried *The Perfumed Garden* to class every day, his reputation would have been ruined, so I crammed the book into my jacket pocket and brought it back to Connecticut." Josh then extracted the book from his satchel and read a few ripe selections aloud. Among the chapters that his friend had annotated, writing "oh, yes" and drawing exclamation marks beside them in the margins, was "Concerning the Causes of Enjoyment in the Act of Generation." "A man who would wish to acquire vigor for coition may," Josh read, "melt down fat from the hump of a camel, and rub his member with it just before the act; it will then perform wonders, and the woman will praise it for its work." Also efficacious was rubbing the "virile member" with asses' milk and the gall of a jackal. "You won't find those drugs on the erectile dysfunction shelf of CVS," Josh said, closing the book. "Only health food stores sell them."

Sunday morning Vicki and I went to the Willimantic Co-op. In the parking lot Vicki found two dimes. "This is our lucky day," she said. In the cooperative we met Josh. Rarely is Josh lugubrious, and the trip to Ohio had slipped from conversation. "You won't believe this," he said seizing us both by the hands and leading us to a shelf stacked high with "Seventh Generation" toilet paper. Printed on the packages was "100 % Recycled Bathroom Tissue." "What sort of person buys recycled toilet paper?" Josh exclaimed. "I wouldn't purchase a roll even if the Dalai Lama was the last person to use it." Also stamped on the wrapper was the statement "No Added Dyes or Fragrance."

"That's meant to reassure," I said when Josh read the phrase aloud. "Reassure, my behind!" he answered. "What's wrong with a little unnatural fragrance in the outhouse?" The next line on the wrapper was "Made in Canada with Imported Materials." "Ye Gods," Josh said. "Never tailgate a tanker truck going to Canada by way of Niagara Falls and the Whirlpool Bridge. Think of the environmental catastrophe that would occur if you smashed into the rear of the trailer and ruptured its tank. The spillage would contaminate the Niagara River and turn Lake Erie into a septic settling basin." Before I could respond, Josh changed the subject and recited an old rhyme that he'd "excavated." Because puns seasoned the verse, he said I'd "love it." "A farmer called his cow Zephyr, / She seemed such an amiable hephyr. / When the farmer drew near, / She kicked off his ear, / And now the old farmer's much dephyr." "You were right," I said to Vicki as we left the grocery. "This is our lucky day. What cheer!" "Maybe," Vicki answered. "Maybe this afternoon," I replied, "we'll see a dragon or meet a woman with braids of green hair."

I would like to wander Paestum and Petra, Taormina, Rhodes and Chichen-Itza. To experience stony ruins, however, I need only roam the woodlands around Storrs. Broken dams and spillways stretch arthritic like claws across small rivers. Along banks mills rise and totter battered and pocked, losing stones. Single and double wall fences waver through forests that were once fields. Foundation holes and root cellars gape half-filled with moldy leaves, and cobble rises bald in the corners of old fields. I don't have to visit sand-strewn Persepolis or Coba and sweltering Mexico to mull the teachings of ruins. Perhaps the wreckage of hopes and farms consoles people, illustrating that everything, both great and small, eventually falls and vanishes. Maybe people who explore forests come to understand that their failures and triumphs are inconsequential, an awareness that is both freeing and comforting. After the last time Vicki and I walked in the woods, we experienced a real, local adventure, one of our own shaping. At Dog Lane Café we bought Senior Cups of coffee. We paid a dollar each for the coffee and considered sharing a piece of key lime pie. A slice, however, cost $7.50. Each pie, Vicki observed, was cut into fourteen slices, making the price of a whole pie $105. "An absurdity," she said, reaching into her backpack and extracting a prune paczki, which she bought that morning at Big Y for ninety-nine cents. Along the lip of the table, we build a cloth wall of coats and backpacks. Vicki divided the paczki, and leaning over we ate it behind the wall, sheltered, we hoped, from the manager's vision. "This is exciting," Vicki said. "Suppose the manager sees what we are doing. What will he say?" "I don't know," I answered, "but we better eat quickly."

The past attracts homebodies more than the future. For such people the past is not lifeless but teeming, even tempestuous. E. V. Lucas was never tempted to lash himself to a pole in order to hear the Sirens, but as a child he recited and didn't forget the quatrain, "The horse bit his master. / How came it to pass? / He heard the good pastor / Say, 'All flesh is grass.'" Edward Clodd, the British banker and sometime anthropologist, was not compelled to travel north of the Caucasus or into Anatolia to experience Cimmerian darkness. In childhood, religion taught him, he recalled in *A Fragment of Autobiography*, to "fear the Lord, the object being to frighten me into being good." Even for venial sins, he was threatened with "eternal hell." "As for heaven the attractive prospect to a high-spirited boy was of a place 'Where congregations ne'er break up, / And Sabbaths have no end.'" The wholesome zest that he said he felt in every limb was "stifled by the maudlin Sunday school hymn—'I want to be an angel, / And with the angels stand, / A crown upon my forehead, / And a harp within my hand.'"

Andrew Lang didn't have to scale the Carpathian Mountains to bring Romany life to mind. He had only to recite a chorus of howling doggerel. The verse described the abandonment of a sick gypsy. "There we leave her, / There we leave her, / Far from where her swarthy kindred roam, / In the Scarlet Fever, / Scarlet Fever, / Scarlet Fever Convalescent Home." Memories of childhood reading are often weepy, a goodly percentage of them with tears of laughter. When he was a boy, Maurice Francis Egan read an account describing the life of Saint Rose of Lima. Because St. Rose grew up in South America, Egan hoped swashbuckling violence would fill a page or two. Egan was disappointed. "So pure was the little saint, even in her infancy," he read, "that when her uncle, who was her godfather, kissed her after her baptism, a rosy glow, a real blush of shame, overspread her countenance."

A person does not have to visit Rome or Barcelona and be distracted by harpies brandishing infants in order to feel hands picking his pocket. To experience felonious, exotic groping, one need only to answer the telephone or open e-mail. Every week I learn that I can buy prescription drugs for a fraction of the price I pay the drugstore. So many universities are eager to award academic credits for my life experiences that I can earn a rack of degrees without hoisting myself out of bed except to write tuition or, better non-tuition, checks. For $4,999, reduced as a special favor for me from $9,999, I can purchase a "Timeless" watch. Turning a crown on the left side of the watch slows time; turning a crown on the right side speeds time, "putting you in control of your life," a flyer states. A socially concerned Samaritan informs me that my credit rating has changed, "a fact that I am sure is extremely important to you," while another benevolent bastard assures me I can become a professional project manager almost without opening my eyes, simply by loosening the threads binding my wallet.

If Adam had not bitten the scarlet pippin, Kipling would not have divided men into two social kinds. All people would have been homebodies. Travel is a bacterial species of work and as such would not have existed had the snake not wormed into Eve's favor. If man had built a permanent home not a handy-man's special in Eden, generations would have strolled leisurely and peacefully through the centuries. "Adventures are to the adventuresome and discovery for the discoverer," W. P. James wrote. Not a single discoverer or adventurer lived in Eden before the apple tree blossomed. Man would not have become ambitious and hitched his wagon to wandering. He would have sheared sheep instead of fleecing people. Time blinkers the memory, however, and the ringing grooves of change cause dizziness. "The Anglo-Saxon race," Robert Lowell noted in exasperation, "has accepted the primal curse as a blessing, has deified work, and would not have thanked Adam for abstaining from the apple."

Kipling's people who stay at home generally treat work as a minor deity and are more content than travelers trudging across the far away. The happy person, Philip Gilbert Hamerton argued, "is satisfied with the present as the present and does not feel that any important change is urgent. The anticipation of future change may overshadow or it may brighten his present happiness, but he looks upon it in either case as remote and is not anxious to bring it about." If forced to choose between old and new, even if I understood the new, I'd choose the old. In part I like the sound of *old* better. It rolls and doesn't bite like *new*, making my nose wrinkle when I pronounce it. Moreover, I resemble the Mary Russell Mitford of *Belford Regis*. I am wondrously happy inhabiting an old world populated by antique people and appointed with aged things. "The world is divided into two great empires of habit and novelty; the young following pretty generally in the train of the new-fangled sovereign, whilst we of an elder generation adhere with similar fidelity to the *ancien regime*," Mitford wrote. "I, especially, am the very bond-slave of habit—love old friends, old faces, old books, old scenery, old flowers, old associations of every sort and kind—nay, although a woman, and one not averse to that degree of decoration which belongs to the suitable and the becoming, I even love old fashions and old clothes."

If Ulysses had remained in Ithaca, he would have stopped imagining the "untravell'd world." He would not have rusted "unburnish'd," but would have discovered interests—common duties and offices of tenderness. Maybe he would have grown beyond being yet another politician endlessly shouting bombastically about thunder and sunshine, dark broad seas, free hearts, and the right to pack pistols in churches. Old books and threadbare scenery would have made his heart leap. He would have donated his togas to the Salvation Army and started wearing blue jeans. He would have braked when he saw a squirrel scampering in front of his car. At cocktail parties he would not have stultified guests by telling stretchers about his college roommate Achilles. When he read about a tornado at breakfast, he wouldn't have looked over the top of the newspaper, snorted dismissively, and described the gales that swept the windy plains of Troy lifting tents and scattering them like leaves.

One day he might have joined Vicki and me at Dog Lane. Moreover, the palace pâtissier would have baked a key lime pie for him to bring to the café. We'd drink coffee sweetened with ambergris and eat the whole pie without being noticed by the manager. Afterward, we'd be bilious and sit immobile until, as the expression puts it, peaches became pumpkins. To while away indigestion we would audit the conversations of people sitting at nearby tables. We'd hear the beginnings and middles of "the damnedest stories." "No puns, no ailments, no grotesque deaths, and, for heaven's sake, no robust medicinals," Vicki would say, has said, and will say again. "I'm not going on a trip any time soon, but I'm younger than you, and my ears are good enough to catch whiffs of life beyond dictionaries and nursing homes." Alas, I know Ulysses would have liked the story about the woman who reported her husband's death to the coroner. "Oh, dear, what did he die of?" the coroner asked, picking up his pen. "Nothing in particular—just plain death," the woman answered. By the by I am sure Ulysses would appreciate my bringing him linguistically up to date and out of the rosy-fingered dawn and winged-words era, explaining that *alas* and *shucks* were sentence connectors and synonyms, both being euphemisms for "Oh, hell," the second a regional variant popular in the Copperhead Highlands.

Fate determined the course of Ulysses's life, and he would have certainly been intrigued by the role coincidence played in the lives of a Storrs couple, Lysander and Lydia Balmford. By coincidence they married at the same church on the same day and ten months later became parents of the same child on the same morning at the same time. Because Ulysses himself was old, the account of an elderly man's visiting a newly-minted doctor for a prostate examination might not have appealed to him. "Doctor," the man said, just before the exam began, "Doctor, I wish you would use two fingers." "What," the doctor replied, "What do you mean two fingers? Why?" "Well, doctor," the man answered, "I always like a second opinion."

In truth I hear all sorts of things, especially when voices don't rise into hullabaloos of syllables. Last Thursday I overheard three people trying to name the horses ridden by movie cowboys. They remembered the Lone Ranger's Silver, Gene Autry's Champion, Roy Rogers's Trigger, and Dale Evans's Buttermilk. They even recalled that Red Ryder rode Thunder and Tom Mix, Tony, the Wonder Horse. But they could not recollect the horse ridden by Hopalong Cassidy. "Topper," I said leaning over their table, "Hoppy rode Topper." I could have added a little buck to their musings by naming a herd of other horses, particularly horses ridden by generals during the Civil War—Grant's Cincinnati, Jackson's Little Sorel, and John Morgan's Black Bess, among stalls of others—but I remained silent. "The men were trotters, not gallopers," I told Vicki later, "and I didn't want to unseat their conversation, so to speak."

I Am Not Unhappy—Part One

In 1990 after reading one of my books, Lockert wrote me. I answered the letter. We became epistolary friends, and for two decades we corresponded, writing three times a year. In June Lockert sent me what he announced as his final letter. He was ninety-one years old. "I am still living after several visits to the hospital," he recounted. "They have diagnosed a fatal illness but they won't tell me when I will die." Only twelve lines long, Lockert's letter was as short as the time he thought he had left to live. "I have enjoyed our correspondence over the years," Lockert concluded, "good-bye." Age had shackled Lockert as it does all the long-lived. At other times of life, place and circumstance manacle people. In the poem "I stumbled into their net of dust," Charles Rossiter wrote, "All those gleaming buildings / that fill the city don't matter, but I stumbled, I admit, / unguided, into that world / I could not call my own."

"These beauteous forms / Through a long absence, have not been to me / As is a landscape to a blind man's eye," Wordsworth wrote in "Tintern Abbey." "But, oft, in lonely rooms, and 'mid the din / Of towns and cities, I have owed to them / In hours of weariness sensations sweet, / Felt in the blood, and felt along the heart; / And passing even into my purer mind / With tranquil restoration." Wordsworth had not seen Tintern Abbey for five years. Both the recollections that quieted the abrasive fret of town life and the landscape that Wordsworth called his own after returning to Yorkshire were fictional, shaped by longing and living. "I've wasted many precious years. Now I'm coming home," a weary everyman sings in the gospel song "Coming Home." In the song home is heaven. Like Wordsworth's abbey, heaven is imagined, not shaped by time and circumstance but an eternal place of healing and restoration.

Experience shapes perception and dream, eventually making all the places into which one stumbles familiar, and to emend Rossiter, even turning heaven into one's own. In Jerome K. Jerome's *Tea-Table Talk*, a minor poet, a Girton girl, an old maid, and a philosopher, among others, whiled away an afternoon mulling a silver service of topics: tartlets, scones, crescents, and intellectual asparagus sandwiches. Among the shortbreads was a discussion of love letters. The philosopher suggested examining love letters written by different admirers to the same correspondent. "It would be interesting to observe the response of the various temperaments exposed to an unvaried influence. It would throw light on the vexed question whether the qualities that adorn our beloved are her own, or ours lent to her for the occasion." One person might address her, the philosopher speculated, as "My Queen" while another might call her his "Dear Popsy Wopsy." "Let philosophers reason and differ about the chief good or happiness of man; let them find it where they can, and place it where they please; but there is no mistake so gross or opinion so impertinent," William Temple wrote, "as to think that pleasures arise from what is without us, rather than what is within; from the impression given us of objects, rather than from the disposition of the organs that receive them."

Surroundings are the scuffed tablets on which imagination draws and erases. Some days when I roam the university campus, I envision a grand opera of trees, not woodwinds of cambium and phloem but instead Teutonic and Wagnerian white oaks, candelabras of tulip trees flickering orange like *Cosi Fan Tutte*, copper beeches dank and tearful as the stony vault beneath *Aida*'s Temple of Vulcan, and then tricolor beeches, witty in pink and green, off to drink Champagne with Prince Orlofsky in *Die Fledermaus*. When lindens bloom, bees sizzle around them gayer than the bohemians in *La Boheme*. On other days, the weedy strut the stage, alder thickets and brambly blackberry, oriental bittersweet and autumn olive. To me they seem Shakespeare's mechanicals, Doll Tearsheet and Ancient Pistol, their canes producing sweet fruit good for fallen humans and sheltering the nests of robins and warblers.

"Today as I was reading in the garden," Gissing's Henry Ryecroft stated, "a waft of summer perfume—some hidden link of association in what I read—I know not what it may have been—took me back to schoolboy holidays." Fragrance, Louise Beebe Wilder thought, spoke "more clearly" to age than to youth. "With the young it may not pass much beyond the olfactory nerve, but with those who have started down the far side of the hill it reaches into the heart." The perfume of mimosa is powdery and light, and drifting through it carries me back to my grandfather's farm in Hanover, Virginia. I ascend Wilder's hill and slid into childhood, the way soothed by sentimental association. Across the sandy drive running past my grandmother's kitchen grew my mimosa. As a boy I was uncoordinated, and the mimosa was the only tree I managed to climb. Often I dozed mornings away perched in a tripod of branches. After rains I searched for tree frogs. On warm afternoons I watched fence lizards sunning themselves on stumps and rocks and buzzards riding thermals, spinning and wobbling like tops. I spent much time pondering, always simple matters, things that adults thought odd but that interested me. One long evening I wondered if Jesus owned any toys when he was a child—metal tanks, plastic half-tracks, and lead soldiers, most unpainted but among them a troop of Royal Bengal Lancers, English Assyrians, their horses pawing the air, bridles gleaming like gold. Did he have braces of cap pistols and a bow and arrows, these last with rubber stoppers at the tips? Did he have spangled chaps and cowboy boots with diamonds stitched across the toes? Did he play canasta with his grandmother, and did he ever lose? What was his favorite stuffed animal? My Nurse Jane Fuzzy Wuzzy, Uncle Wiggily's muskrat housekeeper, was kinder and warmer than any creature loitering about a manger.

Did he read books, and was there a children's hour in the carpenter's shop? Did either of his two fathers read him stories about Uncle Remus, Brer Rabbit, the Tarbaby, the Fox, and Miss Meadows and the Gals? Was either of his fathers as nice a man as my daddy? I doubted that. No one could have been nicer than my father and mother. I wondered if he had a BB gun that he lost deep in a closet after he shot a dragonfly and watched it tumble shimmering like a broken trinket, its elfin music silenced. I wondered if he ever fell asleep hoping to meet Billy Bones and Long John Silver in his dreams. Did he help save Tinker Bell from Captain Hook? Did he go to Sunday school, and if he did, I know he enjoyed coloring pictures of camels more than he did hearing about his holy family. He was almost a normal boy and would have been completely normal if the angels had not pestered him throughout childhood and adolescence, prancing about and on sultry days fanning him with their white feathers. Certainly listening to people talk about the doings of his parents must have embarrassed him terribly.

Mother told me that wild women lived in grandfather's attic. Day after day I rummaged through armoires and trunks searching for women. Although the trunks resembled big loaves of brown bread, their tops roundly pregnant, no women burst forth when I lifted the lids. To assuage my disappointment, Mother told me wild women only spent winters in the attic. In the summer they vacationed in woods and pastures. In hopes of capturing a woman, I dug traps, holes that I disguised, covering them with thatches of grass and twigs. I wondered if Mary told Jesus exciting tales about wild women. Probably not—poor Jesus—if she had, he would have married, inherited the shop, and fathering a tribe of children, would have lived a simple life. He would have been happier and would not have caused so much damn trouble.

In Charlotte Brontë's novel, young Jane Eyre sat cross-legged "like a Turk" in a window seat, studying a volume of Bewick's woodcuts depicting birds. A red curtain shut Jane away from the relatives who disliked and tormented her. The window seat was a perch from which Jane soared beyond domestic unhappiness. My childhood was better, happier, than either the childhood of Jane Eyre or that of Jesus. Life around the mimosa was wondrously varied and promising. Escape never attracted me. To be sure like Robert Louis Stevenson's "little me" in the cherry tree, I "looked abroad on foreign lands"— lands, however, that stretched only down the road to grandfather's dairy and that were familiar and to me as exciting as the faraway because they were rich with life abounding: cicadas yowling, chickens pecking and scooting, Mealy in the kitchen baking a yellow cake, and almost every day black snakes sliding through boxwood, above them paper wasps tending their nests.

In childhood the way to the marvelous was through the ordinary—the other side of a screen door or across a rail fence. Like Alice I explored burrows, not just those of rabbits but those of foxes and groundhogs also. I transformed myself by looking in the mirror and making faces. I rummaged closets and drawers like the Pevensies digging through the wardrobe in C. S. Lewis's *The Lion, the Witch, and the Wardrobe*. In the great hall I became Mrs. Molesworth's Griselda in *The Cuckow Clock*, opening the door to the tall case clock and hearing scampering too shrill for the ears of adults. Age locks magical doors. I have not climbed a mimosa tree or thought about the boy Jesus in sixty-five years. "The world does wicked things to us with its success and routine and morality," the ghost of Marion Kirby said to Topper in Thorne Smith's novel. "It either cheats us with wealth or numbs us with want, steals away from us all the color and wonder of being, the necessary useless things." The utilitarian appoints the adult's days. Pill boxes sit on pantry shelves and tax forms on desks. Such things are rarely "The Door," although the names of the medicines I swallow each day are as exotic as Abdul Abulbul Amir and Ivan Skavinsky Skavar, their effects smacking of William Rands's "The Topsy-Turvy World" in which butterflies court bees and owls porcupines: Diltiazem, Warfarin, Losartan, and Levothyroxine.

Nowadays, most of the nonsense I stumble across is neurological not poetic. My friend Bill is fast sinking into the clogging plaque of dementia. Early in June he had two small strokes. Afterward he spent a month in the Mansfield Rehabilitation Center. Before leaving Storrs in July, I visited Bill every day for two weeks. For forty-three years he taught English, but when a nurse asked what he did at the university, he looked puzzled then said, "You know. You know. The whole shebang," slapping a period after *shebang* by clapping his hands together. Bill's parents were Finnish. One afternoon when Vicki visited the center with me and asked Bill about his childhood, he said he enjoyed "the hot baths," that is, saunas. "Especially," he added, "when girls were there." "I really liked those round things they have, those circles," he said, rolling his hands like wheels above his chest. "I didn't know whether to laugh or cry," Vicki said later. "A mental curtain has slipped the rod," I said, "and Bill says things he would never have said two years ago." Before Vicki and I left Bill's room, he said he liked the nurses and hoped to find a girlfriend "for the next twenty years." "Isn't Bill seventy-eight?" Vicki asked as we left. "Yes," I said then quoted Dr. Johnson, "life protracted is protracted woe."

The fantasy island on which Bill was marooned was a hard, rocky place, as isolated as Nova Zembla. In childhood I explored scores of hidden, isolated worlds. Never was I at a loss for words or being. I delved into *King Solomon's Mines* and later met *She*. I sailed with Gulliver to Brobdingnag and Lilliput. I was Abner Perry's right-hand man when he traveled to the *Earth's Core*. Before Edgar Rice Burroughs I discovered Minuni, the hidden world of the ant men. I hopped from island to island like a passenger on a cruise boat in the Caribbean, touring *Treasure Island* and Jules Verne's *Mysterious Island*, among an archipelago of others. On September 30, my birthday, I accompanied Robinson Crusoe when he washed up on his "horrid island." Defoe's novel became the source of an Antilles of imitators. Generations of boys built huts in backyards, the most famous being Thoreau's cabin at Walden Pond. *Walden*'s appeal is not to youth but to former hut-builders like me, men financially comfortable enough to hanker after simplifying their lives, hoping to escape to a desert place free from endless appointments with cardiologists and endocrinologists. Reading Thoreau provides a glimpse of the road that was impossible to take, the way blocked by love or lust and those familial and social responsibilities that prevent men from appreciating the necessary useless things.

"We must achieve the character and acquire the skills to live much poorer that we do," Wendell Berry wrote. Not only have the characters of people like me hardened amid plenty, but we have aged into medical complexities that force us to live more expansively. Purging the sentimental recollection of hut-building from the bloodstream is difficult, however, and the desire to build often surfaces in late middle-age. Old boys in the easy classes who built huts as children and who were trapped by one or two wild women during extended adolescences often build summer places, getaways in the Smoky Mountains or in Monteagle, Tennessee, on Cape Cod or around Sebago Lake in Maine. They dream of rusticating and digging into the good earth, this last despite realizing that they are not gardening for subsistence but in the forlorn hope of spading up feelings long lost.

Old hut-builders furnish studies in summer homes with spy and crime fiction. Although I have read libraries of each genre, I have almost quit. I don't have mental energy enough to cram my thoughts into Wellingtons in order to wade the abattoirs of blood spilled by Thomas Perry's Butcher's Boy. I'm not a marriage counselor, and I have given up trying to find a wife for M. C. Beaton's Hamish Macbeth. What an odd place Lochdubh must be, its population consisting of hordes of murderers but not a single marriageable female. I have also given up hoping that Bernie Gunther, Philip Kerr's displaced policeman, will escape the field gray cloud of Nazi Germany that shadows him around the globe, and I am no longer intrigued by the rumor that Lee Child's Jack Reacher breaks so many arms and legs, hands and wrists because he is a silent partner in a company called Hominid Orthopedic Associates. As for spy novels, I have written too many first-person books either to have any secrets or to believe that a person can keep a secret. Indeed the pleasure of being party to a secret occurs only when one reveals it, and reveals it not once but serially. No longer do politics intrigue me, and I do not subscribe to a newspaper.

In *The Covent-Garden Journal*, Henry Fielding quoted Robert South, an eighteenth-century divine. "Most of those things," South declared, "that have the mightiest and most controlling influence upon the affairs and course of the world are downright lies." Last month in a coffee tavern I read a wire-service article describing the consecration of a foundling home in Omaha. Inmates of the home, a circuit-riding bishop declared, were doubly blessed by having right-to-life parents who scorned birth control. A photograph showed the bishop in full regalia, wearing an amice, stole, cope, and miter and holding a chalice in his right hand. The bishop was robust and red-faced, and in good catholic fellowship he slung his left arm like a bag of malt over the shoulders of the local priest. The priest was small and parched, shrinking and mole-eyed, and he tottered under the weight. Protruding from the bishop's mouth was a newly-cut, handmade El Rey de Mundo cigar, the band falling off. "Cuban," the bishop said, "its smoke signaling solidarity with the island's true believers, so long prosecuted by this nation's teetotaling, excommunicated, atom-splitting Puritans."

After decades of splashing through the bustle of social life, solitude and isolation are alluring. The shoreline of Crusoe's horrid island beckons rather than repulses. In George MacDonald's *The Princess and the Goblin*, the villainous kobolds once resembled ordinary people and lived above ground. Because of a forgotten dispute, they migrated to the dark underworld of cavern and cave. Living "away from the sun, in cold and wet and dank places," changed their natures, transforming them into hideous grotesques. As their bodies became distorted, MacDonald wrote, so they grew misshapen "in knowledge and cleverness." Success also changes people. Society strips away and turns youthful hut-builders into kobolds comfortable in the social sunlight and the dry air of conformity. In contrast to MacDonald's grotesques, perhaps the only people now who escape turning into kobolds are those who live underground or inhabit the margins of place, something the aged do when they retreat to summer homes. In "The Scholar-Gipsy," Matthew Arnold pondered what wore out men. "'Tis that from change to change their being rolls; / 'Tis that repeated shocks, again, again, / Exhaust the energy of strongest souls / and numb the elastic powers." People eventually tire and forsaking their wearing lives sadly begin, in Emerson's words, "to live in the world after the world's opinion."

I read Thomas Aldrich's stories describing the antics of Peck's "bad boy" when I was a child. The doings of "the Champion Little Devil of America" parasitize the hive mind like an infestation of Varroa mites. In June I re-read *Peck's Bad Boy Abroad*. During the reading, life smiled; high thought melted, and hours became joyous and humane. Convinced that his constitution had been undermined by a surgeon's leaving a tool in his stomach after an appendectomy, George Peck undertook a regimen of travel in order to regain his health. With him he took his son, the bad boy. Because he wanted fellow travelers to think him sophisticated and worldly-wise, Peck collected a stack of adhesive labels on which were printed the names of hotels, ocean liners, and countries. Peck asked the bad boy to paste the labels on their luggage. Peck was near-sighted, and he did not immediately notice that his son switched the labels. Instead of proclaiming that Peck had visited France and Britain, the labels advertised malted milk, green peas, hair restorer, soap, Quaker Oats, and "37 Varieties of Pickles." In Geneva the boy spread the rumor that his father fled the United States because police suspected him of plotting to assassinate the president. As a result, anarchists, dynamiters, and sundry long-haired and wild-eyed folk invited Peck to dine with them and join their bibulous revels afterward. The plan concocted by the bad boy was wondrously absurd and ornate. Because the president enjoyed horseback riding, Peck supposedly proposed soaking the hay eaten by the president's favorite horse in a nitroglycerin solution. On jumping then coming down "kerplunk," the animal would explode, smothering the president under sausage covers and horsemeat. If the president were not dead, he would want to be dead. On learning details of the plan, the anarchists "went into executive session" and collected money to send a compatriot to Berlin to stuff the emperor's horse with feed supposedly formulated by Peck.

Inside the giant pyramid at Giza, the boy yelled, "Whoop-la-much-a-wano, expluribus unum," after which he lit a Roman candle and a giant firecracker. Tourists galloped screaming from the pyramid while resident bats battered their way outside and guides fell to the ground begging "Mr. Allah" to save them. In Rome the bad boy took his father to the catacombs, telling him they were going to a comic opera, "the greatest show on earth." When Peck saw the skeletons, he exclaimed, "Hennery, this is no leg show. This is a morgue." "I told him," Henry recounted, that "his head must be wrong, and I pointed to about a hundred dried corpses, a thousand years old, in a corner, with grinning skulls all around, and told him that was the ballet, and told him to look at the lead dancer, and asked him if she wasn't a beaut from Butte, Mont. And that killed dad. He leaned against me, and said his eyes must have gone back on him because everything looked dead to him."

I laughed then felt melancholy. Once upon a long time ago, I was a very good bad boy. This spring just before I retired, the university made me a "distinguished" professor. Who, I wondered, had I become? My academic career had been platitudinous. I tempered my personality, dulling corners and honing edges into flexibility. I forgot that vulgarity shattered the chain mail of conformity, and I became a courtier. I didn't bow, but I served and was "safe." I never trapped a wild woman, and when I tried, I always set out Havahart traps. I had, in A. E. Coppard's phrase, traveled "the easy smiling roads." I didn't join the festivities of the long-haired. I imagined trickery, but I rarely played practical jokes. I say *rarely* because the week before Vicki and I left Connecticut for our summer home in Beaver River, Nova Scotia, I cleaned out my desk. In a folder I found a copy of a letter I sent twenty years ago to an expert on the writings of John Milton, a friend whose office was down the hall from my office and a man of much learning, considerable charm, and vast earthy experience.

I forged the name of the chairman of the English Department in the letter. "I have a favor to ask," the chairman wrote. "As you are probably aware, Carol's new book will soon be published. In a deft witty fashion, the book explores relationships between males and females. As even the least erected spirit among our colleagues knows, in this fallen world such relationships smack more of man's first disobedience and forbidden (dare I say it) fuck than of the offspring of Heaven's first-born. On the cover of Carol's book— the title, alas, has slipped memory like, I am afraid, those happy realms of summer light—Adam and Eve appear naked except for springs of ivy over their nasties. Most certainly poison ivy—ha, ha."

"The cover's allusion to that Great Argument is clear. Not only do you teach the divine book and cite it incessantly, boring the asses off everybody in the department, but you have in your private life some wide experience in intimate matters. Because you have often bedded down butt naked in those happy fields where p——y forever dwells, I'd like you to be on a celebratory panel with Carol, organized by the Women's Center in conjunction with your English Department. The panel will discuss aspects of the lost paradise focusing on the Hell we moderns have made of Heaven. Your voice's booming out of the abyss would add gravitas to any discussion, 'so what's your point' frightening the reign of chaos and old night. I thank you in advance. Don't think about turning down this opportunity to shine. Shalt thou give law to your chair? Nay. Have a day brighter than the wealth of Ormus and Ind."

The Moving Finger becomes arthritic and eventually ceases to drift beyond safe, smooth margins. I smiled as I read the letter hearing my friend's voice booming, asking me, "So what's your point?" The letter made me melancholy, however. Two years ago on the same day Vicki and I returned from Nova Scotia, my friend was admitted to the local hospital suffering from a virus. For three months our mail had not been forwarded, and we had not read e-mail. Beside my desk sat four boxes of mail, most catalogues and advertisements but buried among them two score forms that had to be completed and letters that demanded answers. I told Vicki I'd visit my friend early "the day after tomorrow." That morning when I went to the hospital I asked the receptionist for my friend's room number. She told me he was no longer in the hospital. "Has he been sent home?" I asked. "Patient confidentiality forbids my revealing that," she said. I then drove to my friend's house. The front door was unlocked. I walked in and called his name. He wasn't there. A neighbor saw me and walked over. "Gene," he said, "died yesterday afternoon. He had a massive heart attack." "Patient confidentiality! So what's your point? The patient was dead," I muttered. "Oh, world, world, world," I thought as drove away, rubbing my right hand across my face.

"Are you, under it all, a fraud?" Frank McCourt asked in *Teacher Man*. Introspective adults interrogate themselves and eventually ask themselves McCourt's question. Most conclude that they have not lived the lives to which they were constitutionally suited. Social life doses taproots with fertilizers and pesticides, the former fortifying acceptable behavior, the latter stunting the unacceptable. Natural living grows out of soils layered with miscellaneous contradictory thoughts, inconsecutiveness, strange actions, and stories of passing. Shoveling away a layer of weedy experiences and replacing it with mulch, say, highly-structured education, homogenizes and fosters seasonal blooming, but it may ultimately produce barren dissatisfaction. In describing Mrs. Wycherley in *The Octave of Claudius*, Barry Pain wrote that "she was by way of being a woman of the world, with the whole world left out." In the final decades of life, high position seems unimportant, and acclaim loses its attraction. Consequently, people often labor to embrace the neglected. Old hut-builders become anti-social and rejecting the dualistic separation of man and nature attempt to weave themselves into the natural fabric. They study the woof and weave of the out-of-doors and become bird-watchers and gardeners. They interpret Matthew's advice, "Lay not up for yourselves treasures upon the earth," as implying that the earth itself, its moths and rusts are mankind's real treasures. Matters once celebrated as contributing to progress and beneficial change now appear to have caused neither. They understand the implications of Aldo Leopold's statement, "Few educated people realize that the marvelous advances in technique made during recent decades are improvements in the pump, rather than in the well."

Frequently people become ecological egalitarians. In *The Forest Unseen* David Haskell argued that all creatures inhabiting the ecosphere were bound together. In discussing a caterpillar's capacity for pain, Haskell wrote, "If we accept the evolutionary continuity of life, we can no longer close the door to empathy with other animals. Our flesh is their flesh. Our nerves are built upon the same plan as insect nerves. Descent from a common ancestor implies that caterpillar pain and human pain are similar, just as caterpillar nerves and human nerves are similar." How nice to be related to a caterpillar, and to recognize the cousinhood, say, of a Lettered Sphinx or a Great Spangled Fritillary, or if not a caterpillar then a dragonfly, maybe a Spangled Skimmer or a Halloween Pennant. How reassuring to be part of a natural chain, not the top link, but just part of the chain. Such thoughts undermine presumption and pride. They break isolation and loneliness and place man in the gnawing, blooming landscape. "O World, I cannot hold thee close enough," Edna St. Vincent Millay exclaimed in a line that is both a heartfelt cry and a guide for a better life.

Haskell studied changes a year brought to a small circle of land on a rocky slope of the Cumberland Plateau. He continued the genre of neighborly or backyard naturalists begun in English with Gilbert White's *The Natural History and Antiquities of Selborne* and embracing scores of other writers including Thoreau. At the end of the nineteenth century, the genre was extraordinarily popular in the United States, its best practitioners being William Hamilton Gibson and Charles Conrad Abbott. "Do not become dissatisfied until you have exhausted your own dooryard," Abbott advised in *In Nature's Realm*. "This has never yet been done. The labors of Hercules were as child's play in comparison. The over-ambitious fool is the biggest fool of them all, and the world is full of them. The rambler that would do justice to his home must be a microcosmic philosopher in so far that he must see how the world works as a whole from the study of the tiny spot before his eyes." According to Abbott, and Haskell, rabbit holes opening into Wonderland pock back-yards. An adventurer does not have to wander afield in hopes of discovering a hidden city of Opar. One can simply walk into his backyard, the screen door slapping behind, separating him from weary convention.

In June I studied portions of several days in Storrs. I began on June 1, a day I labeled Starling Saturday. Starling fledglings had left their nests, and that morning small flocks splattered the yard. Starlings are mimics, and listening to them, Vicki first thought them red-winged blackbirds, reedy and wheezing with song. Young red-winged blackbirds had also left nests, and fledglings clung awkwardly to cattails roughing the edge of Mirror Lake. The weight of the birds bent the plants into quarter circles until the stems began quivering and dropped the birds fluttering into flights spasmodic with ups and downs. Near the island in the middle of lake, a muskrat glided through the water then dove, rippling out of sight through circles of its own making. In an old road worn to dirt pan, hundreds of dying tadpoles turned a drying mud hole into black pudding. At the damp crust of the pan, a Nessus Sphinx moth puddled shaking like a bumblebee. Nearby, caddisfly larvae shuffled the shallows of a small pond looking like tiny rag-and-bone men swaying under bags of greasy sediment.

That morning buds on peonies loosened and spun open into bloom. Cat-kins rained from shagbark hickories, and pollen seeped from the clotted inflorescences of orchard grass in pale, yellow streams. From yellow wood, black cherry, and goldenrain trees, flowers hung in bell towers of chimes. Woods behind my house were musty with the fragrance of maple leaf vi-burnum. Corsages of round-leaf pyrola spread across the damp ground, and naked broomrape blossoms curtsied blushing lavender. A pig's ear mushroom spread cauliflowered into a crinkled cup. Early in the morning, light pebbled gold and green low through the trees along the Fenton River. Branches of mountain laurel swung over the water in white scoops gathering the sun. Above the river bank, sulfur shelf cinched itself around a stump in yellow collars. Four feet away a heavy breast plate of hemlock varnish shelf jutted orange and red from a dead tree, sticking out six inches and circling three-quarters of the way around the trunk. "Oh, what peace we often forfeit," the gospel song "What a Friend We Have in Jesus" laments, "because we do not carry everything to God in prayer." People forfeit peace, not because they neglect the numinous but because they neglect Earth's gifts. The world, as Wordsworth noted in *The Prelude*, is "the place where in the end, / We find our happiness, or not at all!"

A fortnight later I studied the sliver of another day. In the morning I watched a spotted turtle laying eggs in a hole dug into a lip fat above an abandoned gravel pit. A kingbird built a nest in a dead red maple leaning like an airy snag over the pond in the Beaver Meadow. The nest rested in a fork where a branch tilted up from the trunk of the tree. In forsythia beside my house catbirds nested. Cardinals built a nest in the bittersweet strangling the pipe that supported the clothesline behind the house. The vines were thick as my wrist and at the top of the pole flared into scratching tendrils practically forming a hedgerow. In winter robins forged through the vines feeding on the red berries. Inside the garage between the door opening into the drive-way and an inner door leading into the kitchen, Carolina wrens built a nest in a plastic bucket that once contained a hanging plant. The bucket hung six feet off the ground on a nail. A small gray cap woven out of leaves, moss, and bark, the nest lay on the bottom of the basket pushed against the side, the entrance tilting down but leading back and upward into the crown.

We saw the wrens so often they practically became family. The female laid four eggs. The male fed her while she incubated them, usually announcing his arrival and mealtime from a perch in the yew at the corner of the house singing "cheery, cheery, cheery." Initially he delayed flying into the garage if Vicki and I were in sight. Later, however, he became accustomed to our presence and treated us like cousins, slight nuisances but still cousins. After pausing in the yew to study us, he flew into the garage, sometimes landing on a garbage can or the trunk of the Volvo. Often he dropped down and scooted across the cement floor before popping up to the nest. While the female in-cubated the eggs, I did not close the garage door. At night I lowered it part way, leaving a two foot gap between the bottom of the door and the floor of the garage. That satisfied the male, and at five in the morning when I raised the door all the way, I usually found him in the garage. Vicki and I worried that the young birds would not fly the nest before we left for Canada, forc-ing us to leave the garage open. Four days before we set out, the fledglings

abandoned the nest. Later that morning, however, the adult birds sang choruses outside the garage, one perched nearby in a hickory, the other in the
yew. Worried that a fledgling might have tumbled into the recycling bin, I
pulled the bin outside and removed the contents. At the bottom of the bin,
I found a fledgling jumping and trying to spread its wings but imprisoned
by rails of cans. I scooped up the bird. I held it for a calming moment, then
I opened my hand. Unharmed and quick with energy, the fledgling lifted off
my palm and in a low rush flew into forsythia. Shortly afterward the calls
of the parent birds softened. For the next three evenings we heard the birds
calling, not from near the garage, however, but from a grove of hemlocks
across the street. Thinking to search the recycling bin then finding the baby
bird raised my spirits. "You are the Great Nurse," Vicki said. "Yes, yes," I said.

Other ornithological maternity matters didn't fare so well. One afternoon
a down draft of wind and rain banged through the backyard, snapping the
crowns of trees and knocking the hedgerow of bittersweet akimbo, exposing
the cardinals' nest. After the wind died, I searched the backyard with a flash-
light. On the ground I found two baby cardinals, their feathers rudimentary
quills. I dried the birds with a soft towel and put them back into the nest.
The next morning one nestling was dead. The other was alive, though, and
the parents were feeding it. Two days later, it died. Vicki buried the birds in
a ground cover of periwinkle at the corner of the yard. The periwinkle was
blooming, and the flowers formed a purple pall. "I just couldn't toss the bodies in the woods," Vicki said. Sentiment is the highest human virtue and the
progenitor of sundry other virtues, not the traditional seven scarlet virtues,
but virtues more domestic and muted, more livable—call them robin virtues,
kindliness and generosity, tolerance, benevolence and selfless decency, for
example. That afternoon I trimmed the bittersweet. I shredded the cardinals'
nest and spread the makings across the ground in hopes that other birds
could recycle the scraps.

"Everything happens by chance," Richard Jefferies declared in *The Story
of My Heart*, "that is, in defiance of human ideas, and without any direction
of an intelligence." I did not expect a fortnight to elapse between studying
days, but the necessary doings of ordinary life controlled my hours, visits
to mechanics, those who serviced people and cars, and those who serviced
dogs. Twice my fictional friend Josh came to see me. Josh's visits are seasonal. He appears at the end of the school year, bringing with him a sampler
of oddities collected during the term. One bon-bon is always a joke staler
than the catacombs. At a funeral in Lexington, he recounted, a cousin of the

deceased testified. "I'm not much on paregorics," the man began. "You mean panegyrics," a woman whispered from the choir stall. "It don't matter none," the man replied, turning toward her, "they are anonymous."

Josh is never without a wisdom detector, and throughout the year he mines the library searching for bits of lost thought. He dug this year's gold piece out of the pages of Ernest Bramah's *The Wallet of Kai Lung*. "Although there exist many thousand subjects for elegant conversation, there are persons who cannot meet a cripple without talking about feet." Josh also described his latest academic project, digital athletics, a spinoff from digital humanities, the contemporary fad in liberal arts. Digital athletics, he said, would save a national debt of money—no more gladiatorial stadiums and arenas, no more coaches with cardiovascular salaries, no more battalions of trainers and doctors, publicists and graduate students hired to tutor and write papers, no more buying a car dealership of automobiles for assistant this's and that's, all sporting social letter jackets. Only a few scholarships need be awarded, all going to ball-peen nerds. "Of course," he added, "a doctor would have to be on call in order to treat serious injuries, trigger-finger, felon, and carpal tunnel syndrome, among digits of others." Josh is an athletic heretic and refuses to prostrate himself before college sports. "It is a good sign in a nation," Josh said quoting G. K. Chesterton on athletics, "when such things are done badly. It shows that all the people are doing them. And it is a bad sign in a nation when such things are done very well, for it shows that only a few experts and eccentrics are doing them, and that the nation is merely looking on."

Before leaving Josh showed me an article clipped from *Today's Clinician*, a prestigious medical journal. The clipping described the extraordinary popularity of cosmetic ophthalmology in Arab countries, making "its practitioners the most affluent medical professionals in the Mid-East." Because burqas left only their wearers' eyes exposed and sometimes a veil shadowed these, "untold numbers of women" had undergone oculoplasty, that is, eyeball augmentation, this generally accomplished by injections of silicon. Women whose eyelids had begun to droop opted for blepharoplasty. The procedure reduced bagginess in the lower eyelids and trimmed excess skin from the upper. Sufferers from eye spots had pinguecula and pterygium removed from the sclera, or surface of the eye, simultaneously whitening and brightening eyes, making women appear youthful, literally illustrating that "beauty is in the eye of the beholder."

Only in that most fictional of literary genres, biography, is life unified and are actions consistent. Lives off the page are disheveled. Occasionally, of course, page life itself appears rumpled. For the jacket of my most recent book, I provided a sketch of my life. "Pickering and his wife Victoria," I wrote, "live in a modest house in Connecticut with three small rescue dogs and two imaginary grandchildren. 'Damn well-behaved children,' Pickering says, 'mannered and old-fashioned, children who genuflect before their elders and who confine bad language to the dinner table.'" Last spring Vicki and I saw a performance of the Popovitch Comedy Pet Theater. Before the show, hordes of small children scampered about the lobby of the theater. They had hearts and paw prints painted on their cheeks; they hopped and tumbled in bag races, and sitting on huge balls bounced down the aisles. Spring was in the heart as well as in the air. Peach trees blossomed, and daffodils sprung from the ground wearing green tights and blowing yellow trumpets. Phoebes whistled, and towhees gleefully snapped their bills like fingers calling "che-wink." During the show the theater was shrill with happy appreciation as, among other four-legged performers, terriers, a French bulldog, a St. Bernard, and a white cat danced the boards. Vicki and I were the only adults without ties to children in the audience. The "grown-ups" were parents or grandparents although I did spot one or two accompanying aunts and uncles. "You would have been a glorious grandfather," Vicki said after the show. "Even if one of our children had a baby, you are now too old to enjoy it."

An inkwell of blue-blooded thought justifies describing life as it is, not as the page demands it. "The uppermost idea with Hellenism is to see things as they really are," Matthew Arnold explained in *Culture and Anarchy*. Describing life as it is off the page forces one to chronicle the harum-scarum. "To dwell," Heidegger said, "is to garden." Despite the chaotic nature of life and field, new gardeners begin by planning to order and arrange. Green Hellenism comes later. Initially in imagination and in the study, a red brick wall separates plots and the plotted from the disorderly. Boxwood hedges border walkways and discourage careless tramping. Gates inhibit and slow meanderings, both mental and physical, keeping observers on mannerly, tight paths. Stone steps lead down a slope from a terrace to a pool bright with water lilies, butterflies and dragonflies sparkling in the air around it. Urns overflowing with bouquets of annuals sit beside each step. So far the garden is Georgian in structure. Order, however, disappears when I pick up a shovel, much as it vanished when Adam sampled the apple. Under the pressure of indiscriminate affection, artifice vanishes. Like Edna St. Vincent Millay, I love the green world too much to impose order. I like beds rumply with old-fashioned flowers: dark blue Iris; red, almost black hollyhocks; Zinnias; scarlet, tissuey hibiscus; and daffodils rolling in orange and yellow comforters. Here blooms a Chinese dogwood; there a pair of gardenia bushes. No matter the climate, everything blossoms in my imagined garden: a dove tree, Easter lilies, woodbine, wisteria, asters, azaleas, and a hedge of Rugosa roses. Somewhere I find room for a magnolia, a huge bull bay like those that grew on grandfather's farm. Angel's trumpets are out of place but present. Fortune-telling plants circle the trunk of a redbud: four-leaf clovers that bring good luck and daisies that predict the course of true love. I've stocked the garden with efts, toads, and a pair of box turtles. Scattered throughout are bird houses—homes for bluebirds, for wrens, even for a pair of starlings, and for cardinals, a house with a weighty lid that no storm can blow off. In a nook shadowy with melancholy, a tombstone slumps against a wall. Atop the stone a lamb crouches shorn by time. A bouquet of orange lichens blossoms across the face of the stone, making the epitaph, eight lines from "The Three Sons" by John Moultrie, difficult to read: "I have a son, a third sweet son; his age I cannot tell, / For they reckon not by years or months where he is gone to dwell." "I cannot tell what form is his, what looks he weareth now, / Nor guess how bright a glory crowns his shining seraph brow. / The thoughts that fill his sinless soul, the bliss which he doth feel, / Are numbered with the secret things which God will not reveal. / But I know (for God hath told me this) that he is now at rest, / Where other blessed infants are—on their Saviour's loving breast."

   "Here in Corfu," Gerald Durrell wrote in *My Family and Other Creatures*, "anything can happen." Vicki and I had not been to Canada for two years. Before leaving Connecticut, I imagined the impossible, currying my garden into geometric design and writing equilateral, thematic paragraphs. Immediate experience shapes perception, however. The drive from Connecticut to the ferry in St. John was tiring, and Vicki worried about problems arising from opening the house. "The nineteenth century," she said, "wears thin by the beginning of the twenty-first century." Suddenly, I realized that little would startle me and that only the familiar would happen in Beaver River. I was no longer young enough to spend days alone in field and wood. My sentences and thought would dangle and growing weedy would trail off and vanish beneath scrubs of intellectual underbrush. My life was more varied than that of Thoreau, and as a result my prose would resemble an irregular polygon. Our farmhouse was 160 years old, not a hut but a shambling gray presence, the central hall running past parlors and through the kitchen and pantry into a backhouse and a towering barn. Writing straightforward aphoristic prose like that of Thoreau would be impossible in a house in which floorboards buckled and stairwells tilted, dizzying climbers.

During our absence the house became a mouse asylum. A granola of droppings covered floors and tables and seeped into drawers. In the middle drawer of the dresser in our bedroom upstairs, mice gnawed through plastic bags and masticated running socks into a nest. They beat the nest into a gelatinous mound and seasoned it with urine so that it looked like a huge crème brûlée. Vicki discovered similar nests throughout the house, most looking as if they had been shaken out of aspic molds. She found so many nests that she became shrill with exasperation. When I urged her not to let the nests upset her, she asked, "Why do you take screaming so seriously?" Place determines response. Three weeks later, under a slab of pressed wood above the tide line near the outlet of Sandyland Ponds, I found a nest scrabbled together from the feathers of a gull and leafy Irish moss. Turning through the nest were six young mice. "You ought to write a children's book about them," Vicki said when I showed her the mice. "They look so sweet."

In *The Four Ages of Poetry*, Thomas Love Peacock argued that sentiment was "canting egotism in the mask of refined feeling." Words blow page life into dry ideas, pushing writers into bony, untenable stances. Peacock's statement crackles, but it is heartless. Sentiment awakens the feelings and leads to deeds, not necessarily good deeds but deeds that usually soothe the edges of irritation and make living humane. Spiders had spun webs throughout the house, and their droppings speckled the floorboards below the downstairs windows, especially the boards behind the four bays. Suspended in the webs were egg sacks that looked like musty gray peas. Vicki refuses to kill spiders. Indeed, she won't kill any insects except "biters," most commonly ticks, mosquitos, and black flies. In the house she steered female spiders into a plastic container that once held 650 grams of "Great Value Plain Yogurt." In the container she wove the strands of webs supporting egg sacks. Afterward she carried each spider family to the backhouse. There she plucked out the webs and hung them in wooden strawberry boxes. She placed the boxes on the floor of the backhouse, leaning them against a corner wall. Into the boxes she placed seven inch-thin slabs of wood, wide as rulers. The rulers ran diagonally from the bottom of the boxes to the wall of the building. Female spiders used the rulers as walkways to climb out of the boxes. Once on the wall they spun fresh webs and after attaching strands to their eggs raised them out of the boxes and hung them along the wall. Sometimes Vicki was sheepish about her efforts to save spiders. I admired her. Decency is a web, its foundation lines and radii supporting spirals viscid with sappy gentleness.

Small actions reveal more about people than big. Early in the summer Jack, one of our rescue dogs, chased a young hare into the backhouse. The hare wedged itself between a wall and a rough-hewn, handyman's block of shelves. The hare's nose pressed hard against a stud, preventing him from moving forward. To enable the hare to back out and escape, we took the dogs for a two hour walk on the beach. On returning from the walk, we discovered that the hare was locked into place. To release the hare, Vicki and I removed all the tools from the shelves and shifted the shelves. Slowly the hare lopped free, making us feel good about ourselves as we watched it gather its awkwardly long and stiff legs. I have never known anyone who accomplished something society thought "big." Indeed, for me thinking about *big* never brings the socially important to mind, but instead the multitude of unnoticed and unremembered acts that shape and define. In September at Cape Forchu, Vicki found a newly-dead semipalmated sandpiper atop a ledge. The wind was heavy, swishing in currents so strong that they seemed visible. The wind had knocked the bird against a boulder, killing it. Beneath the ledge on an algae wracked beach, a flock of sandpipers was almost invisible among gray stones. Periodically the birds broke from the shore and spun curling over the water, the fabric of the flock tight with only occasional threads unraveling into leaders and trailers. When the birds dipped, they vanished, the murky feathers of their backs invisible against the waves. When the flock swept upward, their undersides broke sharp and white like waves turning and flashing into spray.

Vicki buried the sandpiper above the water line in a sheltered nook. Over the grave she laid a pall bundled together out of sow thistle, goldenrod, and pale New England asters. The mind knows that even the quickest life has a short flight. Even more evanescent, at least to the aged, is wisdom. I ignore the sententious; yet, I stoop to the folly of saving small creatures, especially in the fall when small creatures begin to cross gravel roads: efts, a Fawn Sphinx caterpillar, dozy snakes, and woolly bears chuffing across the lanes. One day I rescued eleven woolly bears and frightened a garter snake into scribbling cursive into a ditch. The next day I rescued thirty-two woolly bears and, alas, unpeeled two red-bellied snakes that cars had crushed into inlay.

Minor changes swell and infect life. In my case changes prevented me from drifting into tranquility and imagining wholes rather than parts. For thirty years on arriving in Beaver River, I raised a mailbox, Box 2610. During the winter I stored the mailbox in the front parlor, laying it next to my walking stick, atop a rug of newspapers. The morning after we settled in our house, I made a deep hole on the other side of the road, pounding a heavy crowbar through the topsoil and into soft peat underneath. In the hole I stuck the metal leg of the box. I set the mailbox up although we rarely received first-class mail, typically four letters in twelve weeks. Presence of the box made me imagine surprises, however. "Who knows what the mail may bring?" I said. The box also imposed routine. On weekdays the mailman reached our house between eleven and eleven-fifteen in the morning. During that time I busied myself in the kitchen meadow, trimming and sawing, always keeping an eye on the road. On mornings when Vicki and I went to town early and I missed seeing the mailman pass the house, I anticipated returning home, hoping as we approached our fields that the red flag on the side of the box was raised. Almost every time the flag flew, the box contained advertising circulars, *The Clare Shopper* or *The Trading Post*, announcing sales stretching along the Bay of Fundy from Yarmouth to Digby, as well as giving the dates and locations of quilt shows, church teas, and fundraising barbeques at fire halls. This past year, Canada Post stopped delivering mail to seasonal residents as well as to people whose boxes stood so close to the road that it was difficult for the mailman to pause without blocking traffic. At the edges of communities, church and bakery parking lots being popular stopping places, Canada Post erected banks of boxes resembling the walls of boxes found inside post offices. Some people whose mail migrated to the lots did not remove the mailboxes standing in front of their houses. A few were set in concrete; others were ornamental, decals of pixies or birds glued to the sides of the boxes. The birds were mixed flocks of blue jays and cardinals. Many boxes were nailed to boards, often cuts of two by fours attached to thick legs at a right angle and which stuck out toward the road, the whole resembling a bent finger. Immediately behind the boxes a petting zoo of animals frolicked atop the two by fours, cutouts of rabbits, cats, pigs, and red barns. Especially popular were ducks with wings that looked like propellers and rotated in the wind.

I suspect that people who resented change did not remove their boxes. The boxes evoked a vanishing rural life or perhaps a life that had already disappeared. Most farms in our immediate area had closed. For years a farmer mowed our fields, taking the hay as payment. Now we paid to have the fields cut, and the hay was left to mildew. "Not having a mailbox on the road is dreadful," Vicki said. "Poor you. You won't survive this. Every morning you used to wait and wait, looking for the mailman." "I will see the box every day," I said. "I leaned it against the wall in the backhouse, number side out." "I assembled the box in the front parlor," I continued. "Somebody else will have to throw it over the stone wall behind the blueberry field." "Get rid of it like you did the wooden box Father built?" Vicki said. "Yes," I answered, "exactly like that."

In the property surrounding the house, change was inexorable and affecting, more soothing, however, than upsetting. Creeping Jenny had spread through the side meadow. The small flowers looked like breakfast bowls heaped with buttery sunlight. Early one morning I stood on the side porch and gazed across the back field. Beyond the snarl of roses, spears of reed canary grass towered metallic, their inflorescences spikes. Swamp candles flickered in a daylight vigil along a stone wall. Meadow fescue spread a purple haze over the field. On my left a pair of red starts foraged larch and broken spruce at the edge of a wood. A yellow warbler landed in an apple tree then flew into a red oak. A song sparrow bounced into music, and a single leaf fell from a willow, kayaking the air. Later I named the corner of the side meadow The Bakery. Shortly after arriving in Nova Scotia, Vicki always embarks on a baked goods odyssey. She buys a sugar cane field of sweets, most of which she eventually throws away, saying she is swelling fat "as a gourd." Among the goods she pitched this year were a chocolate cake from the Farmer's Market in Yarmouth; from Bailey's in Hebron a "dog bone" and six cinnamon doughnuts, the bone being a cruller bathed in a coconut paste; a slice of strawberry-rhubarb pie from Comeau's Market in Meteghan Center; and from the Yarmouth Museum and Historical Society sale, five date muffins, leftovers from a platter of six.

The Bakery was next to a break of meadow sweet and behind a broad band of sensitive fern, its leaves stiff fans of green and yellow. Early in the fall the leaves dried and turning brown and black folded together like the pages of a book held upright and being shut slowly. Eventually the leaflets permed into curls and looked like sawfly larvae. In grass at the entrance to The Bakery grew bog rush, inflorescences bursting shredded from the stems, and wood horsetail, an elegant plant, branches circling the stems in supple tines forming green, watery whorls that wavered gently and dropped nonchalantly. Our dog Jack was an habitué of The Bakery, forever brushing through the meadow sweet, mold and hard crusts not deterring but attracting him.

The early morning quiet did not last and slipped from mind amid the bustle of cleaning and putting the house in order, a chore that took three weeks, the days punctuated by exclamation points. I spent much time outside yanking bales of Virginia creeper out of the Rugosa roses. Many vines were thicker than my index finger. In places the creeper climbed and wound itself into tents, blocking light from canes already wobbly under the burden of age. For three decades I have dug and cut Japanese knotweed. For a week I worked seven hours a day knowing that two weeks later the knotweed would rise resurgent from the dirt, knee and hip high. My back and shoulders throbbed as I worked. Gnats swam across my eyes, beaching themselves under the lids. Black flies crept under my hat and at the hairline sawed into my neck and lapped blood. One day I took an hour's break and walked the property line along the north field. On my return I plucked nine dog ticks from my clothes and hide. Because the ticks felt like small, leathery shingles, I discovered them easily by running my hands slowly down my legs. Although I wore gloves and a sweatshirt when I worked, thorns raked my hands and arms. My "genial spirits," to use Coleridge's expression, failed, and often I wished I had retired with enough money to pay for a gardener. Silently I scoffed at academic appreciators of nature writing who had never pulled knotweed hot summer day after hot summer day, year after year. Only the naïve embraced the agrarian myth that outdoor work ennobled. The thought that the swinging of hand and scythe mirrored the natural rhythms of life more closely, say, than perching on a stool in a bank, seemed suspect—an idea subscribed to by urbanites dissatisfied with their condo and pavement lives and by memorialists who lived in suburbs and while mowing their lawns shaped fanciful recollections of a relative's hay loft. Repulsed by the affluent selves they had become and saddened by the compromises they made for money and position, the comfortably healthy and well-heeled aging often assuage their feelings of guilt and dissatisfaction by devoting a portion of their time to charity work, usually in an exotic part of the globe, often with Habitat for Humanity.

Amid the creeper and knotweed, I longed for, in Emily Dickinson's phrase, the "casual simplicity" of an indoor life. I imagined slumping perspiration-free into an armchair and sipping tea, reading books landscapes away from Wordsworth's nostalgic pastoralism. Alas, life did not permit me to recuperate from outdoor work. After I removed the last big hunk of knotweed, I walked the length of our north pasture. A green orchid bloomed beside the lane leading out to the bluff overlooking the Gulf of Maine, and I wondered if purple orchids were flowering at the bottom of the field. Cinnamon ferns had spread into the damp, and I worried that the ferns had blocked the sunlight, suffocating the plants, forgetting that purple orchids did not appear before mid-August. As I walked the field, I heard the ruckle of pheasants across the stone wall running between the field and the lane. I kicked the ferns aside and grabbing an alder pulled myself up on the wall in order to see the birds. Suddenly I dove into the ground. The wall had collapsed, and I made a heavy two-point landing, one of the points my forehead, the other my left thigh.

The stone that broke from the wall looked like a granite watermelon. I fell atop it, my thigh absorbing the blow, the tumble grinding the muscle atop my leg into gravelly knots.

I could walk, but for three weeks lifting my left foot more than eight inches off the ground was impossible. Ordinary doings were difficult: getting in and out of bed, putting on and taking off my left shoe, and pulling up shorts or trousers. Four days after the fall, a bruise more colorful than Monet's garden spread from my thigh over and behind my knee and down my calf. At its most colorful the bruise had a purple and black center, brown and yellow petals wavering outward, and measured thirteen by eight inches. For a while I mulled stopping the blood thinner I took for atrial fibrillations. "Better," Vicki said, "to bleed to death internally than to throw a clot, have a stroke, and linger in Neither-This-Nor-That Land." The vague and unrealistic hope to write something memorable slipped away. The fall sapped my energy and crushed possibilities. "No more climbing walls," Vicki said. "Act your age. Keep your feet flat and your ideas grounded." Alas, indications that I had rusted already abounded. In Storrs I jogged myself into plantar fasciitis, and I brought two pairs of heel inserts to Canada. I planned to place a set into each pair of my slippers. One pair of slippers was to be worn in the house, the other outside. A chore diverted me after I put inserts in the house slippers. When I returned to the task, I crammed the second pair of inserts into the same house slippers. I didn't notice the mistake immediately. "These inserts are not worth a damn and are dangerous," I told Vicki the next day. "I wobble when I wear the slippers. I wouldn't be surprised if the inserts didn't cause me to fall onto the wood stove and be burned alive."

For a day or two after the fall, I was indulgently splenetic and melancholy. But in the country, in life itself, if a person forces himself to be curious, days enthrall. I hobbled into the Yellow Barn in Port Maitland and paid Rick ten dollars for a Royal Albert cup and saucer. A frieze of Jack-in-the-pulpits decorated the china, five red and green flowers on the saucer and eight on the cup. One of my favorite spring flowers, the pulpits grow in eye-stopping profusion in the wood behind our house in Storrs. I set the cup atop my desk then forced myself out of the house. The game leg slowed my pace. I limped and, pausing, noticed season. Arbors of Indian hemp grew along Cedar Lake Road, the plant's bells blushing from ditches. On rocks above the high tide line at Salmon River lay a newly-dead, young harbor porpoise. Gulls had opened a red gash in the porpoise's belly and raked out its entrails. On the shingles above the porpoise, a pall of seaside bluebells blanketed stones. Trapped in a rocky tidal pool was a fourbeard rockling. The fish was silver and eight inches long with barbels at the tip of its nose. Its first dorsal fin looked like a long, wispy ray, while the second resembled a file of short rays. Near the pool moon jellyfish sagged gelatinous into the sand.

Noticing the milkweed and the rockling, which I had not seen before, almost cajoled me into believing my thoughts quick. I poured tea into the Jack-in-the-pulpit cup and imagined a shelf of decorated cups, not the usual flowered accompaniments of the bite-sized and the crustless—cups gossipy with violets, daffodils, forget-me-nots, and roses, pink with pale green leaves on wristy stems, thorns trimmed. No, on my cups appeared cat's ears, beach pea, and chickweed. This last was a tiny cup, maybe a doll's cup for little girl's tea party. For the rambunctious brother who often crashed tea parties, I put aside a cup decorated with arrow-leaved tearthumb, the flowers in bundles before opening, each looking like a minute milk bottle. Along the stems stretched four rows of sharp thorns, all curved downward to discourage caterpillars and rapscallions.

Hope of describing anything other than wayward, ordinary life disappeared after I fell off the wall. Vicki and I brought our three rescue dogs to Beaver River. On my commenting that the drive from Connecticut might have been easier if we had not stopped eleven times to walk the dogs, Vicki said, "I can't always talk to people." In Canada canine innards work overtime, and every day I paced the kitchen meadow searching for droppings. "We live in Droppingsville not Beaver River," I said one Sunday evening in exasperation. "Be quiet," Vicki responded, "the Gospel Hour is about to begin." Every Sunday for three decades of summers, we listened to the People's Gospel Hour on the radio. I am not a believer, and the program bored me, but our radio only received three stations, and we listened. Although he died five years ago, Pastor Perry F. Rockwood preached the sermon. In July a woman living in Pennsylvania wrote, saying, "I am seventy-one years old, and my husband has moved on to heaven." "When you are seventy-one, I, too, will have moved on," I said to Vicki. "Be quiet. If you talk any more about death, I will whack you on the jaw," Vicki said. What blocked the haymaker was my spilling beet greens on my shirt—a Butterflies of the World tee-shirt. The greens fell on a Scarce Bamboo Page, an inhabitant of tropical Central and South America and on a Belladonna native to Brazil. The Belladonna looked green and blue. My shirt was old and dirt stained, however, and beet juice seeped through the fabric, altering the color of the butterfly's wings.

Aged academics do not explore the intimate movements of a cuckoo clock or discover minute, talkative Indians in cupboards. To emend Charles Lamb, they have "an almost feminine partiality" for old books. They avoid the crisp and the new, preferring pages well masticated, unsightly and grimy, liver-spotted with faded inscriptions crossing them like scars. The hormonal bores me, and for years my bed table companions have been wrinkled. Almost never do I purchase a book published after 1940. In July at the book sale sponsored by the Yarmouth County Museum, I bought three books, paying a dollar for each. The first was the thirty-third edition of *The Pilgrim's Progress*, published in London for C. Johnson on Ludgate Street in 1776. Measuring five and three-quarters inches by three and a half inches, the pages were made from rough rag paper. Woodcuts appeared throughout the book: the "Foul Fiend" Apollyon, the Great Satan, for example, with the wings of a dragon, feet of a bear, mouth of a lion, and belly belching fire and smoke, the rest of his body covered with fish scales. The book's binding was homemade. Bound with the *Progress* were the second and third parts, both continuations, the second the twenty-seventh edition published in 1775, the third the twenty-second edition printed in 1774.

The *Progress* described the obstacles that the pilgrim Christian overcame after fleeing the City of Destruction and This World in order to reach the Celestial City. For almost two hundred years since its appearance in the seventeenth century, Bunyan's allegory had been the most popular children's book in Britain. Christian's journey, the title page explained, was "Delivered under the Similitude of a DREAM." As I held my purchase, I wondered how many children, and adults, had read my copy. What sort of lives did they live and how did they die? How and when did the book come to Canada?

"A Christian Man is never long at Ease, / When one *Fright's* gone, *another* doth him seize," Bunyan wrote, describing the hero's being confronted by lions at the foot of the Hill of Difficulty. The companion of my bookish childhood was Tarzan, not Christian. Tarzan fought lions, but he did not carry a shield quartered by a cross. I was too young and Tarzan too much a child of nature to be seduced by the "Merchandizes" of Vanity Fair, "*Houses, Lands, Trades, Places, Honours, Preferments, Titles, Countries, Kingdoms, Lusts, Pleasures,* and *Delights of all Sorts,* as *Whores, Bawds, Wives, Husbands, Children, Masters, Servants, Lives, Blood, Bodies, Souls, Silvers, Gold, Pearls, Precious Stones* and what not." As an unfallen boy, I made a pilgrimage to Virginia every summer and spent months catching and releasing a fair of animals: cicadas, snakes, lizards, frogs, and turtles—all earthly creatures of great beauty and evanescent joy. I did not fear damnation, only the occasional nocturnal fright caused by the pleasing fiction that bears roamed the nearby woods at night. After dinner my friends and I ran through alleys of cedar trees pretending to be bears, our growls shrill and not at all like the deep-throated, damning roars of the beasts that threatened Christian on his journey. On my grave-stone I'd like two old and familiar lines engraved: "If there is a world above, he is in bliss. / If there is not, he made the most of this."

The second book I bought was a comparatively new release published in 1927 and presented by "Charles" to "Anna" that Easter. The title attracted me, *God and the Groceryman*. I imaged a series of novels featuring God and sundry companions, books like those describing the doings of Tom Swift and the Hardy Boys—*God and the Entomologist*, *God and the Massage Therapist*, and *God and the Teacher*. After trials by wasp and tendon, the heroes of the first two novels were, in Bunyan's words, introduced to Elders wearing shining crowns. Afterward they listened to Holy Virgins strumming harps. The King's trumpeters welcomed them; bells rang, and a sanctified real estate archangel found them a house on a Golden Street, their upscale neighbors not lawyers and hedge fund moguls but "Men that by the Word were cut in Pieces, burnt in Flames, eaten of Bears," and "drowned in the Seas for the Love that they bore to the Lord of the Place." The Teacher did not fare as well. Not a doer or believer, he was a talker able to discourse "on Things heavenly, earthly, mortal, evangelical, sacred, profane, Things past or to come, foreign or at home, essential or circumstantial." On Judgment Day his books and articles served as fire starter. He lost tenure, was demoted, and tossed into the burning lake where he spent eternity swimming from shoreless shore to shoreless shore.

Wrapping *God and the Groceryman* was a protective cover supplied by The Royal Bank of Canada. Sketched on the back of the cover was a commercial pilgrim's progress. At the bottom of the Royal Road, a gang of boys played basketball. Nearby, girls wearing skirts played netball. Words paved the median of the road: "In your Progress along Life's Way the Gateway to Success will open more easily if you save your money." Two-thirds of the way along the road on the right shoulder, a man in an academic robe handed a bouquet to a girl wearing a mortar board and holding a diploma. A few paces farther along the road and on the left shoulder appeared "Choosing a Career." A young man holding a blocked hat in his right hand and wearing a suit and necktie, the suit jacket tightly buttoned, faced an older man sitting behind a desk. At the top and the end of the road gleamed the Commercial Celestial City, rays of light rising above it in a halo. The successful pilgrim passed through the gateway in order to enter the corporate paradise. A beam arched from the gate post on the right side of the road over to a post on the left side. Printed on the beam was the word *success*, the letters thick and substantial as a vault packed with banknotes.

The Groceryman was Harold Bell Wright's thirteenth novel. Among the others were, an advertisement at the conclusion of the book stated, *The Mine with the Iron Door*, "an adventure romance of the Arizona mountains;" *The Shepherd of the Hills*, depicting "the hearts of men and women" in "the clear, inspiring atmosphere of the Ozark region;" and *The Winning of Barbara Worth*, "achievements of human enterprise in a charming love story whose background is an epic of desert reclamation." In *The Groceryman*, Dan Matthews, a former minister but lately "the Rockefeller of the lead and zinc industry—the Carnegie of mining," decided to reinvigorate Christianity. The bane of Christianity, Matthews believed, was the faith's 183 denominations. Instead of accomplishing charitable works, church members contributed to building funds. "If the business men of America do not somehow get a little Christian religion into the business of our country, and if the citizens of this nation do not get a little Christianity into their everyday affairs, national destruction is inevitable," Matthews maintained. "Our great need," he declared, "is to see our good works not as religion but as the fruit of religion." To reform the divisive denominational spirit of the age, Matthews decided to build an ecumenical temple in Westover, a city inhabited by forty thousand people and located in the Midwest, not far from Kansas City, the main office of Matthews's businesses.

Westover was the home of the groceryman, whose parents had befriended Matthews decades before. The town's leading citizens had sunk into the Slough of Despond. They suffered from religious malaise caused by a theological diet of artery-clogging, fatty, pretentious words. Only muscular deeds could strip away the cellulite wrapping their hearts. On Sunday Westover's newspapers printed religious advertisements paid for by churches hopeful of increasing the size of their congregations: "Pastor Seeking to Learn Life's Greatest Kick—offers cash rewards for best answer to the question, 'How is one to get a kick out of life?'" and "Bronco Jack, Here to Hog-tie the Souls of Men—I will ride human herd here and I promise to rope, hog-tie, bull-dog, and scratch the Devil every evening." "Come and Hear Sunshine Jim," a notice urged. "Don't Die on third," the headline of another advertisement warned. The sermon promoted by the ad contained "a number of interesting baseball illustrations." "It is doubtful if any preacher today has as many friends among baseball players as Doctor____."

The absence of active, muscular Christianity undermined the family of Joe Paddock, the groceryman. His daughter Georgia drank bootleg whiskey and, during the course of the novel, almost lost her virtue. His wife, Laura, dallied with Edward Alton Astell, a celebrated one-book novelist. "No one outside of Westover ever heard of the silly indecent thing," Georgia said, "and no one here ever read it, except a bunch of half-baked women he gave autobiographical copies to." By the conclusion of *The Groceryman*, Westover's pilgrims had escaped from the shadow of irreligion and become enthusiastic communicants worshipping at Matthews's temple. Westover itself became a charitable celestial city, the hobgoblins of self vanquished, and Bronco Jack and the slick-fielding Doctor having left for greener pastures and outfields.

God and the Groveryman and the 240-year-old edition of *The Pilgrim's Progress* intrigued me, but the prize of the sale was a worn volume entitled *The Speakers' Library*, an anthology, mostly of poetry, published in 1890 in Philadelphia and held together by twine. "Mother" gave the book to "Willie" as a Christmas present in 1892. On the cover of the book, a maiden, perhaps Calliope, the muse of epic poetry and rhetoric, stood barefoot on the limb of a tree lyric with flowers. A toga rippled like water off the girl's shoulders. Her bosom was slight, and she had a short pixie-like haircut. While her right arm dangled loosely at her side, her left was raised shoulder high, bending at the elbow and extending in front of her chest so that the arm formed a perch. On her wrist rested a small gold bird with a long tail, perhaps a bird of paradise. She and the bird stared into each other's eyes, and her head tilted forward as if she were about to brush her lips across the bird's beak. A dove clung to a limb lower on the tree. Years had worn the color off the dove's feathers, turning it black.

The editor of the anthology, Daphne Dale, hoped readers would memorize selections. She testified that the book contained "nothing threadbare," noting that "it requires no greater effort to memorize a selection of acknowledged reputation than one of doubtful merit." Many poems were lugubrious or inspirational, typically entitled "I Have Drank My Last Glass," "The Little White Hearse," and "Little Joe's Flowers," these last given to a wilting boy. In "Praying for Shoes," "a dirty, barefoot, poverty-cursed urchin" gazed longingly into the window of a shoe store on a dark November day. A lady whose face was as soft "as the gleam of an angel's dream" noticed the boy. The boy was trembling and his lips were moving. When the woman asked the boy what was troubling him, the boy explained that he was praying for shoes. "I was praying God for a single pair, / the sharp stones hurt me so." God answered the boy's prayers. The lady led him into the shop where he was washed, "tended," and his small brown feet shod. Afterward the lady asked him if he was happier now that he had shoes. "Happy?" he replied, "Oh, yes! I am happy! / Then (wonder with reverence rife, / His eyes aglow, and his voice sunk low), / 'Please tell me! Are you God's wife?'"

In the initial stanza of "One Act," Elizabeth Bishop stated, "The art of losing isn't hard to master; / So many things seemed filled with the intent/ to be lost that their loss is no disaster." I have lost a toolbox of academic skills, among them critical intelligence and the toothed inclination to parse and condemn. The loss has not been a disaster. A love of lugubrious and corny narratives remains. Nowadays I rarely judge. "Nature," an acquaintance told me, "is behind the times." "Think of hybridizing and grafting, the innumerable varieties of corn, the endless cultivars of hostas and day lilies. At this moment horticulturalists at the university are attempting to grow black lilies for the funeral market. For gardens atop decks they have already produced rootless carrots, seedless okra, and rhubarb without stems." "If nature is behind the times, so am I," I thought, "I am on a cultural siding." In "The Gray Swan," an old woman accosted a sailor on a dock. Twenty years earlier, she sent her young son, Elihu, to sea on *The Gray Swan*. Elihu never wrote her, and she asked the sailor if her "little lad" was on his ship. With his lips trembling, the sailor asked, "What little lad? What Ship?" The sailor's eyes became misty, and he asked the woman if she remembered removing a kerchief from her neck and tossing it to her son before the ship sailed. On the sailor's calling the boy a lawless lad, the woman protested, saying he was "the best boy ever mother had." When the man asked the woman if she could forgive her son for not writing, she answered, "What I have to forgive?"—whereupon the sailor twitched open his shirt and exposed the kerchief. "My God! My father! Is it true!" the woman cried. "My little lad, my Elihu! / My blessed boy, my child! / My dead—my living child!"

The poem, I told Vicki as I sat at the kitchen table shelling peas, was every parent's lament. "Children vanish. Think of the group who once sat here beside me, shelling a few peas but dropping others on the floor for Penny, the pea dog. You told them to stop. They said they would, but, thank goodness, they didn't obey you." Sometimes loss that isn't literal loss seems more real than actual loss. In "Solitude," Harold Monro wrote, "While you have tided all the things for the night, / And while your thoughts are fading to their sleep, / You'll pause a moment in the late fire light, / Too sorrowful to weep." E. M. Forster said poetry was "means and not end." *The Speakers' Library* was a wonderland of dated verse, poems that in themselves were ham-fisted but that often brought lost recollections to mind.

Many poems were preachy. Other writing made me smile, almost testifying to the healthy advice of Democritus, the Greek philosopher who celebrated cheerfulness and derided pretension. In "Chickens Come to Roost," Ernest McGaffey wrote, "Whether you're over or under the sod / The result will be the same; / You cannot escape the hand of God, / You must bear your sin or shame. / No matter what's carved on a marble slab, / When the items are all produced / You'll find that St. Peter was keeping 'tab' / And that chickens come home to roost." In "The Tale of a Tadpole," a tadpole mused aloud, wondering, "Shall I espouse me a wife?" A wise old frog overheard him and advised him to wait until he was older and had aged into good sense. "Girls change, you know, and the pollywog slim, / That takes your fancy today, / May not be the Polly at all you'd choose / When summer has passed away." The tadpole didn't heed the advice and married a "pollywog fair." By summer's end the bride had matured into a stupid frog "with never a trace of the beauty and grace / Of young Miss Pollywog." For his part the tadpole himself had grown stout and stupid, his vision always focused on his wife's faults. "To all young tadpoles my moral is this," the poem concluded, "Before you settle in life, / Be sure you know, without any doubt, / What you want in the way of a wife."

After the birth of two kittens, one gray and the other black, in "Babies and Kittens," Grandma told tiny Bess, "It will never do to keep them both, / The black one we had better drown." Grandma then sent Bess to bed. The next morning dawned rosy and sweet, and when Bess awoke, her nurse told her to go to her mother's room and "look on grandma's lap." "'Come here,' said grandma with a smile, / From the rocking chair where she sat, / 'God has sent you two little sisters, / What do you think of that?'" Bess looked at the babies for a moment, "With their heads yellow and brown, / and then to grandma soberly said, / 'Which one are you going to drown?'"

"The Ballad of a Butcher and the Dear Little Children" parodied cautionary verse and was a derivative of Mary Howitt's "The Spider and the Fly." At nine every morning a "gruesome butcher" with "a countenance saturnine" stood at the door of his shop watching children walk to school. The children often stopped and looking through the shop door glanced at the sausage machine enjoying "its awful roar." One morning the butcher stood outside his shop and after swearing "horribly" remarked "Life's an awful bore." Some of the "dear little children," he observed, might live to be sixty. "Why shouldn't I save 'em the trouble?" he asked himself. "So he winked to the children and beckoned them in: / 'Oh, don't ye's want some candy? / But ye see ye'll have to come into the shop, / For out here it isn't handy!' / He 'ticed them into the little shop, / The machine went round and round; / And, when those poor babes came out again, / They fetched ten cents a pound." "What do you think?" I asked Vicki after reading her the poem. "When I shop tomorrow I'll buy sausages at Emin's Meat Market," Vicki responded. "Make sure they are spicy," I said, "not incorrigibly bland like the little children."

I Am Not Unhappy—Part Two

"The whole world runs by rhythms I have not learned to recognize," Thomas Merton wrote, "rhythms that are not those of the engineer." What is true for the world is generally true for the individual. Handbooks written by social grammarians attempt to impose the "correctly cold" on speech and life but fail. Society, Matthew Green noted, tries to hedge the "roving mind" with rules. I wonder if it is possible, as Samuel Johnson suggested, to "pause a while from letters, to be wise." Pausing from actual letters may not be possible. Even as I am inclined toward rule-breaking, I wince on hearing the incorrect, an announcer describing "oxes" rather than oxen or a conversation in which a woman said, "Him and me and them was together." Still, pauses occur more frequently as a person ages. Off the page type blurs and wisdom becomes obscure. Many evenings fog rolls off the Gulf of Maine, and the spruce behind the house soften out of definition. Grasses lose their sharp edges, and thought becomes sooty as verbs weaken into the intransitive. An indistinct, ungrammatical beauty remains, however, framed by bay, alders, flat-topped asters, and emotion. Caspar David Friedrich said that an artist shouldn't just paint what he sees in front of himself but "what he sees within himself." The remark applies to writing. A person should not just reproduce what he reads but what he imagines he read, in the process stripping away actualities that prevent one from telling the truth. Memory, of course, influences seeing, and the memory of age is short and long simultaneously, a blend that erases rules and transforms the machine-made into the hand-thrown and irregular.

At times Beaver River seemed a world apart. Our telephone did not ring in Canada. Rachel never fretted about suspicious activity on my credit card. Leslie stopped asking what I believed God thought about gay marriage. My luck turned, and not once during the summer did I win a free cruise to the Bahamas. No one tried to sell gold to my Uncle Coleman, admittedly a hard sell since Uncle Coleman died in 1997. "Senior Living Advisors" didn't urge Mother to move into their continuing care communities. Mother lives only in my thoughts. She died in 1988 and "is beyond the felonious grasp of your goddamn assisted living," I told Denise in May. John did not inform me that my medical alert device was packed and ready to ship, and that commercial Good

Samaritan with access to inside dope from the FBI stopped warning me that a break-in occurred every twenty-two seconds in my extended neighborhood.

Near the end of *Walden*, Thoreau explained that he left the woods because he thought he "had several more lives to live." In Nova Scotia I lived another life, not the one I mulled living before I left Connecticut, however. Place had changed about me; undergrowth clogged the paths I cut years earlier. In the fall lumbermen pruned the boggy wood behind our south field, hauling away dead spruce and leaving traps of branches behind. While skidders rubbed ruts into the damp ground and smashed old stone walls, raspberry and black-berry colonized the newly-opened spaces. When I roamed fields this year, I did not follow old trails but creases worn by small animals, probably feral cats. In the north field grasses slung ropes around my legs and pulling at my knees jerked my stride into stumbles. Thirty years ago I meandered easily and wantonly. Now the north field was tatty with knapweed. Pink and purple and tipped with silver, the flower heads rose straight-backed from urn-shaped involucres that appeared wrapped in military burlap. Roots of the plant dug deep into the ground like hands, the fingers muscular and so grasping that they were impossible to pull, the effort making me forget the beauty of the flowers. Occasionally bumblebees hunkered shaking atop the blossoms of knapweed. In contrast, honeybees had disappeared from all wildflowers, not just knapweed. Not once during the summer did I see a honeybee.

As I walked the fields, twirler or snout moths gusted up from the grass like flakes of white ash. Wood nymphs bobbled into wavering flight before tumbling back to the ground, their wings folding together, transforming them into wood chips. Years ago moths and butterflies swirled like triskelions knot-ted and braided though the hours, illuminating days like illustrations from *The Book of Kells*, the decorated Gospel produced in the eighth century on the Isle of Iona. Like rampaging, book-burning Danes, science had denuded the air, flattening and bleaching the pages of life, erasing monarchs and swal-lowtails. During the summer I saw one red and one white admiral. In past summers I saw hundreds. Wood nymphs and sulfurs were the only common butterflies, the former surviving, I suspect, because it fed low in the shadowed grass, thickets of stems protecting it from tachnid flies. In order to control gypsy moth caterpillars, some years ago scientists introduced *Compsilura concinnata*, a ferocious, non-native tachnid fly, into New England. In addi-tion to gypsy moth larvae, the fly preys upon the larvae of some two hundred native species of Lepidoptera. Pesticides, loss of habitat, climate change—many things aside from the fly could have been responsible for dulling the air. Who knows? Nevertheless, gone from the lights about our house were the moths that swarmed the night, their wings stained glass telling creation stories. On the shoulder of a road, I saw a single Apple Sphinx caterpillar, green and streamlined, and the size of my little finger. That sighting aside, however, no underwings, prominents, or sphinxes brightened evenings or clung to trees during the daylight. The orb weavers that strung platters over window panes and between the stems of grasses in the fields also disappeared. I longed to see yellow and black garden spiders, whose webs shimmered like gold and silver leaf in the morning light, but they, too, had vanished.

On a more comforting note, in the past while pruning I trod on a nest of yellow jackets at least once every summer. This year even though I pulled more Virginia creeper than ever before, I was not stung. A skunk built a den along the lane leading to the Gulf of Maine. During the 1920s and 30s a virus killed almost all the skunks in southwest Nova Scotia. During the past decade the population of skunks has rebounded. Skunks dig yellow jackets out of the ground and eat the grubs. The den seemed to be located on both sides of the lane, one part under a stone wall and the other amid brush folded over roots of a toppled tree. Almost every time I walked past the den, I smelled skunk. To me the aroma was perfume, not simply yellow jacket repellant but an evocative fragrance sweet with quiet childhood memories: squatting beside a farm road watching a mother skunk lead a file of kits along the shoulder or sitting motionless on the ground beside my mimosa tree while a skunk dug for insects, almost at my feet.

The apocalyptic mind focuses on the unknowable future and neglects the known present and past. It imagines hells and heavens, the former a frying pan of flame inhabited by monstrous yet often laughable creatures, the sort of beasts now frolicking in science fiction films, winged sharks, sinners impaled on their teeth, or snakes the size of airplane fuselages, all seats, first class and tourist, occupied by the damned. For people who know they are sanctified, Judgment Day is a happy prospect. They believe white chariots will transport them to the top of Big Rock Candy Mountain, where angels will distribute eternity passes entitling them to everlasting bowls of milk and honey and manna spun into divine cotton candy. For me, however, the Lemonade Spring has dried. Armageddon too often seems a gray, ceaseless dwindling, an emptying that continues when there remains nothing left to empty. Age, of course, has influenced my mind. "With rue my heart is laden," A. E. Housman wrote, "For golden friends I had, / For many a rose-lipt maiden / And many a lightfoot lad." "By brooks too broad for leaping / The lightfoot boys are laid; / The rose-lipt girls are sleeping / In fields where roses fade." Moreover, achievements that social life celebrates now appear evanescent, grassier than grass itself. "The Worldly Hope men set their Hearts upon," Omar Khayyam warned, "Turns Ashes—or it prospers; and anon, / Like Snow upon the Desert's dusty Face, / Lighting a little hour or two—is gone."

Little had changed in the bog beyond the lumbered wood. I had changed, however. Fatigue snapped spring from my step, and instead of bouncing like a dancer through the bog, I crept. Cinnamon ferns grew chest-high. Mounds of sphagnum moss turned the ground spongy and tumorous. Water trickled along paths worn by animals and pooled in cavities created when spruce blew down, prying up roots and lids of dirt. Often I stepped into sinks that clutched my ankles and filled my boots. Limbs sharp as finger bones jutted from dead spruce, scraping my scalp and jabbing at my eyes, impaling my cheeks and eyebrows. Beneath the ferns lay rails of branches and trunks, some slanting up and splintering, others webbed across each other forming hidden rolls of barbed wire. In spaces where trees had fallen recently, shafts of light fell, heating goldenrod into flares and causing New England asters to glow like ground stars, the sight welcoming, lying, fostering the illusion that walking would become easier. "I am a part of all that I have met," Tennyson wrote in "Ulysses." When walking becomes arduous, a person roams infrequently and meets less. Simplicity is not always a virtue. When age pares ambling to the short and easy, not just the rough margin of life fades but life itself can fade.

To infuse vitality into moments, I glutted my weariness, to paraphrase Keats, on the immediate. Six or seven years ago at the end of the kitchen meadow, I planted three shafts of rambling Dorothy Perkins roses. I dug the roses from the foundation hole of a house that collapsed eighty years ago. I did not expect the roses to survive, but they thrived and swept over ramps of knotted weeds and dead Rugosa canes in a pink fog. Corsages hung from the lower branches of a weeping willow, twelve or fourteen blossoms in a bundle. One morning as I looked at the roses, sunlight pushed through the clouds and broke refracted through the dew on the grass. The light cut facets of yellow, blue, and green, transforming the cool damp into jewels, real jewels, not shop-polished fool's jewels. In Nova Scotia discontent, even worry about the environment, is short-lived. On my desk sat a lucky stone. I found the stone above the tide line at Cape St. Mary. The stone resembled Ohio. At the top Lake Erie had spread, washing away much of the state east of Cleveland. At the bottom floodwaters from the Ohio River had drowned some of the low lands north of Huntington, West Virginia. Still the stone looked remarkably like a keepsake Ohio. The stone was small, its longest edge measuring one and three-quarter inches, its height three-quarters of an inch, and its width one and a quarter inches. The stone was granite and to my eye greenish. Shoelaces of quartz wove through eyes and bound the granite. "How do you know the rock is lucky? It looks ordinary to me," Vicki said. "I know," I said rubbing the flat of my thumb along bottom of the stone. Luck cannot be anatomized and may only be a feeling that endures despite circumstance. Maybe the lucky person is he who sees things no one else can see or enjoys beauty that exists beyond literal awareness, for example, the appealing fragrance of skunk, be the aroma close or distant. In "Adonais" Shelley lamented the death of Keats, writing, "Life, like a dome of many-colored glass, / Stains the white radiance of Eternity, / Until Death tramples it to fragments." Both Keats and Shelley died young. If they had lived to my age, cataracts would have blurred their vision and thought, and the white radiance would have been shaded unless they carried lucky stones, planted roses, and in the morning damp looked at the grass and saw the bright unnoticed.

The lucky stone was not in my pocket when I watched a truck "haul" at the Western Nova Scotia Exhibition. Some twenty pickup trucks entered the haul, all of them erector sets of customized pipes, tanks, and bars. Over every truck scrolled decals advertising Seakist, Vodka Farms, Rudder's Seafood Restaurant, Foster Auto Sales, and Rough Country Suspension Systems, among an engine block of others. The trucks had names, christened, Vicki said, by kegs of Budweiser or, for owners a little higher on the Pentecostal scale, by tubs of Bass Ale—among the names, the Aggravator, tides of red, yellow and blue sweeping dizzily over the cab; Smokin' Guns, bright as a Florida orange; Cooter's Joy; The Phantom; and Grampa's Hellraiser, its driver aged and bearded. The bodies of the trucks looked like crabs riding high above the ground on massive panel tires. They burned jet fuel, the noise cracking and sharp-sounding like lightening striking a pine tree. As a boy, Tinker Toys and Slinkys satisfied me. I watched the pulls for a short time. In past summers I might have stayed longer. "No, you would never have enjoyed a truck pull," Vicki said. "Have you ever seen a crèche with a pickup truck leaning over and smiling at the baby Jesus?" "An ox is always present," she continued, seizing my hand and pulling me away. "We have to watch the Sweepstakes Ox Haul." The haul started at nine in the evening and ended at two in the morning. Fifteen teams competed, and despite cataracts in my eyes I recognized oxen and teamsters from previous summers, Lion and Toby, Sparkler and Bright, big as boulders and quiet as myth. "How fortunate we were to see those pulls," Vicki said, as I drove back to Beaver River. "Yes," I thought then quoted two lines from Browning, "The year's at the spring, / And day's at the morn." "Poetry is your lucky stone. You quote more poetry now than in the past," Vicki said, the second sentence in a querying tone. "I don't know why," I answered then continued, "but 'The lark's on the wing; / The snail's on the thorn.'" "Oxen are not butterflies," I mused, "but they are the malleable earth from which butterflies spring."

Poetry is weedy, and it will out, no matter the hoeing and uprooting. While my bed sloped downhill from right to left, every night dumping me in mattress lowlands, Vicki's bed sagged in the middle, opening like a mouth. Vicki called her bed "The Bucket." Despite not going to sleep after the ox hauls until three o'clock, Vicki woke at five. My sleep is always thin, and when Vicki stirred, I woke. "While I was asleep, I composed a poem," she said, "and I can't get it out of my mind." "Write it down," I advised, "and you'll forget it." The poem was short. "Tossed in the sea / In a bucket I be, / Har de har, har, matey." Writing, as it often does, proved soporific. I wrote the poem on a bedside pad, and Vicki went back to sleep. Vicki, incidentally, is Peck's Bad Bedroom Girl. She comes to bed after midnight and invariably wakes me. In Storrs, a small bathroom opens off our bedroom. The bathroom sink is on the wall almost directly opposite our bed, and when the bathroom door is open, light beams into my face. Often Vicki opens the door and shouts, "Lighthouse!" The light revolves as Vicki swings the door back and forth until I am thoroughly and irritatingly awake, causing her to bend over laughing. Before we left Connecticut, Vicki varied her routine slightly. One night after opening the door, she dangled her arms loosely like those of an ape and shouted, "Ogre in the Lighthouse—ahh!" Once I was awake, she closed the door. Before I could fall back asleep, she opened it again. Bouncing up and down and giggling shrilly, she shouted, "Shirley Temple in the Lighthouse—hee, hee, hee!"

Time crumbles the wall separating sleeping from waking, lifting tapestries of lichens off the stones and applying them to the imaginary. In August I dreamed I found a scrapbook in the loft of our barn. The contents revealed the fortunes of a family living in a large farm house similar to our house but whose parlors had been divided into rooms resembling closets. The people memorialized by the scrapbook lived too separate and too near to be close. The scrapbook was forty-three pages long. The final item in the book was a page from a diary describing a young couple in the house who, despite the problems of closeted living, fell in love. The last line on the page read, "Off they rode in the shining car down the shining street." Immediately after reading the line, I woke. I let the dogs out. Afterward I brought wood in from the barn and built a fire in the kitchen stove. I carried slops from the previous dinner across the kitchen meadow and tossed them into blackberry canes beyond The Bakery. Next I brewed a pot of tea, took my pills, and ate a bowl of fruit containing a banana from Columbia, a peach from the Annapolis Valley, and local Yarmouth raspberries and blueberries. The minds of aging people are attics. They spill memories like boxes collapsing and dumping their contents. Clothes slip from racks; locks on trunks break, and people jumble recollections, mussing divisions of time. John Livingston Lowes rummaged through Coleridge's reading in hopes of discovering the sources of "Kubla Khan"—the honey-dewed books that enabled Coleridge to imagine that "sunny pleasure dome with caves of ice." Sitting at the kitchen table I pondered my dream. "From what nook of experience did it originate?" I wondered. No sacred river coursed through my days. I was not an actual or poetic spelunker exploring caverns and couplets measureless to man. In July, however, at an "Antique Barn," I paid fifty cents for an attic remnant, a soiled account book, measuring six by seven and a half inches. The accounts began on "28 April 1806," on page 43, the page on which my imaginary scrapbook ended.

The first owner of the book divided each page into seven carefully ruled columns: Date of Entry, Sum, Debt, Cost, Officer or Sheriff, When Delivered, and Return. Accordingly on "2 Feb 1807" appeared the sum of $6.48, a debt of $4.20, and cost $2.28. The officer was Brewster; the delivery date February 9, 1807, and the return "Satisfied." The debts were all small, and although a few were defaulted or "Unsatisfied," most were "Cleared" or "In Part." The names of the debtors and the people to whom they owed money were familiar and neighborly: Conant, Wheelock, Baxter, Little, Davis, Ames, White, and Brown. On page 98, however, the reckonings ended, and the next sixty-two pages were a scrapbook of clippings sliced from magazines and newspapers by Miss Maria Rogers beginning in 1863. Maria flipped the book upside down and working backward posted the clippings over the accounts. On the inside cover, she wrote her name four times. Thrice she buckled *book* to the end of her name, using the possessive incorrectly, writing, "Miss Maria Roger's Book." Twice she wrote the name Miss Irene Brown, probably a playmate. The clippings were conventional, so much so they smacked of intellectual fetters. The poems Maria pasted in the book were usually religious, earnestly uplifting, and often lugubrious. Some described the weepy loves of maidens and swains. The bruising rapids of life broke the keels of courtships, inevitably bumping one of the lovers into a still emotional pool. There, while life stagnated through decades and the lover's hair turned white like foam left on a beach by high tide, his, or her, affection remained morosely constant.

Titles of the poems revealed their emotional contents. Their milk did not resemble that of Paradise but was instead pulled unpasteurized in "great white pails" from Bet the cushy cow in the old red barn: "Death of an

Infant," "The Messiah," "The Trundle-Bed," "Friendship," and "The Maiden of the Vale." The people referred to by the third person plural pronoun in "They Are Sleeping" lay "in the churchyard cold and gray." "If Mother Were Here!" the narrator lamented, her life would not be "so weary" and "so full of pain." Joys would not wither, and dreams wouldn't "in gloom disappear." "But, O," the tired narrator exclaimed, when her life ended, she would abide "with the angels." Among the heavenly host, she hymned, "Is Mother, sweet Mother, / Who waiteth me there." Happier and rhyming better was "Fadeless is a Loving Heart." "Sunny eyes may lose their brightness; / Nimble feet forget their lightness; / Pearly teeth may know decay; / Raven tresses turn to grey; / Cheeks be pale, and eyes be dim; / Faint the voice, and weak the limb; / But though youth and strength depart, / Fadeless is a loving heart." "Bury Me by the Sea," begged "Woodland Millie" a native of Michigan. "Let me be laid / To rest beside the sounding sea. / Let no spring buds be made / To bloom above me. I would but ask / Forgetfulness. My only dirge shall be / The sea's low moan, now and eternally." "What They Say" was commonsensical not funereal. "'What they say?' Well, let them say it, / Airy echo, fleet as dew, / When they've said it, 'tis forgotten, / They who hear forget it, too."

Maria crinklecut a basket of fillers. An auctioneer trumpeted the merits of a carpet. "Gentlemen and ladies," he said, "some folks sell carpets for Brussels which are not Brussels, but I most positively assure you that this elegant article was made by Mr. Brussels himself." At his death Brigham Young left behind a hundred head of scabby cattle, a pig pen roiling with wild hogs, a barn stuffed with hay, and a farmhouse, its floorboards "sagging under a ton and a half of widow." In his final illness Dr. Chirac, a famous French physician, surfaced from delirium long enough to take his own pulse. Mistaking his arm for that of a patient, the doctor asked, "Why wasn't I called in before? It is too late." "Has the gentlemen been bled?" the doctor continued. When his nurse said *no*, Chirac responded, "Then he is a dead man. He will not last six hours." The diagnosis was correct. Chirac died shortly afterward. Mental wellbeing was the subject of many snippets. "Happiness is like health," one filler noted, "when we begin to nurse it and think much about it, it is a pretty sure sign of its being in a precarious state." Any woman who fainted on being proposed to could "be restored to consciousness," a doctor advised, by her beau's whispering that he was "only joking." Words, another clipping stated, "are little things, but they strike hard. We wield them so easily we are apt to forget their hidden power. Fitly spoken they fall like the sunshine, the dew, and the fertilizing rain—but when unfitly, like the frost, the hail, and the desolating tempest."

A longer clipping and one of two I identified was an excerpt from Joseph Neal's humorous account of Tribulation Trepid in *Grahame's Magazine*. Tribulation was a hypochondriac suffering from undiagnosable ailments. On meeting Tribulation, Mr. Professor asked politely and in passing, "How are you Trepid?" "A great deal worse than I was, thank'ee—'most dead. I am obliged to you—I'm always worse than I was, and I don't think I was ever any better," Tribulation moaned. "I'm very sure, any how, that I'm not going to be any better; and, for the future, you may always know I'm worse without asking any questions; for the questions make me worse, if nothing else does." When Trepid paused to reflate his lungs, Mr. Professor exclaimed, "What's the matter with you?" "Nothing, I tell you, in particular; but a great deal is the matter with me in general," Tribulation continued, "and that's the danger, because we don't know what it is. That's what kills people—when they can't tell what it is—that's what's killing me. My great grandfather died of it, he did, and so will I. The doctors don't know—they can't tell—they say I'm well enough, when I'm bad enough; and so there's no help. I'm going off some of these days, right after my great grandfather, dying of nothing in particular, but of everything in general. That's what finishes our folks."

The other clipping I recognized was an excerpt from Charles Colton's *Lacon*. "We should justly ridicule a general, who, just before an action, should suddenly disarm his men, and putting into the hands of all of them, a bible, should order them, thus equipped, to march against the enemy. Here, we plainly see the folly of calling in the bible to support the sword; but is it not as great a folly to call in the sword to support the bible? Our savior divided force from reason, and let no man presume to join what God hath put asunder. When we combat error with any other weapon than argument, we err more than those whom we attack."

Some clippings told stories, most light and pleasant. In Ophelia Cloutman's "The Blue Stocking," Henry Clinton advised his friend Ned to avoid "Cupid's Trap" and not marry "a literary woman." "Not only are they perfect bores and pests to society," he preached, but they are also "proverbially noted for being untidy in their habits and dress, besides having their heads minus brains, filled with a strange mixture of romance and fiction; and in which their common sense (if they even have any), is completely swallowed up." Advice that fits others often hangs loosely upon the self. As could be expected, Clinton, the literary high-brow and detester of aqua hosiery, fell in love with May Ritchie, the authoress of "the popular and brilliant romance entitled *Estelle De Forest; or the Queen's Secret, a Tale of the French Court*." The couple married, "and to this day, Henry Clinton has never regretted marrying a blue stocking, from whose pen still emanates that divine language of the soul, which has made the name of May Ritchie Clinton, an honored and respected one in the annals of the literary world."

Love flows smoother in prose than it does in poetry. The heroine of Lucy Wallace's twelfth "wisp" from Beechwood was Velona Wheaton, a Tom-boyish hoyden "untamed as a hawk," who loved galloping "up the slopes of ledges" and across mountain tops on her horse Prancer. Velona's life slowed to a trot when a bachelor, "a solemn-faced parson," moved to town and boarded at Widow Smith's house. After climbing "as gracefully as a dancer trips across the ballroom" into a hickory tree where Velona was perched knocking nuts free with a huge stick, the parson, the Reverend Henry Wakeman, introduced her to two loves, that of Jesus and that of himself, without, miraculously, bridling her high spirits. "Our betrothal," Velona recounted, ending the tale, "was a solemn one, but our wedding was joyous. Heaven smiled upon us and we were happy. Excuse me, reader, Henry has just come, and as we are going over to Mother's to take tea I shall have to stop."

Perhaps reading love stories influenced my dream although no one I read about vanished into a distant shining in a shining car. More to my waking taste was the account of Farmer Smith's courtship of Ma'am Jones. The farmer was a widower and Ma'am a widow. One morning the farmer stopped his wagon outside the widow's house, dropping the reins and sitting bent over with his elbows on his knees, this being "the country signal that he wanted to see somebody in the house." Almost immediately the widow tripped out of the house "lively as a cricket, with a tremendous black ribbon on her snow-white cap." The couple chatted until the farmer exhausted his silo of words and asked if the widow wanted to sell any of her cows. "A poor, lone woman like me doesn't know what to do with so many creatures," Ma'am replied, "and I should be glad to trade if we can fix it." The two adjourned to a forty-acre meadow where the farmer alternated looking at cows with glancing at the widow. Unable to decide which cow to purchase, he repeated his visit every day during the ensuing week. "On Saturday when the widow Jones was in a hurry to get through all her baking for Sunday," the farmer was "as irresolute as ever." In contrast, the widow was impatient, for she had "ever so much more to do in the house." The farmer hawed and hemmed, weighing the milking virtues of the brindle cow against those of Old Roan then observing that the Downing cow was "a pretty fair creature" and the short-horned Durham "not a bad-looking beast," all the while sandwiching his comments between staring at Ma'am. "Lor, Mr. Smith," the exasperated widow finally exclaimed, "if *I'm* the one you want *do say so!*" "The intentions of widower Smith and the widow Jones were duly published the next day."

At night the sky above Beaver River is a gloried and storied dome. In August I watched the Perseid meteor shower. At two in the morning I left the house and stood in the blueberry field, my neck cranked back into aching. Most meteors flared like matches then vanished in quick snuffs. A few swished long across the dark, their tails as exotic as Persia. One night a pair of loons called from below the drumlin overlooking the Gulf of Maine, their cries wavering yet joyous. The Gulf itself was calm, the tide low and shuffling. Beneath the stars my casual beliefs, optimisms and pessimisms, seemed ridiculous and not casual enough. Studying the heavens fostered story not thought, story's being true to experience and thought too often an expedient fabrication. Meandering slowly above me was Bootes, the herdsman who invented the plough. After being abandoned by Theseus in Naxos, Ariadne swore she would never again love a mortal. She did not believe Dionysus when he professed his love and revealed that he was a god. When Ariadne refused him, Dionysus took off his crown and threw it into the sky, creating Corona Borealis. Winding through the bright dark was Draco the dragon, who in one tale guarded the Golden Fleece and in another, the Apples of the Hesperides. In many tales Ophiuchus was Asclepius, the god of medicine. One day after Asclepius killed a snake, a second snake appeared and revived the dead animal with herbs. Asclepius became the serpent's pupil and studied the healing properties of plants, creating the science of medicine. Although small, Scorpius destroyed Orion. After Orion boasted that no creature could kill him, Hera used the scorpion to teach humility. Orion clubbed the tiny scorpion to death, not before, however, it stung him fatally. The radiant of the Perseids was Perseus, famous for slaying Medusa, the gorgon. From her blood sprang Pegasus, the winged horse of poetry. Kicked up by his heels was the gravelly, broken-winded newspaper verse collected by Maria, iambic pentameters, their strides snapped by spondees, and heroic couplets, their gaskins strained by sight rhymes. "I had a dream," one poem read, "I thought I was alone, alone; / Oh, it did seem / So far away from home, from home." In the lower world of my study, Draco guarded golden onions, poems the appeal of which was limited to sane, unpoetical natures. Only someone with a lisp and muffled English public school accent should recite "The Unpardonable Sin." 'I cahn't endure the stooped, wude, / Unculchawed chap,—the vulgar boah, / Who weahs in the morning the same pair of twousers / He woah the day befoah. / It makes me mad and vewy cwoss, / With pain and grief I almost woah / To see the next morning the same pair of twousers / He woah the day before!"

Age forces a person to be aware of his body. The aging slip the halter of ideas. Lust slides from the saddle, only to be replaced by the aches of "everything," shoulders, knees, fetlocks, hips, and hocks. Even though I did not shift about as I studied the heavens, my legs wobbled. My gait was unsteady as I walked back to the house. "Ready for the abattoir," I thought initially, but then a bit of consolatory sentimental verse came to mind, its rhythms therapeutic and steadying my step. "So, we'll go no more a-roving / So late into the night / Though the heart be still as loving, / And the moon be still as bright." Frederic Harrison got matters wrong when he wrote, "To stuff our minds with what is simply trivial, simply curious, or that which at best has but a low nutritive power, this is to close our minds to what is solid and enlarging, and spiritually sustaining." What sustains the aged are the trivial and the curious—little matters that awaken appetite for life but do not lead to intellectual insomnia or rest heavy on the lights causing mental gastritis.

Never again, I mused thinking about Byron's lines, would I wander nights watching stars spray the horizon. My morning rovings were also ending. Farewell, I mused, to the oriole, the spring day's meteor streaking orange across wetlands before settling amid the cloudy blossoms of crabapples. Farewell to warblers glittering like constellations in scrubs of alders and winterberry. Farewell to the water-harp of the wood thrush and to scarlet tanagers, feathered Sirius, jewels high in the crowns of trees. Farewell to granite till scruffy with lichens and creek banks mutton-chopped with moss. I thought about places that had drifted from my life. Fall would not find me on the Cumberland Plateau marveling at trees—chestnut oaks, their branches sconces of leaves looking like scalloped ladles; sassafras branching into closets of soiled yellow mittens; the leaves of black gum polished and scarlet, winking sharp at the tips; fleshly Princess tree, its leaves broad and decadent; the plated, ash-burned bark of shortleaf pine; the trunk of white basswood grizzled with sprouts; and then sour wood, its seed pods strung along racemes curving groomed like a dandy's whiskers.

Farewell is melodious and balm-like. Instead of shutting and locking, it opens, and once in the house, I quickly fell asleep, in dream gliding away from the bedroom beside a pair of marsh hawks I saw that morning, the white patches on their rumps cool, their upper bodies blue and slatey and stable. "As I walked through the Wilderness of this World," Bunyan wrote, "I alighted on a certain Place where was a Den and laid me down in that Place to sleep; And as I slept, I dreamed a Dream." My world was tame, not a rough, unmannerly place where temptation soiled and snared. Canes pulled, but rarely did they tear. Occasionally a briar patch forced me to retrace steps, but it didn't cause vertigo or make me ponder Bunyan's question, "What shall I do to be saved?" Dreams did not reveal truths about eternity. Like shooting stars, they simply flared and vanished. When I scaled "the mountain-sides of dreams," I never saw, in Robert Louis Stevenson's words, the land where "parrot islands anchored" lay and where "cockatoos and goats" watched lonely Crusoes build boats. My hut- and boat-building dreams had collapsed decades ago like old tobacco barns, their roofs no longer tenting but sliding broken-beamed, akimbo to the ground. Two hours after soaring aloft with the hawks, I awoke, my eyes wet with tears. The birds disappeared, and in a new dream I crossed a breakwater to a pebbled island. I wore a gray suit and eyeglasses with transparent frames. I was walking to my cremation. What upset me was not impending death but the realization that my father had become confused and losing his way would not be present at the cremation. "Oh, dear," I thought sitting lonely and slumped on the edge of the mattress. Soon afterward, however, I pulled my legs off the floor and stretching out on the bed went back to sleep, this time dreamless.

The next day was sunny, and I wandered a gravel road, a familiar, flat, domestic place, not a wild land pocked by Sloughs of Despond and rumpled by Hills of Difficulty. Purple swept regal over the landscape. Loosestrife rose out of boggy ditches in crenellations. Although fireweed had begun dropping blossoms, isolated patches glowed like cinders. From the flowers white pistils curled out looking like matches, their tips knobby rather than tapered. Purple touch-me-not stood five feet tall. Its garish flowers gaped, almost shouting songs of themselves, very different from the modest touch-me-not, orange and freckled amid the Rugosa roses at the end of the kitchen meadow. Purple veins coursed through the leaves of lady's mantle. Like waterproof medallions the leaves shed dew, the water balling into pearls at the margins. Along the shoulders of the road, clover still bloomed although time had bleached many flower heads. Spikes of fresh water cord grass spread purple through rocks surrounding a marsh. From the spikes pale yellow anthers hung loosely, looking like the teeth of combs. Most knapweed had turned liverish, but here and there tufts remained purple.

I focused on purple and by doing so distorted the roadside. Still, unlike the thinking mind, the eye rarely shutters out the glaringly obvious, a field of goldenrod behind a red barn, a sight to waylay, almost a vision, a scene that makes a person believe he is thinking when he is not thinking, accomplishing when he is still. For years I imagined seeing into the obviousness of things, but that never happened. Beside the lane running out to the Gulf of Maine, tall white lettuce bloomed. Leaves of the plant were irregular, lopsidedly triangular, and looked undisciplined. In a person such an appearance would cause speculation about a life lived rough. The flowers themselves hung downward and tinged with a sickly green seemed depressed and worn, their elastic powers snapped.

For Keats, "Autumn" was the season of mists and mellow fruitfulness. At one moment Autumn sat pliant on a granary floor, her hair "soft-lifted by the winnowing wind." The next she dozed on a half-reaped furrow, a scythe slipping from her grasp. The season was rich with song, not the green lyrics of spring but the quieter melodies of fall. Small gnats mourned "among the river sallows." Hedge crickets sang, and lambs bleated from hilly fields. In Beaver River autumn was also the season of silence and road kill. Drivers raced carelessly and malevolently, reaping, reaping, always reaping: unwinding garter and red-bellied snakes, crushing chipmunks and raccoons, splitting fawns into bags of offal, and knocking flocks of goldfinches from the air, turning autumn into winter's muddy brown. Flickers lay limp-necked in the gravel. The birds often grazed the shoulders of country roads looking for ants. Beyond the shoulders grew hedges woven out of grasses, Queen Anne's lace, alder, and bay. Above the hedges branches of maple, spruce, and white birch leaned over the roads into the sunlight. When startled by cars approaching from behind, flickers rarely bounced straight up. Instead, before rising and flying to the side, distancing themselves from traffic, they looped away from the hedges and limbs, dashing low over roads into the paths of cars.

One morning a snipe tossed itself like a broken roller coaster along the side of the road. I took off my shirt and wrapping it around the bird picked it up. The bird was a beautiful marvel of non-human design. Its upper bill was two and a half inches long, its lower two and a quarter. Pushed high and back toward the rear of its skull, the bird's eyes enabled it to look both to the sides and down along the bill. Feathers on the bird's head resembled a skullcap knitted out of chocolate and buff fibers, this last color binding, stitched around and across the cap. I wanted to save the bird, but its right wing was shattered into toothpicks of bones. "Hope," Emily Dickinson wrote, "is the thing with feathers—/ that perches in the soul—/ And sings the tune without the words—/ And never stops—at all—." For the soft, bloody creature in my shirt, there was no hope. I snapped off the snipe's head and stuffed it into the pocket of my shorts. At home I submerged the head in a stripping blend of Clorox and water. The skull would never perch like hope, but some day, I thought, it would bask in the sunlight on the ledge of the big window in my study in Connecticut, its company other remnants, the shell of a wood turtle, a small, dried flattened snapping turtle, and the skull of a fox, inside this last the shells of two cicada nymphs. Framing a score of paintings on the walls are the skins of a dozen snakes, most shed by black racers.

Education and nurture shape character. Goatish Zeus was nursed by a goat. The funereal furnished the main course of dinner conversation when I was a child. Southerners of my generation did not natter endlessly about ideas. Instead they talked about other people. Acquaintances became stories, actual and fictional, stories with beginnings, middles, and ends, these last not described in whispers but mulled and adorned, usually packaged with exclamatory humor and astonishment. In a sense, the bones that decorate my study are the equivalent of the illuminations found in medieval prayer books. In any case, not all autumn's songs smacked of memento mori; many rollicked merrily toward winter. In pastures spikes of field pennycress dried to seeds. Individual pods were rounded and small, half an inch in diameter and notched at one end. Spikes broke and lay shining in the grass like silver coins displayed on green, shredded paper. Flat-topped asters towered above them flowing white in the wind. Pickerelweed flowered in the cow pond. The plant's stems were supple and twisted about toward the sun, allowing 106 to bloom simultaneously, forming a blue cathedral, the worshippers dragon flies, the spaces between the plants aisles and transepts. At the outlet at Bartlett's Beach, schools of young alewives rushed down from inland lakes and migrated to the deeper waters of the Bay of Fundy. At low tide Jonah crabs hugged the sand attracting hungry black-backed gulls. Four mourning cloak caterpillars attached themselves to the side of the house. They struggled out of their skins twisting like people trying to escape the clasp of muscle-hugging tee-shirts. After a day the pupal cases turned gray, matching the color of the old paint on the house. Apples fell from trees at the edge of the kitchen meadow along the lane leading to the Gulf and beside the stone walls marking property boundaries. Deer grazed on the apples, ironing nearby grasses flat. Groceries in Yarmouth sold sacks of "Deer Carrots" and "Deer Apples," these used by hunters to bait field and wood. "What kind of hunter shoots an animal while it is eating and almost immobile?" Vicki asked. "Man," I answered. "In the South man spreads corn across fields to attract doves. In the Mediterranean, he limes trees to trap song birds. Many things, Thomas Traherne wrote, are bright and 'flow with seas of life like wine.' Man's touch, alas, scorches like wildfire."

Atop the bluff at Bear Cove, I munched handfuls of blackberries. Cotton grass bloomed in the high muskeg, and beneath spruces yellow splashed across the leaves of wild sarsaparilla, dragging brown behind it. In woods thoughts about the doings of man dropped from mind. That night I dreamed I was a notebook, not a spiral notebook coiled and tense, and not a Blue Horse tablet, the sort in which I wrote in first and second grade, on one page copying simple addition and subtraction problems, on the next drawing a pink wigwam, sunflowers growing on each side of the entrance, the petals on the blossoms feathered like arrows. I wasn't a class notebook, eight and half inches tall and seven wide, my boards stiff and marbled black and white, my binding a wrap of masking tape. No, I was a reporter's notebook, four inches wide and eight long, containing seventy lined pages. My covers were soft and flexible; my pages, miscellanies, a description of a leaf falling from a red maple and tacking across the air landing next to a quotation from the *Rubaiyat*, "They say the Lion and the Lizard keep / The Courts where Jamshyd gloried and drank deep: / And Bahram, that great Hunter—the wild ass / Stamps o'er his Head, but cannot break his Sleep."

After the stone wall collapsed beneath me, I became an evening man living in Afternoon Land, a person to whom the *Rubaiyat*'s sense of evanescence appealed, "One Thing is certain, and all the rest is Lies. / The Flower that once has blown forever dies." My left calf bulged, and veins pulsed across it hot and swollen. Vicki speculated that deep vein thrombosis would "knock me off the perch." "So what?" I said, "The man who worries about many things never dies. Ailments invigorate and improve the intensity of life." When my leg throbbed, I sat and read, often forgotten narrative poems, twelfth-rate verse that always raised my spirits. Poor Tommy in "Tommy's Prayer" was a baby when his drunken mother dropped him, crippling him. Now six years old Tommy lived in a cellar at the end of a "dismal alley" where "sunshine never came." His mother despised him, and he was "starved, neglected, cursed," and "ill-treated." He had "not a single friend to love him, not a living thing to love." One day he overheard Jessie, a ragged girl, singing about heaven, describing its pearly gates and streets of gold "where the happy angel children are not starved or nipped with cold." Jessie told Tommy about Jesus. Afterward Tommy begged Jesus to take him to heaven. "In the morning, when the mother came to wake her crippled boy, / She discovered that his features wore a look of sweetest joy, / And she shook him somewhat roughly, but the cripple's face was cold—/ He had gone to join the children in the streets of shining gold."

"It is well to go where the writers of books have been, or to localities as closely akin to these as possible, and bring back with you as many facts as you can carry," Charles Abbott wrote. Field guides expand vision and quicken place, and Abbott advised ramblers to study books then compare their impressions to those contained in the books. "Bear in mind," he warned, however, "that great men often make little blunders, just as little men make great blunders; and sometimes it has happened just the other way, and the dwarf has got the better of the giant." "No really great man ever blindly followed his teachers, or he could never have become great. Ascribe infallibility to the professor, and you become at best but his echo, and condemn to slavery what should be free as air, your own mind." Few people now read Thomas Carlyle's *Heroes and Hero Worship*. Verbal egalitarianism has so spread that the word *hero* has lost definition and jiggles slack as cellulite swaying beneath an octogenarian's bicep. Additionally, only propagandists and journalists label matters *great*, playing the literary equivalent of Pin the Tail on the Donkey. Moreover, Abbott's urging people not to follow their teachers blindly does not apply to the aged. Although experienced ramblers begin their wanderings by consulting handbooks, eventually most are self taught. "They do most by books," Thomas Browne declared, "who would do much without them." Ramblers do not become echoes of professors but echoes of themselves. They lack the strengths of body and mind to bushwhack new patterns of living. Instead they tread familiar byways. Their minds are shackled comfortably to the known, and although they hope to see anew, they only see the old. Often the almost-gone past determines their knowings, generally through recollection or association.

At night toads hunkered in the damp beside the lane leading to the bluff. The toads were fat but not so large as those that clustered in memory, these large and crusty as pie plates, one living at the bottom of steps leading into the basement of the house in which I grew up in Nashville, another in an indentation under a well cover, and always two or three under the stoop and porch outside a grandmother's kitchen. The past rose to my mind mowed and trimmed. In contrast, the present was often overgrown, overwhelming thought: leather leaf around a small bog, snaring and tripping, webs of winterberry and highbush blueberry strung viscous over a boundary line. Nevertheless, some familiar sights although weak as distant echoes momentarily raised my spirits: a porcupine turning his back to me, raising his tail, the needles bristling like the sharp bracts of salsify or in the early morning herring gulls resting on smooth sand and on the top of flat rocks, their wings folded and pinched, making the birds look like gravy boats. Once I could identify all the shorebirds and often stood smiling atop the drumlin, watching and being entertained by sanderlings and least sandpipers skittering in giggles through the skirts of retreating waves. Cormorants beating low and fast over the water slowed my steps as if the distant air fanned by their wings stroked and cooled me. I recognized crabs and barnacles in the shardy droppings of gulls and ruddy turnstones. Now I knew less about shorebirds than I once did. Identities became hazy, and instead of puzzling through the colors of nape and crown, mantle and scapular, I called all small birds peeps.

Losing the names of birds bothered me more than losing the names of people, but both losses were small matters. Time increased the appeal of fog. Almost every day it swelled up from the Gulf and slipped across the land in silver veils. Often the fog's silent rattling awakened imagination, and the thicker the fog, the more I wanted to see. In the clarity of sunshine I frequently ignored my surroundings, in a sense treating them like a blank page. In the mist at night white-topped asters quickened; the caps in the middle deflated, the petals becoming white wheels endlessly spinning. On dense foggy mornings, I often read, the print a guide to the unexperienced. One day I read two of Mary Lou Longworth's mysteries, *Death in the Vines* and *Death at the Chateau Bremont*. Longworth's main characters were Marine Bonnet and her lover Antoine Verlaque, a sybaritic judge who enjoyed good cigars and better wine, among the former, a Petite Corona, Hoyo de Monterrey that "had a long smooth taste that reminded him of freshly ground green peppercorns," among the latter, Pol Roger Champagne and a 1998 Loire Valley Sauvignon that blended a "rich golden color" with a "strong buttery taste." In a one-star restaurant in *Vine*, Verlaque began lunch with champagne and a porcini mushroom tarte, the mushrooms layered "exactly like apples on the famed tartes Tatin." I haven't tasted tarte Tatin, and at night I've eaten on porches under stars but never in a starred restaurant.

Reading the descriptions of Verlaque's meals awakened appetite, and when the fog lifted at noon, I closed Longworth's books and going outside picked blackberries. The canes curved like scythes, their blades serrated fangs. Gathering berries dug bottles of flesh out of my arms and legs filling them with blood. The berries, however, were three star. Moreover, picking wild fruit broadens life, forcing one to bend and twist, to change perspective, to observe and analyze, to hook canes and branches with sticks—all in contrast to watching television, which confines body and attention to a narrow band, politics and athletics astride the peaks of its wave lengths.

After lunch instead of clipping a cap off a cigar, I cleaned the head of the snipe I found shattered on Cedar Lake Road. The eye sockets looked like slices of Spanish olives while the eyes themselves resembled shallots. Clorox bleached and softened the meaty portions of the bird's head into hummus. It also loosened the muscles both on the exterior of the skull and on the interior, so that I could tweeze away nibbles. At dusk rain began falling soft and winy over fields and woods, the fragrance buttery and golden. That night fog was thick, and in the distance thunder stirred like espresso, black in a demitasse cup, the sound vibrating and driving the dogs Jack and Binky trembling to my lap. The next morning Vicki and I lunched at D. J.'s store in Salmon River. We swilled coffee and ate eggs, crispy bacon, and slices of homemade white bread thicker than bookends. For $4.60 we could have added a slice of peach and cream pie to the meal or for $5.90 a slice of chocolate caramel cheesecake. But we did not. We were full. "A four-star meal," Vicki said. "Our kind of starred meal, simple and digestible," I answered. In the side meadow that afternoon, I noticed a lariat of lilac bonnet mushrooms hugging the grass. Caps of the mushrooms were brown and pinkish and were an inch to an inch and a quarter in diameter. From the stem gills swept upward curling the edges of the cups. The center of each cap rose to a lump—a small after-dinner mint, a partially eaten pastille sucked out of shape and reduced to a white nub. While I studied the mushrooms, a cherry-faced meadow hawk landed on my shirt—natural "bling" that crossed the abyss separating man from dragonfly, man from the infinite variety of life that is not man.

That night I wandered the lane. Fog was heavy, and in the beam of my headlamp, the leaves of white clover and blades of grass were light, midday blue. Moisture rolled beady over the blades, making them appear tooled. From the limbs of dead spruce, old man's beard hung moldy while shield lichens gleamed Damascene. Small moths fluttered across my light then dropped invisible onto flat-topped asters. On clear nights midges revolved around my head, silver curls following them making their dizzy turnings glow like sparklers waved by running children. In the fog the inflorescences of meadow fescue were the color of an aged man's palm: dry white but here and there blotched with an atrial pink. Occasionally frogs leaped across the lane, pickerel frogs, yellow brightening the ridges on their backs, and wood frogs, their faces masked and looking prim and censorious. The headlamp invigorated the few remaining Rugosa rose blossoms, injecting pulsating violet into the tired petals, turning them deceptive, making them look like harbingers of another fresh blooming. In the light the retiring green leaves of jewelweed shed their shyness and glowed turquoise, becoming bibs over which the orange flowers shook like bangles. Sunsets along the Bay of Fundy roiled with extravagant colors—oranges, greens, reds skinned to blood, grays as deep as wells, and seams cracking with gold and silver. Beauty catches the eye, but a quiet night snags feelings. Cold becomes warmth and deceives the saunterer into feeling intensely alive, making him forget clammy senescence.

I moved lightly and quietly through the fog almost as if I were floating in saltwater. Out of the fog life was more unsettled. When I returned to the house, Vicki said, "In Tim Hortons today I heard a man say, 'You can't take it with you.' He said it three times in less than a minute." The man was talking to a couple who purchased season tickets for games played by the Yarmouth Mariners, an ice hockey team in the Maritime League. Because the tickets were not cheap, the couple was apologetic about spending their money. "Take it where?" Vicki said. "The dead don't travel often, and when they wander outside their cabanas, they rarely buy souvenirs." "I am tired of platitudes. I prefer poetry," she continued then recited a resuscitating limerick written by Carolyn Wells and lively with ginseng and gingko: "A tutor who tooted the flute / Tried to tutor two tooters to toot. / Said the two to the tutor, / 'Is it harder to toot or / To tutor two tooters to toot?"

Sometimes, I said, prose wasn't platitudinous. Earlier in the week I listened to "This is That," a weekly radio show. An excited announcer informed listeners that the wreckage of the iceberg sunk by the *Titanic* had been located on the ocean floor. Caught in the ice and cinching the identification were a third-class menu dated April 14, 1912, and knife and fork decorated with a reed-and-shield pattern from one of the *Titanic*'s dining rooms. The find, I told Vicki, aroused much commercial interest. Several salvage companies had submitted bids to raise the iceberg, and a travel company printed a brochure advertising undersea excursions and "clear viewings." "Additionally, the owner of a chain of casino cocktail bars proposed recycling the remnant—breaking into it into ice cubes and serving them to the chain's whales, that is, big spending drinkers." The announcement of the discovery paled, however, when an account of the demise of a killer iceberg appeared on the front page of the Halifax newspaper. The iceberg had roamed the northern oceans for at least two hundred years and was responsible for the sinking of hundreds of ships, so many that some oceanographers thought it mythological. In his seminal study of "the literature of the seas," *A Wind's in the Heart of Me*, Richard Wheelock argued that Melville lifted the concept of his white whale from stories about the iceberg. In any case, in July a Russian task force cornered the iceberg in the Sea of Japan as it stalked a container ship bound for Vladivostok. Armed with gigantic mirrors, the task force surrounded the iceberg and focused their mirrors on it, refracting and concentrating the light from the sun. The iceberg tried to float away, but global warming had so weakened its inner shelf structure that escape proved impossible. The execution was done humanely. On board the flagship of the task force were observers from Greenpeace and the Society of Friends, among others.

Also on board lending technical assistance was the warden of the Texas State Penitentiary at Huntsville.

"A sweet disorder in the dress," Robert Herrick wrote, "kindles in clothes a wantonness." Thought is wanton while order is imposed and often starchy with convention and platitude. On the page thought, however, is ironed creating the illusion of order much like a clean, pressed shirt makes its wearer appear reliably predictable, "a team player, someone who can be counted on," as devotees of athletic mathematics express it. Age is more at ease with the random, meandering nature of experience than youth.

"Where is it fled the visionary gleam? / Where is it now, the glory and the dream?" Wordsworth asked. Wordsworth was thirty-four when he completed the "Ode." Although inspiration may be only a fictional palliative paper concept, youth dreads the loss of sudden possibility, the inability to experience inspiration or imagine glory. Unlike Wordsworth, I never lamented losing an imaginary gleam. In truth, I never experienced such a gleam, and I banned *inspire* in all its forms from my classroom, thinking the concept deludingly irrational, a petard burrowing destructively under discipline. And as for dreams, the only dreams I experienced occurred at night while I slept. Recently I dreamed about meeting two boyhood friends whom I had not seen for fifty-five years. Initially I talked to a boy with whom I played baseball and next to a companion on my high school football team. We smiled and described our families. Work had not broken us, and the years had treated us kindly. Although in the waking world both of my friends died four years ago, death had not marred their appearances, and their voices were clear and strong.

I enjoyed visiting the dead. The next day, however, Vicki called the dream "very worrisome." "Let not your heart be troubled," I said quoting John before going outside to pull knotweed, the immortal plant. Three times during the summer I dug and chopped it, and three times stems rose from the dead. If Apollo had been compelled to battle knotweed rather than the dragon Python, he would never have built a shrine on Mt. Parnassus. One of the labors of Hercules should have been eradicating knotweed. He would have failed. In comparison to pulling knotweed, killing the Nemean Lion, the Hydra, and the Minotaur were child's play. Digging and hoeing frayed my temper. To regain control I again subjected myself to the blackberry treatment. I picked a quart and that night covered half of them with heavy cream, and Vicki and I ate them for dessert. The remainder we ate at breakfast, after which I left the house and roamed the headland. The wind was cold and heavy as steel, and I walked slowly, at a human not an electronic pace. In the middle of the lane lay a short-tailed shrew, a feral cat's broken toy. A solitary black-bellied plover looking as if he were wearing a dinner jacket foraged the shoreline. Atop boulders half-sunken in the sand, jaws of northern rock barnacles grinned toothy, fresh and white or aged and yellow. Braids of mermaid's hair, rockweed, knotted wrack, and lank hipster strands of sea grasses clung to the boulders. A bald eagle rode the wind above Black Point, flying away, not, as the gospel song puts it, to a celestial shore but toward a ridge of small clouds. Somewhere below their shadows was a nest high in a spruce.

I watched the eagle shrink to an eyelash then turned and walked back along the lane toward the house. Dew gleamed like melted sugar on the umbels of wild raison, the fruits not yet gunny blue but unripe and cherry red. I stood silently while a pair of yellow warblers chitted through an alder three feet from my face. Apples had fallen and rolled into the lane. They were pinched and cranky, sour and hard, real like life itself, bearing almost no resemblance to the plasticized fruit in grocery stores, lasered and tucked, stuffed with collagen then waxed. Through the crowns of spruce growing behind a stone wall, blue jays and flickers yammered at each other. The racket stopped when a sharp-shinned hawk flew across the lumbered field south of the house and perched in a dead tree, red and buff on a bony white limb. The hawk seemed an emblem of solitude. Of course, achieving solitude is almost impossible for man or bird. The quiet the hawk brought to the field didn't last; the jays gathered and began to swirl around him, rolling over and away whenever he dove at them, eventually chasing him away.

Later that day I plucked a woolly bear off Route 1. "Do you realize that I probably saved your life?" I said, addressing the caterpillar as I ferried him over the shoulder of the road and set him down in distant brush. "In the beginning was the Word," John recounted, but words were now so corrupted, I thought, that preserving the life of a small caterpillar accomplished more than all the great talkers achieved in their babbling years. The realization made me splenetic. The dark mood lasted only a moment. A cloud of sulfurs scudded over a newly mown pasture and transformed dark into light. The sulfurs were the first I saw during the summer. Mulling "what man has made of man" grieves the heart, as Wordsworth put it. In contrast, the golden butterflies raised my spirits. Too often man tries to measure and in the process destroys. Too often words blind and smother, especially when plastered over the breathing world. "Our language," Charles Abbott wrote, "is too accommodating in the matter of high-sounding phrases." Chances are that when "you" hear "grand generalizations," you "can set the speaker down as more full of words than wisdom." Perhaps the best that a person can do is observe then resist the temptation to fabricate meaning; simply notice a bed of rattlesnake fern in the damp atop the bluff at Bear Cove, the leaflets lacy and brightly green in the glancing sunlight of late afternoon, or the branching inflorescences of Canada goldenrod stretching and beckoning, calling "come here" in the breeze. But no matter the fever caused by the sentimental homesickness of long years and its accompanying desire for a place, the flowers were not lights shining in a window of an eternal home. A sight may lift the heart, but it is not, as "Precious Memories" puts it, a sacred scene. At its best such sights are gloriously profane.

At times I envied people certain that following the natural led to the sacred. A hundred and fifteen years ago in *The Roadmender*, Margaret Fairless Barber testified that she had lost her once voracious appetite for books. "Their language," she explained, "is less plain than scent and song and the wind in the trees; and for me the clue to the next world lies in the wisdom of the earth rather than in the learning of men." *The Roadmender* was remarkably popular and reprinted thirty times in ten years. Barber wrote that she could not recall a time when she did not love the Earth, "this mother of mine with her wonderful garments." "In the earliest days of my lonely childhood," she stated, "I used to lie chin on my hand amid the milkmaids, red sorrel, and heavy spear-grass listening to her many voices, and above all the little brook which ran through the meadows where I used to play." Barber said the brook trailed through her whole life at last losing itself "not in the great sea but in the river that maketh glad the City of God." "Valley and plain, mountain and fruitful field; the lark's song and the speedwell in the grass," she hymned; "surely a man need not sigh for greater loveliness until he has read something more of this living letter, and knelt before the earth of which he is the only confusion." Barber and I were very different. Relatives as colorful as Christmas stockings crowded my childhood, and although an only child, I was never lonely. Moreover, I lacked Barber's ability to glimpse the numinous beyond the beauty of the natural. The living letters I saw did not form words and, alas, like theological Burma-Shave signs direct passersby to a celestial city. Still, the letters ran like cursive and were alive and animating, and that was good enough.

Near summer's end on the beach at Cape Saint Mary, I found a mourning cloak butterfly partially buried in sand. Wind toppled the insect down from a dune onto the beach. I scooped up the butterfly, blew the sand off its wings and thorax, and to warm it cupped it to my chest. The insect revived, and I carried it across the dunes and released it in a meadow. The butterfly trembled folded on my palm for a moment, then it opened its wings and flew off, away from the beach. "A symbol," Vicki said. "Of what?" I asked. "I don't know," Vicki said, "but clearly something good." During the Middle Ages butterflies were emblems of the human soul, dragging through dirt for scores of years as caterpillars then pupating in dark shells before breaking out of their chrysalises transformed and flying into the "beauteous heavenly light." Two of the four mourning cloak butterflies that hung cocoons on the house turned into butterflies. Predatory wasps, not sin, parasitized the other two caterpillars. "Two out of four plus one rescued from the cloying sand," Vicki said, "better than could be expected." That night Lyra was bright in the sky. On it Orpheus played the music of dreams, and stones rolled down mountains in order to listen. On cold August evenings, looking into the sky loosened the threads of ordinary living for a moment, and I almost heard Orpheus coaxing notes out of the harp.

Thoreau was thirty when he left the cabin at Walden Pond. He explained that he had other lives to live. He was young enough to attempt to live according to some of the advice he pondered. I knew I didn't have much more of this life to live, never mind other lives. Late in September lightning struck the tallest spruce in the windbreak across the side meadow. The lightning burned down the tree, stitching in and out of the heartwood, peeling bark, and raking out splinters, tossing some of them twenty feet away from the trunk of the tree. Unlike the tree I am not broken, but time has wormed through me. Throughout the summer I hesitated before sitting on the ground. In order to stand after sitting, I rolled onto my abdomen like a beetle righting itself in the dirt. Once on my stomach I spread my legs and arms then pushed up, slowly rising into a crouch. Unlike limber Thoreau, I was reluctant to give advice or pontificate. "It is well," Charles Abbot wrote, "to think little of those who think little of the earth." Thinking well of man, rather than individuals, was impossible. Age made pondering the earth and man's place on the earth more conscious, less spontaneous, and simply grimmer. To shed pessimism and push myself up into optimism strained back and mind.

In "The Hungry Heart," Edna St. Vincent Millay described her appetite for life, writing, "My heart, being hungry, feeds on food / The fat of heart despise. / Beauty where beauty never stood, / And sweet where no sweet lies. . . . .It may be, when my heart is dull, / Having attained its girth, / I shall not find so beautiful / The meager shapes of earth." Three hours every day I roamed field and wood hoping to scrub away plaque, to prevent dross from clotting perception and blocking appreciation. Sliding into conventional observations comes easily and naturally. "Too much life, like too much gold," Sara Teasdale wrote, "is sometimes hard to hold." I struggled to notice meager shapes, seeking, I hoped, in Whitman's phrase, "primal sanities." In the evening I listened to the jingle of crickets, in the brown early morning, the calls of great horned owls. I watched a minute cone-shaped snail, probably a *Carychium* exile, circling a leaf of wild raisin, eating the edges and reducing the diameter of the leaf. Attached to the trunk of a dead spruce was a hemlock varnish shelf fungus, ten and a half inches wide and swelling out seven inches from the tree. The starched underside of the fungus rose to a pouched lip. Beyond the lip was a smear of red looking like lipstick. A storm drove a meadow vole into the barn where it bundled about the foundation searching for a dry snuggery. A hare crouched immobile beside a ditch, its ears cocked and its fur red and brown like cranberries over-ripening on a headland bog. After a long rain a three-legged doe appeared in the kitchen meadow. The doe's right front leg was withered and looked like a wrist, the hoof a vestigial hand dangling loosely at the end.

By the beginning of fall frost had settled on bay leaves, and in the farmer's market in Yarmouth, bakers sold pumpkin pies. In the sphagnum bog, winter slippery cap mushrooms blossomed green. The small caps of the mushrooms tilted lumpy to the side like homemade biscuits. Chanterelles rolled wavy into yellow and orange. As green sheets of ferns wilted out of definition, red became more noticeable: redgill webcap mushrooms, hawthorn berries, rose hips, and jowls of berries bending branches of mountain ash. The caterpillar of a brown headed owlet fattened on the leaves of an aster. The moth of the owlet is brown and looks torn from a monk's cowl. In contrast, the caterpillar wears carnival dress, its clothes decorated with black, white, red, and orange medallions, yellow streaming down them in enameled drippings. So long as a person roams, his heart will not become gray, no matter the fat in the actual food he eats. In September Vicki and I stopped at a roadside farm stand. The farmhouse had collapsed inward into drab desuetude. Inside the barn tools rusted out of identity. Cars abandoned a generation ago became pigeon roosts and chicken coops. Shingles clumped over woodpiles that fifty years ago had been sheds, and a tractor leaned off its tires, its axle broken. The farmer sold jams, writing the names of each variety on strips of tape stuck to the sides of the jars. He sold blueberry, blackberry, strawberry, and then my favorite, "Raspberry I Think." We bought six jars, the "I Think" to be opened and served on my birthday. "Your birthday surprise," Vicki said as she put the jars on a shelf in the pantry.

In "The Eagle and the Mole," Elinor Wylie wrote that if a person could not live as an individual, free like an eagle apart from the "lathered pack," then he should burrow underground like a mole. "If you would keep your soul / From spotted sight or sound, / Live like the velvet mole; / Go burrow underground. / And there hold intercourse / With roots of trees and stones, / With rivers at their source, / And disembodied bones." Only in the word-shaped landscape of the page can a person bore to roots or splash about in baptismal sources. Holding intercourse with deep phantasmagoric wonders is possible only to the deluded. But that is all right. Instead of digging for roots, a person should embrace trunks. Thomas Browne was right when he wrote, "We carry with us the wonders we seek without us." Every morning during summer's last days, I dressed just as sunlight began whispering in the east and walked through the south pasture into the lumbered edge of the boggy woods. The woods had been lumbered because groves of spruce had died and fallen across each other rotting like smashed rail fences.

The week of the Harvest Moon was the season of crane flies pronging across lawns and of woolly bears bumping across dirt roads, these last turning me into a ferryman. Flocks of birds slowed to driblets. Most of the stragglers foraged alders: myrtle and bay-breasted warblers; northern parulas, their backs green as privet; an alder flycatcher, a Canada warbler flicking its tail, all accompanied by fussy, domestic chickadees. Beside the boundary between wood and field, grouse clucked, and along the shore crows yammered cacophonously, sounding like people pushing and jabbering, dissatisfied with their lots in life. I smelled the barn-stall fragrance of deer and at dawn listened to their nervous wheezing snorts. The deer harvested wild raisin preventing it from spreading like eczema across the lumbered field.

Here and there towered brush piles of skeletal limbs and branches. From a distance the piles looked like the unruly hair of an old woman, a person living naturally, not trying to dye herself out of season. Stumps sprouted feathers of turkey tail. In the field I wore Wellington boots and long trousers. Grasses were high and dripping with dew, and my trousers quickly became soaked. I tried to appreciate the wet September cold. I toyed with language in hopes making *clammy* appealing. I failed. Every morning I faced west. When the sun rose, it warmed my back. My chest remained chilled, and in fact the contrast seemed to force the cold deeper into my bones. A forehead of thin, weary spruce separated the boggy wood from the field. Lichens white-washed the bark and then peeled into flakes. Lower branches had snapped into ladders of snags. At their crowns the trees spread into brushes of scouring needles. In the field itself saplings had room to grow, and they yawned broad looking like Christmas trees. The trees were hybrids of black and red spruce. They weren't white spruce. Woodsmen say that crushing the needles of white spruce produces a noisome aroma. I crushed and chewed handfuls of needles. They brought holidays to mind and palate. The flavor refreshed me. My taste, though, is not to everyone's tongue. Not only do I like snuffing skunk on the wind, but barnyards invigorate me, the fragrance of hay and cow manure an aphrodisiac lifting mood.

I chewed paths across the field, breakfasting on blackberries, occasionally blueberries, and always wild raisins, afterward brushing my teeth with leaves of lance-leaved goldenrod. Two apple trees grew at the corner of the field. I did not know the variety and dubbed them Farmer Apples. The fruits were small, about half the size of my fist. Skins of the fruits were yellow freckled with brown and blotched with red. One morning after "breakfast" I ate seven apples, "all natural with no wax and no hint of pesticides," I told Vicki. Of course daybreak gourmandizing can scour the innards, something that isn't a nuisance if one is near fistfuls of sphagnum moss. On the days I was in the field, elsewheres disappeared. I forgot parochial truculence and my sour loathing of political Babylons, their corridors smoky with gun-made men, hog-eyed statesmen—war-mongers and sottish lickspittles—for whom "man's inhumanity to man" caused rejoicing not weeping. What I could not escape was my shadow. The floppy hat atop my head and the walking stick I carried to steady my steps were always apparent, making me look like a puppet, freed momentarily from handlers and strings but still, I knew, a puppet. In the field I was silent. Even my thoughts were taciturn. In part the field resembled drawers of an attic dresser, moldy with old sweaters, unkempt, forgotten, spooling backward out of form and use into fragile skeins of wool, mothballed and mouse-ridden—clothes that lurked on the lip of familiarity, bringing dead family members to mind. Who, I wondered, wore the cable-knit sold by Langrock's in Princeton, the tennis sweater with bands of blue and red wrapping the waist, or the toggled shepherd's cloak, its wool thick and itching?

Across the field asters grew in bundles, many toppling over: New York and New England, their petals blue and lavender, flat-topped and bristly white with yellow buttons in the middle, and wood asters, their petals irregular and snaggled, needing a floral dentist. A crazy quilt of grasses patched spaces rubbed bare by lumbering, among others reed canary, fowl meadow drooping languidly, and red-top, the inflorescences wispy and lolling against each other, forming low clouds delicate as mist. Rushes were bright green and soft although they tapered to needle-like ends. Deciduous trees had not been cut. Most were saplings, however, a few white birches and then stands of yellow birch, the bark gleaming and peeling burnt orange. Brambles grew head high then curved over, barbed and forbidding. Ferns splayed and collapsed into hedgerows, the fronds of bracken blackened and those of cinnamon ferns bronzed and hardened out of suppleness into fragility. Almost every morning small flocks of cedar waxwings settled in the tops of spruce at the edge of the field. The birds groomed and dozed in the sun. Occasionally they woke and fluttered into a mountain ash laden with berries. After eating fingerlings of berries, the birds returned to their perches and sunned themselves back into sleep. "A good life, maybe the best," I murmured, standing immobile and almost asleep myself. Only the zinging of minute mosquitos kept me awake. One morning a Canadian darner cruised the brush beside me. "He will scatter the mosquitos," I hoped, but the dragonfly was intent on patrolling its territory and paid no attention to the mosquitos. Another morning a doe and I studied each other. The doe flicked her ears but eventually realizing I was harmless returned to cropping shoots of raisin. A Red Admiral butterfly settled on a flat-topped aster, the only Red Admiral I saw during the summer. In past summers, butterflies swarmed across days like soft crayons dabbing hours with color. I wore crisscrosses of paths across the field, but I knew that they would quickly slip unblocked out of form like the sweaters I found in the attic dresser. I marked the ground, but I knew that a year would erase my weak scribbling everywhere except perhaps on the page. But that, too, is all right. Though the world casts us away, to emend John Gould Fletcher's verse, "there will dawn and sunrise . . . And the leaves dancing / Over the hill."

"Did all those hours in the south field lead to any epiphanies?" Vicki asked in October as we drove back to Connecticut. No man with a bum leg and a halting intellect jumps easily to conclusions. "No," I said. "Doesn't that make you unhappy?" she asked. "I'm not unhappy," I said then recited Wendell Berry's "The Peace of Wild Things." "When despair for the world grows in me / and I wake in the night at the least sound / in fear of what my life and my children's lives may be, / I go and lie down where the wood drake / rests in his beauty on the water, and the great heron feeds. / I come into the peace of wild things / who do not tax their lives with forethought / of grief. I come into the presence of still water. / And I feel above me the day-blind stars / waiting with their light. For a time / I rest in the grace of the world, and am free."

When the Harvest Moon was full, I stood in the blueberry field behind the barn and studied the sky, first with my left eye then with my right. When I stared with my left eye, the moon seemed a sphere carved out of mother of pearl. My right eye transformed it into three cloudy water marks like those left atop tables by damp glasses. In the middle of the sky was the thickest mark, but above and to the left was a second circular mark. Below and to the right curved a third mark. "No, I'm not unhappy," I repeated. "I have been part of the summer's quiet passing. I have seen things aslant and that's exciting for a person my age." "I tried to capture place and mood, but that is difficult, maybe impossible," I continued, "and of course I couldn't escape the lure of terrible books and worse poetry. But no matter the strivings for accuracy and truth, words, as T. S. Eliot wrote in the *Four Quartets*, 'strain, crack, and sometimes break.' They slip and 'decay with imprecision' and won't 'stay in place.'"

"Do you think anybody will read what you wrote?" Vicki asked. "Maybe," I said then quoted Uncle Remus, lightening the tone of our conversation, "Hog don't know which part of him will season the turnip salad." "If congressmen studied Joel Chandler Harris, they wouldn't meddle in the affairs of so many tarbaby countries," Vicki said then asked, "Does anybody read Uncle Remus nowadays?" "No," I said. "Doesn't that make you unhappy?" Vicki asked. "A little," I answered, "but that will vanish when I get home. Before unpacking I'm going to inhale a bottle of Wilfred Mulliner's Buck-U-Uppo and not the A grade for human invalids either but grade B invented for animals in India. Too often elephants, P. G. Wodehouse wrote, turned tail and ran away after sighting a tiger, disrupting the favorite pastime of sporting maharajahs. One teaspoon of Buck-U-Uppo administered in its morning bran mash, Wilfred Mulliner declared, 'will cause the most timid elephant to trumpet loudly and charge the fiercest tiger without a qualm.'" "Have you ever heard of Mr. Mulliner, the brother of the pharmaceutical genius? You can find him in *Meet Mr. Mulliner* or in the bar-parlor of the Angler's Rest," I continued without waiting for Vicki to reply. "Literary critics could learn a great deal from the conversation of Mr. Mulliner and his friends. Just the other day the friends analyzed *The Vicissitudes of Vera*, a movie in which a mad professor tried to turn a girl into a lobster."

"Oh, Lord, that's not my kind of story. What's next?" Vicki asked, "More icebergs? Such tales make chills run up and down my spine." "You are not the only person to whom the movie doesn't appeal," I said. "I don't like stories like that," one of Mr. Mulliner's companions said. "They aren't true to life." "By the way," I said to Vicki just as we crossed the Connecticut border, "did you hear about the man who swallowed a bottle of Allen's Hair Restorer, mistaking it for a pint of ginger brandy? Not long afterward he felt a little *down* in the mouth." "Great God!—that's got to be the cream of the crap," Vicki exclaimed. "No more. No more—ever!"

Would that I could modify my chat to please Vicki, but altering the bent of my wordy nature is impossible. I cannot, in Jesse Wills's words, break the bindings of my "stifling crust" and be newly and wide awake. "When marked out by destiny," Ernest Bramah wrote in *The Wallet of Kai Lung*, "a person will assuredly be drowned, even though he passes the whole of his existence among the highest branches of a date tree." Nevertheless, since returning home, I have spent many solitary hours silent and free in the grace of the world. I roamed fields plumed by goldenrod and silvery in the sunlight. I shivered under damp shadows blanketing the ground beneath hemlocks. I saw snowbirds tumble like leaves across the ground and catch in brambles. Cardinals and blue jays waved like college pennants, and a heron stalked the shallows off a low bank of the Fenton River. Cords of oriental bittersweet turned the thin, bare branches of gray dogwood orange and red—the small trees bright and cheerful, growing beside the river and indeed appearing in the river itself, the water erasing some of the trimmings but only slightly dimming their gay reflection. I hummed with squirrels as they bounced across the yard like vaudeville tunes, bounding gaily from stump to brush pile and from trunk to limb. I watched deer mince across the yard and clip the yews growing in front of our house. During a short visit to Tennessee, I marveled at Nepal grass rugging through disturbed woodlands and listened to a pair of pileated woodpeckers call reassuringly to one another, their high whinnying warm and natural, almost a symphony.

In the Nashville newspaper, alas, I read about a melancholy rooster who suffered from hen-nui, but I haven't described the bird's plight to Vicki. At Christmas Vicki is always in good Champagne spirits. Maybe that'll be the time to mention barmy barnyard matters. Perhaps I'll even quote one of Harry Graham's *Ruthless Rhymes for Heartless Homes*, say, the first verse of "The Children's 'Don't.'" "*Don't* tell Papa his nose is red / As any rosebud or geranium, / Forbear to eye his hairless head / Or criticize his cootlike cranium; / 'Tis years of sorrow and of care / Have made his head come through his hair." If that doesn't appeal to Vicki, I'll forge on, reciting, "When wilful little Willie Black / Threw all the tea things at his mother, / She murmured, as she hurled them back, / 'One good tea-urn deserves another!'" In any case most words go down smoothly after a Double Magnum. But if the verse catches in Vicki's craw, no matter, the poems make me laugh. Even if Vicki doesn't cachinnate, the lines will cause her to shake her head in wonder, not necessarily appreciative wonder, but a healthy, invigorating seasonal wonder.

Not until conscious life ends do wonder and feeling cease. Thirty-five years ago, the first year Vicki and I were married, I taught in Latakia, Syria, a place we loved but a place that had drifted out of affection, and thought, until last week when I received an e-mail from a former student. Attached to the e-mail was a photograph of the title page of *The Second Penguin Book of English Short Stories*. I had signed the page for my student, writing, "May your life bloom like the small, happy flowers on the green hills." "Dear doctor," my old student wrote, "Today I was searching in my library for a book to teach my son English essay and it was my pleasure to find precious words written on my book by you hand when you were teaching me at Tishreen University in Latakia Syria. After I saw the words I began to look for on the net to keep in touch with you because you have somthing good inside me. I hope you are fine and hope you colourful life. Hope I meet again. My son is now fourth year English literature in the same university of me and I am trying my best to fill his mind with some of the precious information taught by You."

The letter from bleeding Syria awakened, as the gospel song puts it, precious memories, simultaneously making me melancholy and joyful. On the page my life is wanton and disheveled, foolishness coloring one moment, bathos the next, heartache others, but no matter the inconsistencies or more accurately because of them my one living has been, as Thoreau put it, a happy gift. In *The Autumn Holidays of a Country Parson*, Andrew Boyd said that while certain trees ought to be pruned regularly, apples and Irish yew, for example, other trees should not be trimmed, among these birch, beech, oak, and weeping willow. Human beings, Boyd stated, needed "a great deal of pruning." "Like odd habits, the rudiments of worse habits need every now and then to be cut off and corrected. We should all grow very singular and ridiculous and unamiable creatures, but for the pruning we have got from kind and unkind hands from our earliest days." Rigorous grafting determines the savor of apples, making some sweet, others tart. In an apple orchard trees share a field and grow in rows. I was an only child and had fields to myself. When I was a boy, my parents spared the shears, and I spent days alone cantering libraries and pastures. As a result, I grew like Boyd's willow, sprawling and disheveled, frequently dropping branches and paragraphs, odd twigs sprouting from limbs. For readers who like lawns and pages curried, picking up my trains of living may be tedious and inconvenient. For me, though, under the shade of a willow, if I'm not the barky tree itself, life blooms bright like the spring crocus, popping up amid tumbling strings of green, the bulbs planted so long ago the flowers seem to appear spontaneously and unplanned, startling and certainly not pruned, but pleasing and in a vague liquid sense flowing in natural disorder.

Much time has now passed since I left Nova Scotia. Fall has gone. Winter has come to Connecticut. Mirror Lake is an eye of ice. The banks are eyelashes of brown cattails. Deer have chewed rhododendrons in our yard into crinkled shanks, and turkeys pick through bare spots in the wood behind the house. A person never gets quit of himself, and I have succumbed to the tyranny of small duties, shoveling the drive and raking snow off the roof of the study. Yesterday Lockert's daughter Dolly wrote me from North Carolina. "Daddy died earlier this evening at home," she began. In the envelope she included a letter she found on Lockert's printer. The letter was four lines long. Lockert wrote it late on the afternoon before he died. "Yesterday," the last lines stated, "was sunny and no breeze. The beach was crowded like summer." I showed Vicki the letter. "I saw a flock of robins today, and I heard a titmouse whistling," she said. "Summer will be here before we know it, and cardinals will appear around the house. Please don't let them build a nest in the yews by the front stoop." "I won't. I promise I won't," I said then asked, "What should I do if I see wrens in the garage?" "They are messy and are a nuisance, but they make me smile. Just leave them alone," Vicki said.

Reunion

This fall I attended the fiftieth reunion of my class at Sewanee. I had never been to a reunion before, but Vicki said I should go. So near the end of October, we flew to Tennessee. We stayed a week, spending much of our time roaming Sewanee's "Domain," thirteen thousand acres atop the Cumberland Plateau. During mornings we hiked the Perimeter Trail and the new Caldwell Rim Trail. We climbed up and down bluffs, sweating through Shakerag Hollow and out to Piney Point. We leaned like threshers against saplings and pushed through brush around massive blocks of sandstone. We explored dry fire lanes off Brakefield Road, descended slippery stones down Morgan's Steep, and pulled ourselves up and through the stone tunnel at Proctor's Hall. Except for the cackling of pileated woodpeckers and the thin rill of falling water, the forest was silent. The woods were a garden, and we talked little except to note the honeyed variety of trees: yellow sassafras, starry sweet gum, black locust, hickories and maples, chestnut oaks, their foliage paddles needled with holes, walnut, basswood, red cedar, sandy short-leaf pine, and big leaf magnolia, the leaves battered violins, the bodies warped, the fingerboards split, worn out by accompanying the deep musical fragrance of flowers during spring. Our mazy motion slanting through trees and beside bluffs gap-toothed with limestone caves did not transport us to romantic chasms. For a moment, however, the turmoil of living vanished. Our heartbeats slowed, and delight was quiet. We did not stumble upon Coleridge's Abyssinian maid strumming a dulcimer and singing of Mount Abora, but at the Memorial Cross overlooking Hawkins Cove, we came upon a bagpiper playing "Amazing Grace." The man had once been a school teacher. "I gave teaching up for music and play the bagpipe for a living. I perform at weddings, corporate receptions, and parties at country clubs," he said, "but mostly I play for God. That's what I am doing now. I know God hears me."

After the reunion I thought about Emerson's writings. His essays read like chapters from commonplace books. His sentences are epigrammatic and snap so sharply they discourage mulling. They propel the young and the underread into decided opinions, more often than not into agreement. Age, however, unmuzzles pondering. Once the crack of words slumps into silence, age unravels the loops in Emerson's thought and neutralizes their stinging certitude. In "Self-Reliance" Emerson famously wrote, "Whoso would be a man must be a nonconformist." The statement appeals to youth apprehensive that joining society's "joint-stock company" and shaping living to the wills of others destroys individuality and natural inclination. The fear exists despite youth's inability to define individuality or recognize natural inclination. For old stagers who, unlike the young, see life through the closing shutters of years, nonconformity often seems the font of ill humor and, at worse, despair.

Emerson's call for an original relationship to the world ages and has aged poorly, both in the perception of people as they grow older and on the pages of other, later writers. "It is common to talk of originality as the distinguishing mark of genius," William Mathews wrote in 1881, "when, on the contrary, it is essentially receptive and passive in its nature. Its power lies, not in finding out new material, but in imparting new life to whatever it discovers, new or old; not in creating its own fuel, but in fanning its collected fuel into a flame. All the thought, the stuff or substance, of a new poem or essay, is necessarily common place. The thing said has been said in some form a thousand times before; the writer's merit lies in the *way* he says it. We talk, indeed, of *creative* intellects, but only Omnipotence can create, man can only *combine*." Escaping the shell of conformity is impossible in writing and thinking. "The world of books has become like a congested churchyard," L. P. Jacks wrote in *Realities and Shams*. "Every grave we dig disturbs the resting-places of the buried generations. We cannot stir the ground to plant a tree or a rose-bush but the spade turns up the jawbone of a prophet." Even if a person so resists accommodating his living to the demands of society that he appears original, the originality is only momentary. "Man is an imitative animal, and so strong is the instinctive feeling to follow in the footsteps of others," Joseph Neal wrote in *Charcoal Sketches*, "that he who is so fortunate as to strike out a new path must travel rapidly, if he would avoid being run down by imitators."

"Self-Reliance" appeared before Emerson was forty years old. At Sewanee my classmates were over seventy. If Emerson had been among them, afterward he would have written, "Whoso has reached seventy must be a conformist." Most of my classmates were doctors, lawyers, bankers, and owners of businesses. In general people who attend fiftieth reunions are satisfied and at ease in the world. They have lived long and well enough to be comfortable with and simultaneously oblivious to the demands of society. At Sewanee we were serving our end-time genially and had perfected the art of doing little. We agreed with Mark Twain's quip that the only better way of spending a holiday than lying under a tree reading a book was lying under a tree without a book. We had aged not simply beyond disruptive thoughts about "badges and names" but also beyond catchpenny idealism and acrid realism. In G. K. Chesterton's phrase we suffered, if we suffered at all, from "a fanaticism of moderation." The ailments of age did not darken mood, and nodding to expediency came easily. We talked more about friendship and family than about society. We did not argue. We paid closed-lip service to the ancient advice that arguing with a fool accomplished nothing aside from convincing bystanders that two fools were present. On no subject did we try to change another's mind, long ago having realized changing a mind involved serious surgery and no matter the skill of the neurologist always failed. We resurrected "Precious Memories," telling old, old stories, not of the Gospel but nevertheless of love and fondness. Like persimmons we had broken from ambition and the top branches of the tree of life and had been grounded long enough to rot into sweetness.

My favorite tale involved Freddy Russell and my classmate from Nashville Allen Wallace. For sixty-nine years Russell was a sportswriter for the *Nashville Banner*. He was also a legendary prankster. One Saturday in the spring of 1974, Russell and his wife hosted a brunch at their home prior to a Vanderbilt-Tennessee basketball game. Attending were Clay Stapleton, Vanderbilt's athletic director, Alexander Heard, the university's relatively new chancellor, and Wayne Sergeant, who had just moved to Nashville to publish the *Banner*. After the party had been going for twenty minutes, there was a loud knock at the front door. On the steps stood a boisterous man in a black-and-white striped shirt and wearing a whistle around his neck. Although the man appeared to be a basketball referee, he was actually Russell's and my friend Allen Wallace. "I just wanted to come by and say hello before the tip off," Allen announced. The referee's appearance startled Sergeant, who whispered something to his wife. "You could tell," Russell reported later, that "he was probably saying, 'Does this really go on in the South? A basketball official's coming by a sportswriter's home before the game?'" Another of Russell's friends who was in on the joke then took Allen in hand and steered him about the room so everyone could hear what he said. "Listen," the friend said to Allen, "we love your coming by here. We're going to eat in fifteen minutes, and we'd like you to stay and eat with us." "Oh, no, I never eat before a game," Allen answered, scrutinizing the bar before declaring, "I wouldn't mind having a little vodka on the rocks, though." The friend gave Allen a double, after which Allen worked the room, talking to everybody, drinking, and discussing officiating. At this time Alex Heard became considerably exercised and vanished into the library, taking Clay Stapleton with him. "Clay," Heard said, "even if we should win, this is not good." After some more intense schmoozing, Allen looked at his watch then addressing Russell said loudly, "I have got to get to the game, but, how about fixing me one more for the road." Allen then took his drink and left, not before assuring guests at the brunch that the outcome of the game wasn't in doubt, in the process leaving Vanderbilt officialdom fooled and deeply concerned.

"What is commonly called success," A. C. Benson wrote in *At Large*, "has an insidious power of poisoning the clear springs of life because people who grow to depend upon the stimulus of success sink into dreariness and fullness when that stimulus is withdrawn." Benson's statement did not apply to my classmates at the reunion, most of whom had pruned disturbing stimulus from their lives. Moreover, the sympathetic views we took of ourselves and each other banished dreariness. Anecdotes and the times they reflected seemed silly, yet magically and alluringly innocent. For people young enough to be ridden by ambition, life might seem real and earnest. For our part we lived in and for fictions. When Joe got his new "used" Volkswagen Beetle in 1959, he took it for a spin around his hometown in Iowa. Before turning down the backstretch toward his house, he stopped at the local doughnut shop to celebrate. Instead of parking outside, however, he drove through the open front doors up to the counter and ordered a half dozen glazed doughnuts. Receiving and paying for the order proved easy. Unfortunately, reversing and turning were more complex than Joe imagined, and he was still shifting gears when the police arrived. The police hauled Joe off to jail, but since his antics were not fueled by drink but simply high adolescent spirits the sheriff lectured him then telephoned his mother and asked her to fetch him. "No," she said, "staying the night will be a good driving lesson. If Joe gets hungry, he can eat the doughnuts."

"We talk of 'creative' minds," Mathews reiterated, "but this is only a figure of speech, for man can create nothing—he can only select and combine." "The week at Sewanee was enjoyable, and I suppose you'll jot something down about our hikes and your classmates," Vicki said after we returned to Storrs. "But now that you are no longer teaching, what else will you write about?" I retired in September, and students vanished from my life. When I taught, all students, not just those in my classes, seemed individuals. Their lives were storied, and from them I culled paragraphs. After I retired, bright, skipping Alice and rough-around-the-elbows Bob became indistinguishable members of a faceless *they*—an oppressive group disassociated from me, one that clumped together in pushy, almost frightening clots in halls and on sidewalks. Worried that the withering of the university world around me would so reduce the number of things I could "combine" that it would cause my mind to atrophy, I considered writing a murder novel. "I didn't kill anyone until after I stopped teaching," I began. "Although I had long wanted to become a social sewage plant and process cell blocks of criminal sludge, I restrained myself while I was in the classroom. I took teaching seriously and did not want to set a bad example for children." I wrote no more. I decided to call the book *The Broken Chalk Mystery*. Unfortunately, the title brought childhood and the Hardy Boys to mind, novels like *The Disappearing Floor*, *The Secret of the Lost Tunnel*, and *The Shore Road Mystery*. No matter the magnums of blood I spilled, I knew I could never write a book as exciting as *The Sinister Signpost* or *The Crisscross Shadow*. In hopes of broadening my life so I would have more material for pages, I signed up to run the Manchester Road Race on Thanksgiving morning. I had not raced in a year, and on learning that I was running, my friend Raymond gave me a Death Chip, a metallic band that a runner attaches to a shoelace. Printed on the band were my name, address, and telephone number, "so the undertaker," Raymond explained, "will be able to identify your body." "I know that your memory is failing," Raymond continued, "and if you survive the race but forget who you, are the chip should remind you, that is, if you remember to look at your shoe." When the race began, the temperature was thirty degrees. Fifteen thousand people registered to run, and 12,879 ran. I did not reach the starting line until the race had been underway for eight minutes and thirty-two seconds. Feed lots of pumpkin-shaped people and picket fences of friends holding hands surrounded me, and I could barely twitch until after the race was half over. Still, I finished thirty-fourth out of seventy-eight in my division, that is, males aged seventy to seventy-four. "Did you collect a cord of paragraph fuel?" Vicki asked when I returned home. "Oh, yes," I said, "a hearth tub of lightwood."

The object of a walk, Robert Lynd wrote in *The Blue Lion*, was to find a good place to sit. "When you have found this," he advised, "you return to it day after day, and, instead of attempting to make your way round the world, sit down on a tree-stump or on the grass and allow the world to make its way round you. This, I think, is the only way in which to see the world. If you make yourself part of the procession, you cannot see the procession. To do this, you must be content to be a silent spectator, and in time the procession will surely begin." Lynd's advice was good, particularly for a guy chilled and exhausted from racing through the streets of Manchester, Connecticut. The first place in which I sat was the university library. Almost immediately a procession of quotations ambled past. Leading them in stuffy tweeds was a remark made by G. K. Chesterton, "The two things that a healthy person hates most between heaven and hell are a woman who is not dignified and a man who is." Next in more colorful dress adorned with jade ornaments and stitched together with silk ribbons strode a saying of Ernest Bramah's Kai Lung, "There are few situations in life that cannot be honorably settled, and without loss of time, either by suicide, by a bag of gold or by thrusting a despised antagonist over the edge of a precipice on a dark night." The shade of the seventeenth-century divine Thomas Fuller approached, moving at morality's slow pace and reading aloud from *Good Thoughts in Bad Times*. On having his shoes stolen, Nicias, a philosopher, said, "May they fit his feet that took them away." At a glance, Nicias's remark appears good natured. "But there was that in it," *Good Thoughts* recounted, "which poisoned his charity into a malicious revenge. For he himself had hurled or crooked feet, so that in effect he wished for the thief to be lame." Harlequin appeared next and infused bounce into the procession by asking, "Why did the sight of fiddle strings upset the cat?" On my, and Fuller's specter, remaining silent, Harlequin answered his own riddle, "Because they made him think his death would probably result from violin-ce."

Implied in Emerson's urging people to live "in harmony with Nature" and in Thoreau's hectoring advocacy of "Simplicity" was criticism of materialism, the critique seasoned with shakings of sentimental primitivism—a hankering for times better and more honest because they were simpler. As I sat nondescriptly in the library like a responsible conformist thinking about Emerson and half in agreement with his criticism of social life, along came Gerald Gould and *The Return to the Cabbage*, a volume containing Gould's attack on primitivism. Gould noted that savages delighted in putting on clothes while only civilized people dreamed of taking them off. Separated from "the great Heart of Nature," many people assumed that cruder, barer lives were "more natural—more just and apt to the essential but undiscoverable core of humanity." Such people believed that leading less complicated lives calmed body and soul. True placidity, however, could never be found, Gould wrote, "among subtle, various, self-torturing men" or among "self-conscious, self-assertive, self-inhibiting animals," and "certainly not among the roars, croaks, whines, shrieks, moans and gibberings of hill and farm and jungle." To return to Nature and thus achieve a better life, a person, Gould advised, should study vegetables, in particular, cabbages. "They do not sweat and whine about their condition; they do not lie awake in the dark and weep for their sins," Gould explained. "They do not make me sick discussing their duty to God; not one of them is dissatisfied . . . not one is demented with the mania of owning things; not one kneels to another, nor to his kind that lived thousands of years ago; not one is respectable or unhappy over the whole earth." "O new age," he concluded holding the cabbage aloft, "I present you with your ideal."

Once I noticed the procession, slipping its presence was impossible. The gang followed me into my study at home and appeared when I turned on my computer. A former student wrote a blog in which she cited statements she remembered my making in class two years ago. "Ending a sentence on the word *though* is not a big deal, but I wouldn't end on *horseshit*" was the first good counsel she recalled. I occasionally refer to equines when I am not in Emersonian mode, but I don't recall that particular grammatical advice. Supposedly, I observed that "on the Fourth of July, little boys light sparklers and run through the dark spelling bad words in cursive." "Forget all this writing stuff," I may also have suggested, wisely, I must add, "and study caterpillars. Study salamanders. Study butterflies. You'll be happier." When asked if I was the nicest person in America, I responded, "Well, I am, but God Almighty don't say so in public." Overstatement becomes the classroom, and because the last remark was so exaggerated, I probably said it. What I certainly read to the class one morning, and which I wished the girl had remembered, was advice Charles Colton gave in *Lacon*: "Always suspect a man who affects great softness of manner, an unruffled evenness of temper, and an enunciation studied, slow, and deliberate. These things are all unnatural, and bespeak a degree of mental discipline into which he that has no purposes of craft or design to answer, cannot submit to drill himself. The most successful knaves are usually of this description, as smooth as razors dipped in oil, and as sharp. They affect the innocence of the dove, which they have not, in order to hide the cunning of the serpent, which they have."

Of course, my remarks pale beside the astonishing procession of articles that describe the oddities of ordinary living and that appear daily in newspapers across the country. The *Boston Globe* reported on the unsuccessful pursuit of a gay bigamist. The man had husbands in both Connecticut and New York. To escape prosecution, the man fled to Utah from which, the paper reported, it was doubtful he would be extradited, "in light of the state's long history of tolerating, even supporting, polygamy." In Athens, Georgia, the *Banner-Herald* described the failure of environmentalists to replace showers in locker rooms at the University of Georgia with bidets. Unlike showers that wasted "rain forests of water," flushing a bidet consumed only one-eighth of a gallon, although the head of the local chapter of the Green Party, Sherrod Dormer, conceded that a bidet could be overused and abused. "Not, I hope," she hurriedly and "somewhat red-facedly" added, "by our proper student athletes." After much debate the faculty senate at the university vetoed the plan because of the objections of female athletes, two of whom testified that "we are American, not French." In contrast, male athletes overwhelmingly supported the switch, this despite a promising running back from Nahunta straining his thoracolumbar fascia when he bent over, mistaking the sample bidet in the locker room for a water fountain.

In Wartrace, Tennessee, the *Shelbyville Times-Gazette* reported, a "Christian" grocer was arrested "for breaking the Seventh Commandment and committing adultery of the comestible variety." Taped to the entrance of the grocery and hanging throughout the store were verses of gospel music. Above the front door appeared, "I'm not ashamed of Jesus / Who died on the Cross for me. / I'm not ashamed of Jesus / Who suffered on Calvary." Over the meat counter hung, "I can't take a heart that's broken / Make it over again. / But I know a Man who can. / Some call Him Savior, Redeemer of all Men. / But I call Him Jesus, for He's my dearest friend." By the entrance to the lane leading to the cash register stood a sign reading, "He could have called ten thousand angels / To restore this world and set Him Free. / But He died alone for you and me." The reporter was more waggish than he should have been, writing that the grocer "kept a bible up his sleeve." For my part, I was sympathetic to the grocer. A supermarket chain had undercut the grocery's prices and pushed the store almost to bankruptcy, this when the man's familial responsibilities were extraordinarily heavy. Not only did the grocer have three children and an invalid wife and her aged mother living with him, but he was also supporting his widowed sister and her two young children, one of whom suffered from childhood apraxia of speech. Living in this world for others while simultaneously living in the next world for the self has never been easy, certainly not for the poor, not even for the financially comfortable. In any case, the man purchased barrels of corn syrup and used it to adulterate honey, maple syrup, and orange and apple juice, among others. He cut olive oil with sunflower oil and mixed so much sawdust in granolas that the reporter declared him to be "a cereal adulterer."

After middle age, words prefixed by *re* dominate a person's days: retirement, reunion, and remember, among others. Acting and thinking in new ways becomes impossible. Instead, one repeats patterns established through recent decades of living, and the final years of life function as coda to the fugue of being. Often the aged return to habitual activities not to recapture lost youth, but in hopes of resuscitating ache-less moments and of losing self-consciousness in activities so familiar and simultaneously so diverting that time seems to pause. My days of finding pleasure in Childe Harold's "pathless woods" and not worrying about losing my way ended thirty years ago. Only the unfledged, and the silly, discover rapture on Harold's lonely shores. While their offspring are young, daddies roam beaches with children and shovel periwinkles, limpets, whelks, and moon snails into red plastic buckets. Once children forsake sand for school, parents retreat inland. They occasionally picnic near a beach, but usually they stay close to home, digging and planting in the yard. Later, when their backs begin to throb, they lose their trowels and ponder moving south. Few people are actually muscular enough to shoulder the detritus of years, and so they, and I, don't move but instead take sunny vacations. To escape the bony grasp of winter in New England and the chillier season of Christmas alone in Connecticut, I booked a month of cruising the Caribbean with Holland America, something I had done thrice in previous years.

Vicki and I sailed on two ships, a fortnight on the *Prinsendam* followed by two weeks on the *Nieuw Amsterdam*. The first cruise began December 22. The second ended January 19. The ships traveled 6,980 nautical miles or 8,027 statute miles. Although the ships sailed the same seas, the cruises were different. The *Prinsendam* was smaller, carrying slightly less than 800 passengers, while the *Nieuw Amsterdam* carried 2,100. Moreover, while both boats sailed from Port Everglades, the *Prinsendam* stayed at sea for two weeks before returning to Fort Lauderdale. In contrast, the *Nieuw Amsterdam* returned after a week, disembarking and taking on new passengers, thus breaking the cruise into two self-contained loops or, in fact, distinct cruises.

Because the *Prinsendam* was comparatively small, it stopped at islands that large cruise ships could not visit, islands new to Vicki and me, St. John, Bequia, and Terre-de-Haut. Moreover, the *Prinsendam* lingered in ports longer than the *Nieuw Amsterdam*, steering the interest of passengers toward the islands and life beyond the ship. On the *Nieuw Amsterdam*, stops seemed secondary to shipboard activities, a mélange of the slight, ostensibly appealing to the inhabitants of retirement communities: among others, bingo, karaoke, games of trivia, wine-tastings, drawings for slivers of tanzanite, duty-free sales of cosmetics and tobacco, and talks pitching the virtues of acupuncture and, as an advertisement for the ship's greenhouse spa put it, "our sought after selection of skin-perfecting, body-bettering serums, slimmers and smoothers." Both boats, for example, stopped at Grand Turk at eight in the morning. By two-thirty, passengers had to be back on board the *Nieuw Amsterdam*, and shortly before three in the afternoon the ship throbbed away from the dock, its generators jittering, suffering the mechanical equivalent of atrial fibrillations. The *Prinsendam* did not sail until after five, the extra hours warfarin, freeing passengers from the rack of pulsating time and giving them the leisure to explore.

During the stop on Grand Turk, Vicki and I rented bicycles from Oasis Divers on Duke Street, paying $10 each for the day. We rode to the lighthouse four miles away at Northwest Point and afterward meandered the roads webbed around North Creek and the Town Pond. On Grand Turk small donkeys once delivered water to houses and pulled carts loaded with salt to the docks for export. Their descendants now roamed the island. Some fourteen curried the lawn surrounding the lighthouse, jennets grooming, foals nuzzling and sucking, and two jacks displaying their endowments. "Impressive," Vicki commented. I did not respond. The donkeys had worn trails through the heather and prickly pear along the bluff at the point. People also walked the trails dropping bottles that once contained Bambarra Rum. I picked up three bottles and dumped them in the recycle bin at the lighthouse. Off the point, rock ledges curdled lumpy under the surface of the water, and the ocean was a mottle of green and blue. Unfortunately, around the eastern edge of the point, currents poured into each other producing a pool swirling with plastic detritus. The sight darkened the day for a moment, but then a pair of Gulf fritillaries bobbled past distracting me.

After bicycling Vicki and I swam at Pillory Beach. There we collected a wallet of inflated sea biscuits and watched a great egret pick through brush above the sand. In Cockburn Town we drank Turk's Head beer and munched conk fritters and cracked lobster at Olivia's stand. While I ate, a well-fed, rusty brown bitch with nipples pulled into the size of corks fell asleep between my feet. Across Front Street a Geiger tree red with blossoms looked like a Christmas wreath. From a retired minister at a souvenir stand opposite St. Mary's Anglican Church, Vicki purchased six straw coasters. A ring of small shells, probably Atlantic bubbles, formed the border of each coaster. Vicki also bought me a blue souvenir tee-shirt. Swimming sewn across the chest and through green seaweed were three fanciful tropical fish striped orange and red, yellow and turquoise. Below the fish appeared "Turks & Caicos." The print notwithstanding, the shirt was made in Honduras, and the coasters probably came from the same place. Also on Grand Turk Vicki bought three hand-sized paper mache saucers. The saucers were a patchwork of colors. My favorite saucer resembled a crazy quilt of blocks. Purple snails pulled themselves across a brown rock. Seaweed wavered tremulous in pink and yellow waves, and orange dots spotted the shingled carapace of a turtle. During the month Vicki and I collected few souvenirs, all small and inexpensive. To a vendor on the boardwalk in Samana in the Dominican Republic, I paid six dollars for a mysterious wooden creature. "A curiosity for the study," I said; "since visitors never mention my books, this will give them something to talk about." Mahogany and three inches high, four long, and one and a half wide, the creature had the general shape of a tailless dog. Woodcuts turned its sides and back into those of a zebra while its head looked like that of a turtle, the beak, however, rounded and flattened, the mouth a thin smile, the eyes round wells. For her part Vicki purchased a miscellany of little items, mostly presents, among others, in Samana a diminutive wooden turtle that actually looked like a turtle and for our daughter Eliza the contents of a small jewelry box, sea shell earrings, and a bracelet beaded with mahogany. Hanging from a silver link on the bracelet was a dark wooden fish, a chiton pasted to its back, the mosaic on the shell softening the wood and floating the fish up into the light. On Bequia Vicki picked up a grocery cart of carry-bags stitched from sacks of chicken feed, the contents processed by East Caribbean Feeds in St. Vincent—for pullets, layers, and broilers. "Useful for shopping in Willimantic," Vicki said. She also bought a serving dish made from half a calabash. "Bob" had scraped away much of the gourd's rind but left it thick on the bottom, the remnant shaped like a hawksbill turtle. I didn't shop on Bequia. Nevertheless, I carried complimentary souvenirs back to the boat, dog droppings thick between the treads of my hiking shoes. In St. Lucia Vicki paid a dollar for a glass painted with fanciful red hibiscus blossoms. Nestled among the petals was a blue hoopoe, the feathers on its head raised into a crown, the shafts black, the barbs white. In Mexico she paid five dollars for a small yellow ceramic bowl covered with red peppers, and on Grand Cayman, she bought two weightless wooden rings carved from date palm nuts. The rings had been shellacked and painted simply, caramel splotched by vanilla decorations, dots and wobbly rectangles.

Among the pleasures of roaming, Charles Conrad Abbott declared, was the possibility of an "unexpected occurrence, a sort of gathering grapes from thistles." The grapes we plucked when away from the *Prinsendam* were often pinched and moldy, but they satisfied our appetites. In Cockburn Town a sign taped to the front window of Munchkins Bakery on Market Street announced "Beer Available." "An all-purpose bakery," Vicki said when I walked out of the shop holding a slice of chocolate cake and two doughnuts. The sign delighted us, but the doughnuts were too thistly to eat. They were so stale that only soaking them in beer would have made them palatable. Dogs are not as particular as people, and just before we boarded the boat to leave the island, Vicki fed the doughnuts to an ancient dog sunk to rib and pelvis. "My good deed for the day," Vicki said. "I am glad you found Munchkins."

On Holland America, the unexpected is the expected: the chocolate feast by the pool late one night or escargot and baked Alaska for dinner at least once, nothing like the happenings on the Orient steamer that Maurice Baring took from Tilbury to Fremantle just before World War I. One morning as the ship was traveling down the Red Sea, Baring wrote in *Round the World in Any Number of Days*, a stoker, "a Maltee, went mad, owing to the heat, and jumped overboard." The steamer stopped but could do nothing as, Baring recounted laconically, "the sea is full of sharks."

For reading people, trips are in great part printed words. In Key West across Fleming Street from Key West Island Books and the Amazing Cakes and Creative Bakery was Living Dolls, a sporting house. "Full Nude. You Get Naked Too," words pasted to the window proclaimed; "One on One and Couples Welcome. Outcalls Available. Menu of Services." "I suppose the spécialité de la maison is flank steak," I said. "No," Vicki replied, "pulled pork." Around Mallory Square on the Key West waterfront, homeless men and cats lived rough. The men cared for the cats, in the process softening their own hard lives. Bound by rubber bands to a wrought iron fence at the town side of Mallory Square was a cardboard sign reading, "Help Our Kitty's Have a Merry Christmas." Chained to the fence below the sign was a wooden box into which passersby could drop contributions for the cats. "Do you think the money really goes for Puss 'N Boots and not Ripple?" Vicki asked, holding two dollars in her hand. "Yes," I said. "Put the money in the box."

In Port Elizabeth a sign informed tourists that the De Bistro restaurant was an international franchise located in New York, London, Paris, and Bequia. In Antigua amid the grounds of St. John's Cathedral, a high fence of rusted iron spikes surrounded a raised stone box tomb. Leaning against an end of the tomb was a scrap of cardboard ripped from a packing case. "This End Up," printing on the scrap urged, the words bookended by arrows pointing skyward. The cardboard was upside down, however, and the arrows pointed at the ground. "Oh, dear," Vicki said, "not the direction the family hoped the departed would take." "Who knows?" I said. "Wills determine the attitudes of families." After a warm morning of exploring old San Juan, Vicki and I shared a mound of ice cream in Café Galleria on Cristo Street—three varieties of ice cream, chocolate fudge brownie; coffee, coffee, buzz, buzz, buzz; and chunky monkey. The café sold Ben and Jerry's ice cream and was sugary with sloganeering American optimism. Printed outside on the door of the café was "Love, Peace, and Ice Cream." Inside, uplift twisted serpentine over the walls, coiling into phrases like "Relax. Just Love" and "Be True. Be You. Be Brave." Sweet thoughts often bring sour thoughts to mind. I frowned, but before I slipped into cynicism, Vicki spoke. Vicki can read my lips even when I don't move them. "Be quiet. Don't spoil the day," she said. "The ice cream was tasty and invigorating. Now I am going to buy two cappuccinos. They'll be good, too."

People turn themselves into tablets. Through the customs building in Port Everglades, a woman pushed an old man in a wheelchair. Sticking out between the man's teeth was the soggy remnant of a panatela. On the man's head sat a green baseball cap; scrolling across the crown in white letters was "Over the Hill." For several days on the *Nieuw Amsterdam*, a passenger the size of a *Mola mola* wore a shirt on the chest of which was printed, "I Survived Anorexia." Akin to words glimpsed are words heard. In Charlotte Amalie on St. Thomas, a huckster stepped out of Post Office Alley and spoke to Vicki as we walked along Veteran's Drive. The man was a talking sandwich board. "Pardon me," he said staring at Vicki's feet. "I can't believe you are wearing those shoes. Last night Oprah Winfrey hosted a special and said those shoes really went well with the jewelry I sell." Vicki looked puzzled then smiled. I chatted with the man until he spotted another tourist and addressed her, repeating the remarks he made to Vicki. "When two or more cruise ships are docked, I say those words at least two hundred times a day," the man told me, adding, "they work. The number of people they entice into my store would startle you." Beside the lighthouse at El Morro Castle in old San Juan, a man compared his wife to a scatterbrained young dog he'd tried to train to fetch the morning newspaper. The wife maundered about the castle aimlessly, from the husband's point of view. "You're like a puppy," the man said. "You sniff a stick then pick up a rubber ball, and I never get my damn paper."

Robert Louis Stevenson compared "natural talk" to plowing, saying good conversation ought to turn up "a large surface of life" rather than dig "mines into geological strata." Vicki and I are practically an island unto ourselves. Almost never on a cruise have we crossed the main deck and become chummy with other passengers. No one we have met on a cruise has sent us a Christmas card. Even when we ate meals with other people on the *Nieuw Amsterdam* and *Prinsendam*, conversation rarely rose on thermals of words to the altitude of anecdote. Much was spoken but little soared. Still, some statements clung like remoras to memory. "Come here. I have something to tell you," a woman said as Vicki and I ambled through the Lido Restaurant on the *Nieuw Amsterdam*. We had not seen the woman before, but since she motioned to us crooking the index finger on her right hand, we obeyed her command. "Never," she said, lowering her voice and looking around, swiveling her head carefully before continuing, "never trust a hornet." I nodded and said, "Thank you." "Was that wit?" Vicki wondered as we walked away from the woman. "No, age," I answered although short declaratives are frequently purloined. Josh Billings's quip that some people's brains are located in their heads has appeared in many conversations, usually masquerading as spontaneity. On board the ships, however, age, not plagiary, affected much that I heard. A retired brigadier general asked if I were related to the Pickering who led the famous charge at Gettysburg. I considered pointing out that my last name ended in *e-ring*, an internet matrimonial, while the name of Lee's lieutenant ended in the gustatory *ett*. The general was old and had long been hors de combat, however, and I didn't want to confuse him or embarrass his wife, who managed their cruise like a good quartermaster, so I simply said, "No."

Humor forever slips the managed care of libraries. Raconteurs slather fresh vocabulary on tales like pancake makeup in order to make them appear youthful. Crow's feet, however, crinkle over them like dusty spider webs, and instead of bounding into jokes the tales remain that more ancient thing, the jape. An old lady was being shown the spot where the Confederate General Stonewall Jackson fell during the Civil War, a comedian recounted during a show one night. "Goodness me! No wonder," the old lady replied. "Heavens! It's so slippery there I nearly fell myself." On the *Prinsendam*, an entertainer appealed to British travelers by quoting, but not acknowledging, Charles Colton's statement that "while an Irishman fights before he reasons and a Scotchman reasons before he fights, an Englishman is not particular as to the order of precedence, but will do either to accommodate his customers."

"I call that a barbed-wire dress," a man said commenting on the skimpy outfit a woman wore to a formal evening; "it protects the property but it doesn't spoil the view." "Personal injury lawyers held a convention at Pompano Beach last week," a man waiting in line for a dinner table informed people standing nearby. "The lawyers didn't swim much. The only time one of them went into the ocean, a shark chased him out of the water," the man continued. "What a shocking lack of professional courtesy! I imagine the shark's finny compatriots must have dis-sandbarred him." In describing a prominent Republican politician in South Carolina, a man with whom Vicki and I once shared tea with on the *Prinsendam* said, "He is descended from a long line of men who found wives at family reunions." "Oh, that's nothing," a woman sitting across from us drinking stout black tea remarked. "Last week I read in the *Daily Post* that the fathers of forty-six percent of our present congressmen married their first or second cousins."

Vicki and I chatted more with the drivers of the taxis and vans we hired to take us around islands than with our fellow travelers: Dwight, Angel,

Alfredo, Marlene on Grand Cayman who talked nonstop, informing us about "everything" in an English peculiar to herself and that we could not understand, and then James on Barbados. James did not obey the port's rule and wait in the taxi line at the cruise dock. Two years ago he approached us as we walked down Princess Alice Highway and seduced us into hiring him for the day. James was charming and good-natured and a little creatively crooked. He was so memorably sunny that months after the cruise when Vicki and I recalled jaunts around the Caribbean, he slipped into the conversation. "I wonder where James is now," Vicki said this year as we left the port, the taxi line vanishing behind us. Almost immediately, James appeared. He remembered us, not simply that he drove us in the past but that we were from Connecticut, that I taught school, and that Vicki loved animals. James looked the same, the only noticeable difference being that his smile was brighter, this because over his front teeth he now wore a grill decorated with "diamonds and rubies," the stones forming dominos. Drivers told us stories getting matters slightly wrong. Arthur, for example, drove us from Castries across St. Lucia to the Mamiku Gardens on the East Coast. Near the garden in the heights above Dennery was Bordelais prison. Fer-de-lances infested the forest surrounding the prison. The snake was endemic to St. Lucia, but Arthur said that the government imported the snakes from Africa and scattered them about the woods in order to discourage escapes. The plan was successful. Because prisoners were frightened of venturing into the forest, officials were able to hire fewer guards, thus saving money. Twice before on St. Lucia, people had told me about the importation of fer-de-lances, both times noting with approval that snakes were less expensive than and a green alternative to electrified fences and concertina wire.

Passengers on the *Prinsendam* differed slightly from those on the *Niuew Amsterdam*. Not only did the cruise on the *Prinsendam* last two full weeks, but each week was more expensive than a comparable week on the *Niuew Amsterdam*. Probably because passengers spent more on their holidays, they seemed to "invest" more of themselves in the trip. They appeared more cultured, ignoring the jangle of onboard activities and not so much taking as selecting the cruise because the boat stopped at islands that intrigued them. Moreover, a goodly percentage of the *Prinsendam*'s passengers were Canadian or European and had long planned their travel. In contrast, the one-week cruises of the *Nieuw Amsterdam* attracted Floridians, people not buckled to airplane fares and schedules, retirees quick to purchase tickets at reduced prices and able to leave their condominiums at a whim's notice. At times the boat seemed populated solely by groups taking vacations from gated communities. A great majority of these passengers were women. In a group of nineteen that I met, only a single person was male. One afternoon a woman and I entered an elevator on the second deck at the same time. On the next deck the door opened, and three other women joined us. "Heavens," one exclaimed, "what is that wonderful fragrance?" I smelled nothing. "It's my perfume," the woman who got on the elevator with me said, extending her wrist, passing it around like a serving dish. The other women bent over and sniffed. "Wonderful," one said. "It's Panache," the woman said. "I order it from London." The elevator stopped again, and all the women got out talking animatedly. Once the door shut and my ride continued, I wrinkled my nose and breathed analytically, snuffing the four corners of the elevator. The air was stale, and aside from a touch of carpet cleaner and a whiff of outsole, I couldn't detect any aroma. After breakfast one morning, a krill of bling appeared on tables beside the Lido pool: wallets, shirts, pendants, hats, watches, key chains, scarves, necklaces, and bracelets, everything costing ten dollars or less. Immediately schools of sharks swept open-pursed across the tables. The first school consisted of forty-three women and two men. Later, when the shops on the promenade deck held an open house, the numbers were more balanced, consisting of thirty-seven women and five men, the men probably attracted by flutes of champagne—vinegary but free.

When I booked the weeks on the *Niuew Amsterdam*, I didn't realize that the cruises were devoted to the finals of Holland America's seaborne version of *Dancing with the Stars*, a popular television program. During the cruises "celebrities" from the program appeared and danced, causing astonishing turmoil and excitement. I had not heard of *Dancing* or the celebrities. One morning I paused at the doorway to the showroom and overheard a speaker declare "motion equals emotion," a remark that garnered wild applause from the audience but drove me into the freshening air on deck. Stomping and banshee screams answered the cruise director every evening when he asked, "Are you happy?" The noise was so loud that before attending shows I stuffed wads of Kleenex into my ears. In truth, however, many passengers booked the cruise in order to dance, observe dancing, and meet stars.

Being an outsider can make a person hypercritical. After a week on the *Niuew Amsterdam*, many passengers struck me as cartoonish. A few who "lived to dance" and taught dancing looked desiccated and too blond or too red haired for their ages. Their noses and chins were sharp, and their hair often stood up straight in dry quills. Vicki called them woodpeckers. Other devotees of *Dancing with the Stars* were overweight television addicts. They wore bikinis and spent hours lounging in deck chairs around the sea view pool. When I glanced down at them from the panorama deck, they resembled walruses beached on a rocky island in the Aleutians. Brown and hairy, their pods swollen around them, the males looked like old bulls, detusked but seamed with scars, their shoulders and backs greased and roiling with rockweed and kelp. "The Perils of Obesity," Vicki said later, quoting Harry Graham as we walked the promenade deck, "Yesterday my gun exploded / When I thought it wasn't loaded; / Near my wife I pressed the trigger, / Chipped a fragment off her figure; / 'Course I'm sorry, and all that, / But she shouldn't be so fat."

Twice during the cruise the staff of the *Niuew Amsterdam* staged fashion shows on deck. I watched the first show. The celebrities and several of the boat's resident dancers pranced around the sea view pool dressed in hothouse outfits. The clothes had been worn by or were similar to those worn by performers on television. Music appropriate to the costumes accompanied the models as they circled the pool, the tango, the samba, cha-cha and merengue, among others. The dresses were farragoes of mesh, ruffles, beads, sequins, netting, appliqués upon appliqués, and fluffs of neon ostrich feathers—red, blue, pink, green, and yellow—clothes not suitable for kitchens, pantries, or basement washing machines. The models wore high heels that looked like bits, but instead of tapping into thought they simply clicked on the deck. The women seemed store-bought flowers, their long, bare legs taproots pulled from the soil and scrubbed into sterility, their bodies gift wrapped in tissue paper and sold, not in florist shops, but in Price Chopper groceries. As the models danced through the parade, their breasts and bottoms quivered, shaking like fruits about to break from cankered twigs. After the show ended, I leaned against the railing of the deck and watched masked boobies waltz the air, elegant in black and white. Tilting and swinging, never jabbering or twitching, they suddenly folded into pikes and plunged, pursuing fish in the water below, above them cumulus clouds billowing silently into melody.

Such moments were disappointingly rare. The farther the ships traveled from Florida, the fewer the birds. A flock of black skimmers congregated on the seaward lip of Mallory Square in Key West, their bills smears of orange lipstick making the birds appear gossipy. At Port Everglades an osprey soared above the Intercostal Waterway, and turkey vultures glided into the scrub beside North Ocean Drive. Little blue herons tapped through the hedges of West Indian Jasmine planted above the New River in Fort Lauderdale. Near the Lauderdale Marina grackles scavenged boardwalks, and terns tossed themselves about like confetti. At sea and amid the islands, the number of birds decreased. Off Cuba, red-footed boobies culled flying fish disturbed by the ship. Mockingbirds and bananaquits foraged brush on Little San Salvador Island. Tri-colored herons crept along the shoreline of Town Pond on Grand Turk. On Terre-de-Haut cattle egrets shared a rough hillside with goats, chickens, and iguanas. A green-throated Carib shimmied through an orchid tree in the Mamiku Gardens on St. Lucia, and a pair of frigate birds greeted the *Prinsendam* when it sailed into St. John's Harbor in Antigua. Aside from the fashion models whom Vicki said did not resemble flowers but flightless rails, I saw no birds out of the ordinary, if, of course, flying creatures can ever be called ordinary.

Idle people, Laurence Sterne wrote in *A Sentimental Journey*, went abroad for one of three reasons—"Infirmity of body, Imbecility of mind, or Inevitable necessity." Although most passengers on both cruises were aged, they didn't travel in order to keep tuberculosis at breath's distance as Englishmen did in the eighteenth and nineteenth centuries. Travelers didn't expect to recapture the capacities of youth. At best they wanted to awaken curiosity and momentarily separate themselves from the routines of ordinary living. Passengers were not nomads or people eager to delve into strange cultures. Slight differences in the surfaces of places—a fresher breeze and a little more light—satisfied their and my expectations. Moreover, shipboard life was almost familiar. Its divergences from the timetables and customs travelers experienced at home were not striking enough to dislocate and make people uncomfortable. As for necessity, I've never met a passenger fleeing the constabulary or trying to creep into the Caymans in order to withdraw funds from a secret bank account. On the other hand, imbeciles gathered every night in the casinos, particularly the casino on the *Niuew Amsterdam*, smoking and cackling like starlings. Moreover, every day a goodly number of people whose taste flickered at low wattages admired the kitsch for sale in the boats' art galleries.

Two days before I left Storrs, my friend Josh commented on the sales of my books. "You should be proud," he said. "You've perfected writing the unread." "Not the unread, but something much better," I replied. "I've perfected writing the unwritten. My volumes are scandalously cheap. Moreover, if a fellow drops a copy on the floor, picking it up won't rupture his bosom. At night he doesn't have to turn a light on in the bedroom and waste electricity in order to read one of my books. Moreover, the tales are salubrious. The paragraphs are not kennels housing apparitions of blue devils and black dogs. Never do the plots cause hypertension, blister the affections, or worry a person into hives. And when the reader finishes a book, recycling is easy." I believed my rejoinder would sweep Josh's remark out of mind. I was mistaken. Three or so times during the cruise, his statement unexpectedly popped into thought. As the old saying describing a cat's misbehavior puts it, Josh's comment "crept in, crapped, and crept out," soiling moments and making me susceptible to misanthropy. While gale force applause rising from the showroom triggered one spell, the yard-sale canvases hawked as high art caused others. "Take care that the mind does not become too fastidious and refined. It is not a blessing, but a hindrance in the work of life," the nineteenth-century divine F. W. Robertson cautioned, good but difficult advice to live up to. In any case, Vicki and I may not be typical cruisers. We don't buy paintings. We have never gambled, and not once in the two hundred days we've spent on cruises have we bathed in a ship's pool. Once our exploration of an island ends, however, we generally swim on a beach, during this trip at beaches named Pillory, Princess Margaret, Dickinson, and Enterprise. On St. Thomas, we swam at the beach tucked into Secret Harbor, after which we guzzled "Lime in the Coconut" at the Cruzan Beach Club. Our favorite beach was Pompierre on Terre-de-Haut, a white, sandy bay with coconut palms splaying above it in rich green falls and goats suddenly drifting close, cadging scraps.

Feeling almost at home even though one is far from home becomes more important as a person ages. The unknown and the unexpected disturb rather than challenge. College reunions are now associated with the phrase "old home week." At a reunion, an alumnus experiences the continuities of friendship and place, even though the place may have changed radically since the alumnus last visited. In Fort Lauderdale, Vicki and I spent two nights in the Riverside Hotel on Las Olas. Leaving Storrs at four in the morning and flying from Hartford exhausted us, but when a receptionist greeted us by name in the hotel lobby, our energies quickened. We deposited our bags in our room, left the hotel, and ambled along the New River. The familiar sights boosted our spirits: royal and cabbage palms, live oaks, Poinciana with its filigreed leaves, inside stone pots the sepals and petals of bird-of-paradise blooming sharp, the flowers looking like orange Swiss Army Knives, and then women leashed to condo dogs, most of which looked like white muffs. I stood on the porch of the New River Inn and watched a train clatter over the river on tracks owned by Florida East Coast Railway. The engine was diesel, but as flat and box cars, coal carriers, and tankers banged past, I recalled the steam engines and trains of childhood, the Norfolk & Western rolling through Hanover, Virginia, in the black night, whistle crying and headlamp weeping light; the N. C. & St. L., muscular, rods driving, wheels rolling and flexing, as it pounded along the trellis crossing West End Avenue near the Sulgrave Apartments in Nashville. The appearances and appointments of cruise ships don't appeal to me, their lines sagging under decks stacked too high, blocked, and stretched wavering, their velour interiors glitzy with imitation art nouveau. As trains attract me, their cars splotched and tattooed with graffiti, so in ports I noticed the workaday: a tugboat with nine tires strung along each side, in Bequia, *Geronimo* and *Melino*, old hulks, rust spreading across their blue hulls like eczema, and in Barbados, the *Tropical Unity*, a small, gray container ship, cranes hovering over and picking at it like long-mandibled insects.

As sights along the New River invigorated us, so did eating familiar food at familiar places, chicken pesto sandwiches at the Gran Forno Bakery and breaded alligator at Fifteenth Street Fisheries. At the Downtowner Saloon we split a Jack's Burger and a sampler of beers, my favorite being Funky Budda's Floridian Hefeweizen, which smacked of cloves, although Vicki insisted that it tasted like Lapsang Souchong tea. Two nights later the Santa Pub Crawl occurred. Hundreds of people dressed like Santa and his helpers wandered down Las Olas eating and drinking. Some helpers had extraordinarily toasty constitutions as their outfits looked too skimpy for the hammering and gluing that occurs in toy shops at the North Pole. Indeed, even on a warm night in Fort Lauderdale, wearers risked frostbite. Vicki and I sat on a bench across from the Riverside and ate ice cream as we watched the parade, Vicki eating a hazelnut-mocha gelato and I a cup of Dominican chocolate from Kilwin's. As we munched, a high-spirited girl wearing a jewelry counter of sparkly bracelets, green elf cap, red tights, and boots with fluffy white faux fur tops skipped across onto the sidewalk and hugged us, saying, "You are so adorable." "Nuts," I muttered. "Not many," Vicki said misunderstanding me, "Not enough to justify the price of this gelato. But wasn't that girl sweet?" Alas, a week later in Bequia, a market woman greeted me saying, "Hello, papa."

"Age," Vicki said, "is in the eye of the beholder, not in the being of the person beheld. Remember you are an exornati" (Sewanee's name for graduates who have lived long enough to attend a fiftieth reunion). From the market woman we bought lunch, paying ten dollars for chicken, rice and beans, macaroni, salad, and bottles of Presidente beer. We sat on a stone wall and ate, our companions a grackle and an unwashed yellow mutt. "A chicken hound," Vicki said, "a breed not registered with the Kennel Club but strong-jawed and a capable, enduring dog nonetheless." One of the signs of a real gourmet, M. F. K. Fisher wrote, "was a complete lack of caution." Once Vicki and I left Fort Lauderdale, we became gourmands. Off the boat we shed the "weight of uncomfortable caution" and foraged the streets: eating curried goat and sweet and sour fish in George Town, at the Roti King on St. Mary Street in St. John's, munchy, pale balls composed of ground split yellow peas, flour, and tamarind sauce, and from a country woman on the dock at Cruz Bay, a package of Torments of Love, round, doughy beignet-like pastries sweetened with fruit pastes, coconut, banana, papaya, or guava. In Samana, we ate at Pico Pollo Yiya, an open café-like restaurant. The restaurant was empty aside from the cook, a waitress, and two shoeshine boys sitting nearby on the curb of Marina Avenue. In the kitchen I found a fresh red snapper. The cook fried it, and Vicki and I ate it with rice and beans, drinking two liter bottles of Presidente beer. Afterward we walked across Marina. While Vicki shopped for souvenirs, I dozed in the sun and watched pelicans dive into the bay. In Bridgetown we wandered behind St. Peter and Paul Catholic Church, momentarily getting lost. We were the only people on the street who looked "like us," and Vicki became nervous. "If somebody frightens you, run," I said, "and don't worry. I will be streaking ahead, damn far ahead, yelling for help." "You bastard," Vicki said. "I hope you get mugged." Vicki's mood mellowed when I discovered Yvonne's Bakery. We bought four pastries that resembled Lithuanian nut rolls, two stuffed with raisins and almonds and two with coconut. The pastries were thick and heavy, but they were light on the palate and were the best sweets we ate in the Caribbean.

At a closet-like grill on a back street in Playa del Carmen, we ate tacos composed of cheese, refried beans, and spicy pork, eye-wateringly hot. I threw up several times that night, but no matter, the tacos tasted better than any I'd ever eaten. The most unpleasant food I tasted was a drink in Florida, however. The *Nieuw Amsterdam* docked at Port Everglades for a day at the end of its initial week of cruising. Vicki and I spent the day ashore roaming the Broadwalk at Hollywood Beach. At Josh's Organic Juice Bar, I drank an Egg Fruit Smoothie. Made from egg fruit, bananas, and coconut water and meat, the smoothie was the color of an egg yolk and tasted like musty clay. It was also a bowel scourer sending me scampering to the lavatory in the Welcome Center. Vicki and I liked Hollywood, however. Early in the morning the beach was bare, but by noon umbrellas had rooted and bloomed looking like a field of windflowers. Also thriving at midday were old men. Scores of bare-chested, barrel-bellied, bung-naveled, ancient boys paraded along the Broadwalk. All reeked of sunscreen and sweat, the fragrance stronger than that of durians. Their shoulders were scaly and covered by husks of hair, making them bristle like pineapples. "Not pineapples," Vicki said. "They look like walking merkins."

Time has cleared my life, grubbing out the stumps of athletics and politics, superstition and common sense. People who once loomed like rocks have been reduced to pebbly fill. Although I have lost most of my root hairs, and hair, and although newsprint cankers my feelings, interest invariably buds in the presence of plants, some of which I've never before noticed and some of which I have known as long as college classmates. Attention sends out runners. The tar spots of years pale and, sappy as it sounds, metaphorically and literarily, life flowers spilling good cheer through days. In rain forests, in cities weeviled by cars and on beaches crowded with the grumpy and the disheveled, suddenly I recognize a tree and feel an unexpected exhilaration. When I saw the long threaded twigs of casuarina or leaflets of neem combed and falling parted along midribs, no longer was I a tourist dissociated from place and feeling. My spirits bounded when I noticed gullet-like pods swaying on tamarind, smelled the cheesy fruits of Indian mulberry, recognized testicular breadfruit, or imagined the leaf blades of silver palms folding and spreading, silently shuffling the wind into notes too high for my hearing.

Rhythm and pace forsook me, and I stumbled when I saw white frangipani, Tecoma's golden bells, concert bands of trumpet trees brassy with pink or yellow blossoms, and just above high water, Portia tree. Clinging to this last tree's branches were pouches of dried brown fruits and hibiscus-like flowers, the petals wrinkled and thinly lustered. Paradoxically, stumbling made me both blink and open my eyes, enabling me to avoid thorny, snagging catch-and-keep vine and forcing me to notice white passion flower winding through platters of sea grape. Pausing, I saw coral vine, or chain of love, curling pink across hillsides and bougainvillea cushioning itself atop jumbie bean, turning an abandoned lot into a garden. Thunbergia appealed to me more than any other vine, scrolling over trellises and shrubs, and scaling walls and the sides of buildings. Masses of trumpets blossomed on the two most common varieties, dark blue on scrambling sky flower and light blue on Bengal clock vine. When asked the local name for thunbergia, islanders shrugged unknowingly. On Terre-de-Haut the vine carpeted the front porch of a house, tendrils of blossoms dangling and rising endlessly in blue constellations. The owner of the house stood in the side yard feeding sheep. On my speculating about the name of the vine, the man stared at his porch for a moment then said, "I just call it flower."

Vicki's and my favorite ramble during the cruise was in the Virgin Islands National Park on St. John. We hiked the Reef Bay Trail as it descended to Reef Bay, starting from Centerline Road five miles east of Cruz Bay. The trail was slightly over two miles long and wound through damp and dry forests following a Danish cart road collapsed into ankle-twisting gullies. A park ranger led the way. At the bay we swam to a boat that carried us back to Cruz Bay, circling the southeast coast of the island past Chocolate Hole and the bays, Fish, Rendezvous, Grand Cruz, and Turner. Appearing potted, brome-liads flourished high in trees. Termite nests clumped around limbs looking like bulbous, crusty wens, their epidermises stretched but strong enough to stop the nests from rupturing. From the nests shelter tubes trailed down the sides of trees to the ground. A black gongolo millipede crawled through litter on the forest floor, its legs moving in waves. When held, the millipede emitted an orange liquid that smelled like iodine and burned my nostrils when I sniffed it. Great trees grew beside the trail. Beneath their crowns, my pretensions—hopes, fears, achievements—were meaningless, an awareness that lowered my blood pressure and comforted me, allowing me to saunter and avoid the temptation to impose distorting significance.

The heavy buttresses of kapoks billowed like sails, and the knobby rem-nants of broken branches stuck out from the trunks looking like carronades. Around them faces shifted in an absence of design. "Smile, O voluptuous, cool-breathed Earth!" I said to Vicki, quoting Walt Whitman, "Earth of the slumbering and liquid trees!" Across the limbs of massive mangos, colors melted, flowed orange, then hardened brown and black before melting and flowing again. The tracks of spikes that circled sandbox tree were responsible for another of the tree's names, monkey-no-climb. While the trunks of bay rum trees ripped tan and sinewy, the leaves were dainty and frivolous, their fragrance reminiscent of Old Spice, more appealing than the meat inside the seed pods of West Indian locust, which smelled like rotten banana. At the bottom of the trail, hundreds of hermit crabs dragged through the wrecked buildings of a sugar mill. Swaying from ceilings of the buildings were brooms of Jamaican fruit bats. Emerson did not go far enough when he wrote that Nature "wears the colors of the spirit." Just as true is the statement that Na-ture colors the spirit. Later that day when the *Prinsendam* sailed from St. John, the sky was a palate of grays and silvers, metallic then milky and yellow as sunlight burst through bodices of clouds. After dark the clouds drifted away; the sky was clear, and the moon rose, almost full. "A pretty good day," I said to Vicki as we stood on deck looking up at the stars. "A pretty darn good day," Vicki said, repeating the phrase and for emphasis inserting *darn*, a word more sincere and less mindlessly reflexive than *damn*.

As we left Mamiku Gardens in St. Lucia, Arthur handed Vicki and me each a leaf from the air or leaf of life plant. The leaves were a panacea for a pest house of human ills. They cured cancer, healed abscesses, blocked coughs, lowered hypertension and cholesterol, stymied the rot of diabetes, and purged rank bacteria and harmful worms from the intestines. Not only did the leaf awaken flagging appetites, one for food, another for intimate doings, but it also reversed aging. Plantlets sprout from the edges of the leaves. Arthur instructed us to press the leaves between the pages of a book. "Take them home and plant them. After the plants grow, pluck leaves and dry them. Make tea out of the leaves if you get sick," he said. "When you get better, you will remember St. Lucia." "Is taking the leaves into the country legal?" Vicki asked while waiting to clear customs in Fort Lauderdale. "Who cares?" I said, "Customs, the Food and Drug Administration, the Center for Disease Control, the President of the United States—not one of them gives a hoot in hell about the leaves or us. The only people who might be upset work for drug companies. Our leaves will put them out of business." The leaves are now in our kitchen in Storrs planted in small plastic cups. Outside the house snow is a foot deep and walking is hazardous. The temperature has been below freezing for eleven days. Ice lies piled against the banks of the Fenton River looking like loaves of white bread, ripped open, the slices tossed haphazardly onto the ground. The limbs of hemlocks are teary with snow, and the woods are silent, the shadow of a crow passing above the trees the only movement. At night the sound of snow plows growling never ends. The kitchen, however, is a warm and quietly affectionate place, a nursery of small succulents.

In and Out of It

Leslie Stephen said people should read Emerson's essays as Emerson read his predecessors, "for stimulus or inspiration." "We are not to take his philosophy for a system of truths," Stephen cautioned, "but for a series of vivid intuitions." Most people are taxonomists. They prefer law to intuition and are reassured by rule and definition. Literary critics analyze and recombine Emerson's thought and in the process rarely fail to fabricate system and coherence. Religions attract crowds because, as Clutton-Brock put it, they attempt to set people "above custom, above the need for reasoning, above ethics." Religions create fictional worlds that are comfortable because they appear stable. A great part of the lure of fiction and non-fiction is that they both are molded and thus fictional. "The advantage of literature over life," Jerome K. Jerome wrote, "is that its characters are clearly defined, and act consistently. Nature, always inartistic, takes pleasure in creating the impossible." Actual human life, J. H. Shorthouse stated in agreement, "does not group itself in stage effects" or "arrange itself in elaborate plot."

The intuitive is misty. Because intuition cannot be touched or seen clearly, people distrust it and often defer to weighty actuality. "The trouble with us English," George Grossmith wrote, "is that we are seldom thoroughly happy unless our amusements take a tangible shape. We must have some blatantly outward and visible sign of the fact we are enjoying ourselves." People are urged to focus and narrow their lives if they wish to succeed. The true critic, John Addington Symonds wrote, "divests himself of idiosyncratic whims and partialities." He does so to "enter with firm purpose into the understanding of universal goodness and beauty." Stripped of personality, bound by the chainmail of purpose, and seeking elevating universals, Symonds's critic is a cartoon riding through books to do battle with originality, intuition, and vibrant, intemperate life, his vision confined, limited by the Great Helm into which he forced his thought. "To know one's own business, with quiet persistence to forward it, and to mind nothing else," Coventry Patmore wrote grayly, "that is the true way to carry on the work of life." The life Patmore describes is impossible and unpleasant to live. More often than not, Grossmith's tangibles are abstract or mercurial. For most people, the real thing, Robert Lynd wrote, "is the unreal thing of the moment—the bus on which we are riding, the office to which we are going, the dress-tie that has gone crooked, the fox-trot that is stumbling in our ears, the bad wine we have given a friend, . . . the newest play and the newest player, the overdraft at the bank, and all the round of work, amusement and appetite."

What is in mind and attention one moment is out the next and then, perhaps, suddenly back again. Solving a simple geometry problem is pleasurable, and reassuring, because the steps are logical and deceptively skeletal, nothing like parsing a day's sprawling hours. In his *Notebooks* Samuel Butler wrote, "How loosely our thoughts must hang together when the whiff of a smell, a band playing in the street, a face seen in the fire or on the gnarled stem of a tree, will lead them into such vagaries at a moment's warning." Stability and balance are achievable only on the page; even then they seem forced. Silence, Henry Graham wrote, "is often the wit of fools as well as a virtue of the wise." The balance of Graham's quip undermines its wisdom and reduces its wit to the forgettable. Often the attempt to mortify the swing of mood or idea seems absurd—the prim aunt who legendarily defined *junction* as a place where roads separated, not met or, worse yet, merged.

Temperance is not a lively subject. Practically the only people who live temperately are octogenarians, time having unwound their vitality, causing their pendulums to quiver rather than swing broadly between "in" and "out." In *Culture and Anarchy* Matthew Arnold celebrated "spontaneity of consciousness." He also praised the desire to see things as they are. Doing so, he wrote, required "a balance and regulation of mind." Spontaneity of consciousness and regulation of mind are at odds. Inspiration and intuition arise, more often than not, from spontaneity rather than from temperate balance. Indeed, achieving balance undermines the possibility of intuition, reducing a person simply to being rather than being in or out, rather than seeing and thinking aslant.

Last month in Manchester Vicki and I saw the movie *The Grand Budapest Hotel*. The screen did not hold my attention, and shortly after the film began I left Rave Cinema and entered the Old Winter Palace Hotel in Luxor. A bright oriental carpet spread magically across the lobby; above it hung a chandelier, its arms dangling then turning up, curving around elbows, ending in fists of lights. Vicki and I stayed in the hotel in 1979. Few other people were in the hotel. We had been married for less than a year, and every morning I stuck a scarlet hibiscus blossom in Vicki's hair. "Brown and long then not gray and short," I muttered. "Shush," Vicki said leaning over, adding, "you don't want to disturb people." "Okay," I said and left my seat again and returning to Egypt roamed Karnack. From a vendor crouching at the feet of a statue of Osiris, I bought an iron replica of the desert cat deity Bast. For years Bast sat on a shelf in my study, but then she became lonely and wandered upstairs to Eliza's room, where she became best friends with Kitty, a small stuffed kitten and the closest companion of Eliza's childhood. Kitty now sits on the pillow on Eliza's bed, and Bast on the corner of Eliza's bedside table. The two felines have become buddies, "cats of a fur," I say, though Bast is hairless and affection wore Kitty's coat off long ago. The buddies talk and meow through the dark. Bast tells fairy tales about old days in Upper Egypt. Kitty is a good listener and is quiet and soft spoken. Every so often when Bast tells a story about Horus or Isis, Kitty says "my word" or "heavens." During some nights, though, usually holidays, Kitty does most of the talking. She describes her life and the life of our family when Eliza and her two brothers were young. She tells Bast about summers in Nova Scotia and living in Western Australia. She describes how frightened she was the night Eliza left her outside by the woodpile and how relieved she was when I found her the next morning. Sometimes I hear Kitty murmuring, but I don't dare listen outside the bedroom door. I couldn't bear to hear Kitty's stories. My life and sentences are tidy and comfortably dry. I am old and not strong enough to endure a heavy wash of sweet recollection.

Yesterday morning Vicki and I drove Eliza to the airport in Hartford. She was flying to visit Stanford in California. For the past three years Eliza has lived in Berlin. This fall she decided to attend graduate school and get a Ph.D. in English. "Like you, Daddy, and Grandpa Dudley," she explained. "It's in the blood." "But," I wrote her, "I'm taking blood thinner. It also doubles as rat poison. Read the label and beware." I then quoted Agnes Repplier: "Everybody is now so busy teaching that nobody has any time to learn. We are growing rich in lectures, but poor in scholars, and the triumph of mediocrity is at hand." I said that books were better companions than professors who talked about books. To support my contention I quoted the editor James Payn. "Small literary people are seldom good company," he wrote; "they talk literature too much, and though it is the best shop to talk about, shop is always better left alone." Eliza had not heard of Payn or Repplier. She ignored my concern and applied to graduate schools. In March she flew to Connecticut from Nashville. Vanderbilt awarded her a fellowship, and she had traveled from Berlin to visit the school's English department. A person should not live through his children. Attempting to do so lumbers a child with too great a burden. But, oh, I wanted Eliza to attend Vanderbilt. My father majored in English at Vanderbilt, and Nashville was my hometown.

In quiet moments I imagined returning to Tennessee and spinning out my days near family and old friends. "We could live at Sewanee," I told Vicki, "and drive to Nashville and see Eliza. Every time I went to the cardiologist, we could meet. Or, better, she and Travis could drive to Sewanee and spend nights with us. They'd love hiking the Cumberland Plateau and going to craft fairs. And when I died, you could bury me in the old graveyard at Sewanee, or if the people already sleeping there blackballed me, you could bury me in the family plot in Carthage. That would make me so happy." "She's not going to Vanderbilt. She's going to Stanford," Vicki said, "and, happy or not, for God's sakes, don't tell her that you want her at Vanderbilt."

I didn't mention my wishes, and by the end of Eliza's stay in Storrs, I knew she'd attend Stanford. After leaving Eliza at the airport, Vicki and I drove to Dog Lane Café in Storrs and bought senior cups of coffee. As I sat with the coffee in front of me, I mulled comings and goings, the ins and outs of life. Early one morning, I bounced into my parents' lives, but late one afternoon I drifted away and married Vicki. Shortly afterward my parents died and left me, but then my children came and stayed for years brightening all the pale hours. Now they had gone building separate lives, leaving Vicki and me to fill days with words. "Thin and stale," I thought, "as leaves in the fall." Eventually, I'd go then Vicki and. . . . I did not complete the thought. The truth is that no person can revisit his past without feeling melancholy and sensing that the landscape of his life has been despoiled. In any case, a waitress turned on the café's speaker system and started playing music. Suddenly, I heard Wilson Pickett singing "In the Midnight Hour." I know more songs than most teachers. California and Stanford vanished from thought, and by the time midnight rolled away, I was riding with "Mustang Sally." In memory, youthful jaunts with Sally or Bess or Patsy were lively. If a prim great aunt had found out about them, she would have behaved like Florrie Forde and sung "Hold Out Your Hand, Naughty Boy." I'd try to change the subject by asking my great aunt if she knew the price of the doggie in the widow. If she ignored that enquiry, I'd ask when the little hen would lay an egg for tea.

Florrie also sang "Goodbye Dolly Gray," the music hall song first popular during the Boer War. Dolly's beau heard the bugle blow and left her. When the regiment returned and marched with their drums rolling, Dolly's lover was not among them. "The one you love so well," the song reported, "fell with his face toward the foe." After the sweet, the old saying states, comes the sour. Definitions are temporary, and as time passes differentiating the sour from the sweet is difficult. How vastly different "Dolly Gray" was, I thought as I sat in the café, from Creedence Clearwater Revival's Vietnam anthem, "Bad

Moon Rising." "Don't go around tonight" is good advice because someone, usually the government, is fomenting trouble. But that mattered little to me since, as the gospel song says, I "ain't a-going to study war no more." "Some glad morning," I knew, "I'll fly away." "You coffee's getting cold," Vicki said interrupting the medley playing through my mind. "What are you thinking about?" "The dream Eliza had last night," I said. "She saw a colony of wombats gorging themselves on cheese." "What kind of cheese?" Vicki asked. "Eliza wasn't sure, but she thought it was cheddar, probably New Zealand cheddar. She was positive it wasn't Wensleydale or Duddleswell."

Words and surroundings change quicker than human nature. In lower Nidderdale in Yorkshire in the nineteenth century, *kelterments* were odds and ends of questionable value—admittedly the stuff of my essays but also of literary criticism. Life, I almost wrote Eliza this afternoon, is getting and losing. It has little relation to the partial and polemical criticisms fashionable today. When literary criticism ceases to have much to do with the lives of bright, ordinary people and uses words that such people cannot understand, it is trivial and absurd. When study kills rather than quickens and serves as midwife to stillborn boredom rather than ardent joy, it is contemptible. If critics were less learned, they might understand more. If they had poorer memories, they might write better. All his life, Havelock Ellis testified, he had "been casting away" knowledge "gained from books about literature" in hopes of "coming to literature itself." "Do those statements apply to literary study at Stanford?" Vicki asked. "Probably," I said, "they apply to practically all graduate programs in English in the nation." "You sound bitter and self-pitying," Vicki said. "No, just tired," I answered getting up from my desk; "I'm off to take an agrypnia," a Nidderdale word for "a watching or dreaming slumber," that is, a nap. Books color days more than they make a room. To *pickeroon*, Nathan Bailey's *An Universal Etymological English Dictionary*, published in 1721, stated, was "to go a plundering or robbing." As a scribbler, not only am I a Pickering, but I am also a resourceful pickerooner, adept at plundering and plagiarizing.

Early in the year vagary led me to explore Bailey's *Dictionary*. I unearthed a tag sale of kelterments. *Teenage* did not refer to an awkward stage of life but was instead brushwood for hedges. *Colibus* was "the humming Bird, which makes a noise like a Whirl-wind, tho' it be no bigger than a Fly: It feeds on Dew, has an admirable Beauty of Feathers, a Scent as sweet as that of Musk or Ambergrease." Along with words Bailey explained proverbs. Of "The Belly has no Ears," he wrote, "This Proverb intimates, that there is no arguing the Matter with Hunger, the Mother of Impatience and Anger. It is a prudent Caution not to contend with hungry Persons, or contradict their quarrelsome Tempers by ill-timed Apologies or Persuasions to Patience. It is a Lecture of Civility and Discretion, not to disturb a Gentleman at his Repast, or trouble him with unseasonable Addresses at Meal-time." In describing "I talk of Chalk and you of Cheese," Bailey wrote, "All the Impertinence in Conversation, Commerce, or Business, is represented by this saying, where by the Company do not make a Harmony in their discourse, nor keep to the Point in Question."

Although surroundings do not change human nature, they can briefly affect mood. I am especially influenced by bookish surroundings. In January I read John Donne's last sermon, "Death's Duel." The sermon dressed the moment in somber morbidity and from the perspective of now, not the seventeenth century, was intemperate. The whole world, Donne said, was a universal graveyard. Life itself was but a week of death, "seven periods of our life spent in dying, a dying seven times over." "Our birth dies in infancy, and our infancy dies in youth, and youth and the rest die in age, and age also dies." Youth, he elaborated, does not rise out of infancy or age out of youth like the phoenix out of the ashes of a previous phoenix but like "a wasp or a serpent out of carrion, or as a snake out of dung." Youth was worse than infancy and age worse than youth. Youth thirsted after sins that infancy knew not; and "our age is sorry and angry, that it cannot pursue those sins which our youth did." Because so many calamities accompanied every period of life, death was an "ease to them that suffer." Passages from death to death ran through all periods of life. Birth, Donne declared waving the shroud, was "an issue from death, for in our mothers' wombs" we were effectively dead because we didn't know we lived. There was no grave so close or prison so putrid "as the womb would be" if we "stayed in it beyond our time or died there before our time." "In the grave the worms do not kill us; we breed, and feed, and then kill those worms which we ourselves produced. In the womb the dead child kills the mother that conceived it, and is a murderer, nay, a parricide, even after it is dead."

To counteract Donne's dark anatomizing, I swallowed a dose of homeopathic poetry, the last lines of Thomas Warton's "The First of April, An Ode." The verse was promising and green and described resurrection not burial.

> Fancy, with prophetic glance,
> Sees the teeming months advance;
> The field, the forest, green and gay,
> The dappled slope, the tedded hay;

Sees the reddening orchard blow,
The harvest wave, the vintage flow:
Sees June unfold his glossy robe,
Of thousand hues o'er all the globe:
Sees Ceres grasp her crown of corn,
And Plenty load her ample horn.

Poetry blows life into the embalmed. Many poems resemble Butler's whiffs and are geegaws, or as Bailey defines, *trifles*. For my part I prefer to think such verse *nonpareil*, a sugar plum, according to the *Etymological Dictionary*. In Eaton Stannard Barrett's *The Heroine*, a lively gal sang a ditty bemoaning the absence of Theodore, her lover. "Alas, well-a-day, woe to me, / Singing willow, willow, willow; / My lover is far, far at sea. / On a billow, billow, billow. / Ah, Theodore, wouldst thou couldst be, / On my pillow, pillow, pillow." I was not montigenous, that is, born on a hill literally or intellectually. Nashville is in a basin, and I grew up roaming wetlands, observing unreal things of the moment, one following another "scimble scabble," "hanchumscranshum." I am not sure if the child is the father of the man, but certainly once a dictionary is in my hands, the pages usually stretch and flip over to other pages. Bailey's dictionary cautioned readers against setting foxes to keep geese. "This Proverb," the dictionary explained, "reflects the ill Conduct of Men in the Management of their Affairs, by entrusting either Sharpers with their Money, Blabs with their Secrets, or Enemies or Informers with their Lives; for no Obligation can bind against Nature: A Fox will love a Goose still, though his Skin be stripped over his Ears for it; and a common Cheat will always follow his old Trade of tricking his Friend, in spite of all Promises and Principles of Honor, Honesty, and good Faith."

Blabs are intemperate and lively. They have gumption enough to be dishonest and unreliable. They stimulate and keep a person from settling in or out. How nice to know that the real Henry the Eighth, at least the only Henry worthy of song, married the widow next door. She had been married seven times before. Not one of her previous husbands was a Willie or a Sam. All were Henrys, making Henry the singer Henry the Eighth. Actually, much conversation quickens life. In discussing Elizabeth Barrett Browning's poetry, Edmund Gosse said that sincerity was "the first gift in literature." The statement is preposterous as sincerity may actually be the first gift to good humor. Recently Vicki ate lunch at Taco Bell. She had a chicken burrito and a soft drink. When she paid the bill, she noticed that the clerk had forgotten to charge her for the drink. When she pointed out the oversight, he said, "No disrespect ma'am, but seniors get their drinks free." "I didn't think I looked that old," Vicki told me later. "I couldn't decide whether to laugh or cry, so I laughed." "A hearty diet of boiled beef and carrots would have reddened your face and made you look younger," I said to Vicki, lyrics of the music hall swinging into mind. "Then you would have been charged for the soda."

Last week a reporter interviewed me for a magazine and asked what part luck had played in my life. The question torpedoed my spirits. Initially I opined that luck was responsible for every success I enjoyed, as "small as they were." But then I back-tracked and suggested that some people created luck or at least "conditions in which luck could root and grow." I explained that I didn't drink, smoke, gamble, or drive fast. I was frugal. I married well, and I wasn't a whoremaster. I noted that I wasn't sensitive and didn't care what people thought about me. I said I got up at five in the morning and every day spent eight hours at my desk writing. After that spasm of words I broke down and recanted again, attributing my successes to luck or DNA, as moderns dub luck. Lastly, I pointed out that I was smarter than practically everyone else. "That's obvious," the reporter said. "Huh," I muttered. "But how can I be responsible for that?" I asked and sagging deep into my chair ended the conversation, rising only to warn the reporter that since spring was approaching, he should not let a robin die in his grasp. If a robin wings out in a person's hand, I told him, that hand will turn white and start shaking, and the person will eventually die from the creeping palsy.

Often conversations refloat the spirits. Two weeks ago David and I ran outside for the first time since December. The run tired me, and as we ran up Bonemill Road, my pendulum stopped swinging and settled on "out of energy and life." But then David spoke. His remark invigorated me, and my pace increased, not mechanically tick-tocking but skipping erratically. "What hymn is always sung at the funerals of Christian proctologists?" David asked. On my breathing too hard to think of an answer, David answered the question himself. "Holy, Holy, Holy," he said, sprinting ahead. "Zolch," I shouted then youped, a *zolch* being a mock-angry exclamation, and *youp* meaning yelp. Perhaps I should have exclaimed "By gok," a minor oath, but my head was shogging, that is, moving jerkily. Once I caught David, we subjected *The Rich Man's Guide to Heaven* to a close literary reading. Our analysis was thorough and publishable despite being short because all the pages in the book were blank.

David and I have spent ninety-five years in classrooms urging students to enjoy literature. Our houses resemble hornets' nests combed with shelves weighty with books rather than cells of fat larvae. As a result, our conversations run to reading, the pace of our talk always faster than that of our jogs. Last Tuesday lying atop a table in the reference section of the university book store was *The Dictionary of People Who Died on Their Birthdays*. More interesting and thicker, I said near the fag end of an eight-mile run, was the dictionary's companion volume, *The Encyclopedia of People Born on Their Birthdays*. "What do you think?" I asked David. "Will it sell as well as *The Wit and Wisdom of Judas Iscariot*?" "Don't stamp on thorns if you are not wearing shoes," David replied, his answer capping our run and fittingly surreal as we bent over panting. We looked more like cashew nuts than humans with our heads bowed and dripping, stomachs sagging uncorseted, and hands plastered to our knees, splinters of pain forking through our lower backs, causing our legs to quiver.

Emerson, Stephen wrote, cared "nothing for consistency" and was "content simply to see." What I often see are sentimental and comic operas. Consistency leads to dogmatism and constructs systems that exclude vivid and not-so-vivid intuitions. Consistency focuses vision and classifies. It denatures play, undercuts the elevated, and pinches ideas. It banishes mystery and reduces the meaning of poetry to the explainable. Last night I read Charlotte Elizabeth Tonna's description of the evening primrose, which begins: "Flower of eve, the sun is sinking / Far beneath the western main, / Thirsty shrubs the night dews drinking, / Moon beams stealing o'er the plain, / Stars are trembling through the sky, / Flower of evening ope thine eye." The poem is minor; yet, it made me imagine wandering July nights. I will spend this summer on our farm in Nova Scotia. In the moonlight evening primroses are white. I will stand atop a drumlin overlooking the Gulf of Maine, primroses at my feet, and before me a silver ladder of moonbeams stretching runged across the low waves.

Hanging in There

"Unless a man is a born fool," James Payn, an English novelist, wrote near the end of the nineteenth century, "he knows, after fifty, the worthlessness of all pretense. He doesn't wear tight boots, or cultivate the nobility. He is content with his own position, and has learnt that an ounce of comfort is worth a pound of swelldom." Time tempers zeal as well as pretense. After fifty, Elder Eagle Peabody recounted in a dime novel published in 1910, almost all the "Grace Running Brethren Following the Footsteps of Jesus" moved from Amen, Alabama, across Patawucky Creek to Lower Amen. There they worshiped in the chapel of the "Grace Walking Brethren." Zeal is youthful and explosive, lean and as sharp as a grain sickle. Middle age is easy and comfortable. Running becomes walking, and as a man grows fat, his temper never overloads and causes regrettable short circuits. Three weeks ago I ran the Willi Whammer, a half-marathon following streets and trails in and about Willimantic, Connecticut. Three hundred people registered for the race, but the weather reduced the number of runners to two hundred and sixty-two. At the start the temperature was forty-three degrees; a wind blew peevishly, and rain fell in a scraping drizzle.

At seventy-two I was the oldest runner. I ran twelve-minute miles and finished ahead of thirty participants. For most of the race I ran alone with no other runners in sight ahead or behind me. I got a medal for finishing second in the seventy and above age group. I expected to finish first, but a newly-turned-seventy, barely-weaned ringer won the group, beating me by a disrespectful forty minutes. "Second and last," my friend David said later. As training I jogged six miles a day, five days a week, for two months—not a rigorous regimen but the best my creaky self could manage. I jogged with David, who was once a nationally ranked runner. David is now seventy-eight, and age has brought him back to my side and pace. While we jog, we chat. Actually, I do the talking and David the listening. I run like I write, steadily and mechanically, almost anonymously, all the while chuckling. For two months prior to the race, I got up early and started writing at five in the morning. Every day in the week, despite jogging's breaking weekdays into halves, I wrote for at least eight hours. Essays do not write themselves; they are written.

Writing is a solitary activity. It is not good for the body. I put on weight when I write. When my mind balks before the rails of an idea, I leave the study and roam the house. Almost always I visit the kitchen. I open the refrigerator or rummage shelves in the pantry. Invariably I eat—crackers, hummus, peanut butter, dark chocolate, grapes, oranges, granola, raisins, anything that comes to hand quickly and unconsciously as I try to spur nouns over the writing hurdle at my desk. Writing is also antisocial. In the morning as I sit on the edge of the bed before plunging into standing, pain pools in my right shoulder, laps up my neck, then washing down my spine eddies across my hips. After I have spent three or so hours writing, my back throbs again, and I become irritable. I look out the window and notice the green world—not sublime sights but little things, tumbleweeds of forsythia, a Japanese magnolia delicate as a harp, or the blue sky brushed with cumulus clouds. At the edge of the wood behind the house, the white rib cage of deer claws upward out of leaves like the tines of a rake. Small creatures have carried away most of the carcass, leaving one leg and the spine of the deer behind. What remains is being gnawed clean by ridged carrion beetles, so many beetles that they remind me of an audience crammed into a popular theater, every seat occupied, row after row, rib by rib. Thoughts about what man is doing to nature then ratchet through my head like the aches that drench me before I get out of bed in the morning. Jogging does not cure the pain I feel when I ponder the crooked six-penny ways of humans, but it distracts and transforms me from a critic into an appreciator. "Look at those weeping cherries. Look now; the blooms won't last long," I ordered David the last time we ran toward the graveyard on Spring Hill Road, after which I polished a tarnished line from *Hamlet*: "The beauty of the world, the paragon of spring, and oh, what these flowers mean to me."

Rarely do I reach conclusions either running or writing. Conclusions are fictions appealing to the young and the inexperienced, not to people my age. Among old or "advanced" people, Edwin Muir wrote, "one observes a strange contradiction: the existence in one and the same person of confidence and enthusiasm about certain aspects of life along with diffidence and pessimism about life itself. The advanced have made up their minds about all the problems of existence but not about the problem of existence." Clearly Muir knew few runners. In a race, knees and ankles cause problems but not existence. Runners are not optimistic or pessimistic; they are simply runners. In Willimantic, spectators stood in the rain and rang cowbells. When I drew alongside, they shouted, "Hang in there," "You can do it," and "You can make it," hospice remarks, spoken only to the lagging, making me think my wonky heart would collapse and a garden would soon bloom atop my stomach. "Goldenrod, hollyhock, and zinnias for color, and Easter lilies for their smothering holiday fragrance," I thought.

During the run, my mind posted from sentence to sentence much as my pencil does at home. As I ran on Kingsley Road then along the Airline State Park Trail, I thought about the White Salamander, an evangelist from Sphoon, Mississippi. When the Salamander preached, he donned a white robe and a white turban encrusted with a costume-jewelry mine of sapphires and rubies. In every peroration the Salamander urged congregations to sympathize with the plights of their neighbors, and for two or three hundred yards, I worked on one of his favorite remarks: "In the heart of every Christian is a hear and an ear." I had trouble polishing the statement, so I gave up and thought about the ceramic parrot the Salamander carried to revivals, setting it on a table beside the pulpit. The parrot was eighteen inches tall and except for a reddish crest was white. The Salamander was an amateur ventriloquist. If he balked at a rail and became unseated during a sermon, he "threw" his voice to the parrot. Immediately the bird gibbered and screeched. Sometimes it ground like a rusty hinge, other times it howled like a dog, the noise lasting until the Salamander settled on the saddle and vaulted back into his sermon.

On Cards Mill Road, I remembered my friend Kent's describing the architecture of university buildings as "Early Laundromat." On the Frog Bridge, Christopher Morley's word for embarrassing questions came to mind, "inquirendoes." A woman standing in a driveway looked familiar. She was probably the clerk at Big Y who told me that so many older customers frequented the grocery between ten thirty in the morning and two thirty in the afternoon that employees referred to the hours as "White Hair Time." As I crossed Main Street at the foot of the bridge, I recalled that while David and I were jogging on the university track last month, a stranger approached and spoke to David. The man recognized me, too, and later I asked David the man's name. "He is one of my many close friends whom I do not know," David answered. As I ran down West Avenue, I thought about the correct use of *who* and *whom* and sundry other contemporary grammatical noirs, *lie* and *lay* and *I* and *me*, for example. Two nights ago at dinner Vicki said, "I can agree with her but never with she." Who said, I wondered as I passed behind town hall, that "politics does not make liars of us; it makes us believe lies." On the straightway trailing down Valley Street, I mulled threadbare sentences that once passed for wit, the comment, for example, made by a listener in hopes of silencing a noted raconteur, "I've known that story since it was an anecdote swaddled in one-syllable words."

As I turned on to Pleasant Valley Road and passed the ten-mile marker, I forced myself to think in paragraphs. I hoped that they'd be painkillers and separate my head from my cramping legs. Because I read and appropriate widely, plagiarism interests me. J. C. Squire believed that a writer could slip the "charge of imitation" if he fulfilled one condition, "that is that he should be more himself than anybody else. If he really *is* any good, we may identify things he owes to other people, but we shall *feel* his individuality all the time." Of course, by the time I reached Mansfield City Road, I decided that I fulfilled Squire's single condition, leaving aside any consideration of good. In hopes of distancing myself from the throbbing miles, I then thought about my past—boyhood years in Tennessee and Virginia, days when I galloped lightly, never tiring and reading for fun not for the page. "One of the best things in the world to be is a boy," Charles Dudley Warner wrote; "it requires no experience, though it needs some practice to be a good one. The disadvantage of the position is that it does not last long enough; it is soon over; just as you get used to being a boy, you have to be something else, with a good deal more work to do and not half so much fun.

Suddenly boyhood ended, and I crossed the finish line, not with a chaplet of flowers around my brow, but, as spectators invariably say, "looking good." To impress Vicki I straightened my back and dropping my arms pulled them back and forth along my sides like coupling rods on a steam engine. For a few strides I even managed to get both feet off the ground at the same time. Unfortunately, Vicki missed the show. I finished twenty minutes before I predicted I'd finish. Rain streamed down, and to keep from getting soaked Vicki sat in the car, rather than stood beside the finish. No matter—a man handed me a mug with the monogram of the Willimantic Athletic Club emblazoned on the side. I filled the mug with Long Trail Ale and collected the medal for finishing second in my age group.

Thomas Wentworth Higginson said that libraries were writers' tool chests. As a writer ages, he must learn, Higginson wrote, "to take what he wants and to leave the rest." Life itself is a chest. A person shuts his eyes, reaches inside, and grabs whatever his fingers touch. Happenstance determines what he seizes. After the race, I received a packet containing an extra-large running shirt, a coupon for a second mug of beer, and a handful of advertising flyers. "Follow the Ice Cream Trail!" one flyer urged, listing and providing a road map to forty-two ice cream shops in Eastern Connecticut. Another flyer promoted a "Wealth Management" group, explaining to the reader that "education and understanding of your financial situation is vital to your success." A third brochure described the Mediation Center of Eastern Connecticut.

The center offered "divorcing couples an alternative to bitter legal battles" by building "on the positive aspects of the couple's relationship." "Generally speaking," Vicki said when I showed her this last brochure, "divorce isn't good for a marriage."

Although runners bolt tubs of ice cream between races, rarely do they amass wealth, and their divorce rate is much lower than the rates of landscapers, college deans, and aerospace engineers. Running isn't amenable to courtship as lungs, not hormones, are responsible for practically all the panting that occurs during a race. Moreover, busyness makes people conventional, and dull. Runners do not gallop romantically into the lives of strangers wrapped in silk capes and seated atop rearing stallions. Instead, they trot past wearing twee shorts, wheezing, and bent double looking like old bobby pins. Moreover, endlessly taking off street dress and putting on running togs then taking off the togs and putting street dress back on doesn't leave runners energy or time enough to sashay through extramarital wardrobe changes four or five times a day.

The life of a runner is not without poetry and appetite, however. After the race Vicki bought two loaves of bread from a woman sitting under a tent, "Fresh Rosemary and Black Olive Tapenade Bread" and "Ten-Penny Multi-Grain Beer Bread." From the NoRA cupcake truck, the name an abbreviation of "North of Rapallo Avenue," a street in Middletown, we purchased an oven of cupcakes. The names read like verse: Ginger Pear and Raspberry Lemonade, Goddess, Honey Bee, and Strawberry Rhubarb, Black and Blue, Irish Car Bomb, Cherry Lime Rickey, and Dulce de Leche. After purchasing the quatrain of sweet iambics, just the thing to quicken tired minds and bodies, Vicki drove us home. I showered, and we went to Dog Lane Café, where we drank a gallon of hot coffee and ate bowls clotted with shrimp and sausage gumbo.

An acquaintance and former runner noticed us and walked over to our table. I told him I ran the half-marathon in Willimantic, and we talked about races. "When a rich man dies," he said, "people ask, 'How much did he leave in his will?' When a runner dies, people ask, 'What was his best time?'" He said he often saw David and me jogging past his house on Davis Road. Runners toss rank and ceremony aside and talk at ease in the presence of other runners. "David and I are identical twins," I said. "Not many people realize that. When David was a child, a railway train clipped him flipping him over and over. He has had two score plastic surgeries, but as you can clearly see from your front door, the operations were miserable failures." I then described the brochures I found in my race packet, and we talked about the role of chance in life. "My first cousin teaches philosophy at Illinois State in Normal, Illinois. He is not pleasant, and few people like him. Fifteen years ago he came up for tenure," the man recounted. "The two best academics in the department vehemently opposed granting him tenure. On the day the vote on his tenure was scheduled, a small tornado passed through Normal. No one was hurt, but trees fell on the garages of the two hostile professors. The trees destroyed the cars of both men, preventing them from attending the debate. A quorum of teachers made it to the meeting, however, and at day's end the department voted to tenure my cousin, the count going in his favor by one vote. Tenure by tornado—real happenstance." "Do you believe that story?" Vicki asked later. "Sure," I said, "many of the best tales I know are imaginary creations, rooted in truth as well as in lies and exaggeration. When I tell people that I finished second in my age group in the race, I won't tell them that the group contained two people. People will look at me and say, 'Wow, way to go. You really hung in there.'" "Not revealing the number in the group will perpetuate a species of lie, but that doesn't matter. It certainly won't matter to runners, most of whom are charming, habitual liars." "Yes," Vicki said, "not self-serving dissemblers, but sweet liars, fudgers sugaring their times, people with modest bank accounts who rarely need divorce mediation."

Happiness

"The American," James Russell Lowell wrote, "is nomadic in religion, in ideas, in morals, and leaves his faith and opinions with as much indifference as the house in which he was born." Time changes people. The seasons of life do not revolve like those of the year forever rolling the familiar back into mind and place. Instead, the seasons form a chain. Although the links are woven together, the climate of each link varies slightly from that of every other link. Matters that make twenty-year olds happy bore octogenarians. Conversely, what makes the aged clap their hands rarely appeals to mortgage-paying householders. A month ago Vicki and I thought our dog Jack was about to cross the Rainbow Bridge and bed down on Kibble Street in Pooch Paradise. Jack ate something foul, and for two days afterward he was plugged and barely able to walk. Whenever he stood, he stretched then collapsed. When I was a boy, a neighbor poisoned Pup, one of my favorite dogs. Jack's symptoms resembled those of Pup. "I don't expect to find Jack alive," I told Vicki when I left the bed to go downstairs on the third morning. I was mistaken. The kitchen floor was awash in poop. "Hallelujah," I shouted to Vicki, "Jack has recovered! There is dog shit everywhere!" Thirty years ago, no matter my affection for the resident pet, discovering the kitchen had become a canine privy would not have inspired a verbal jig. I would have used the s-word, but it would have been prefaced by "oh," and the exclamation point at the end of the phrase would have underscored exasperation, not glee.

At the beginning of *The Trembling of a Leaf*, Somerset Maugham described the Pacific Ocean. Usually, the ocean was gray and rough, he said, boisterous and capped with white crests. "It is not so often that it is calm and blue," he continued. Then "the sun shines fiercely from an unclouded sky. The trade wind gets into your blood and you are filled with an impatience for the unknown. The billows, magnificently rolling, stretch widely on all sides of you, and you forget your vanished youth, with its memories, cruel and sweet, in a restless, intolerable desire for life." For the aged, despite living inland amid the doldrums, early mornings are not calm. Aches clamor boisterous and cloudy, and the soft exterior of a capsule is the first blue one notices. Occasionally, I kick against Time and restlessly hanker for a wind to lift me above the familiar and blow me into a romantic unknown. This restlessness does not last beyond breakfast sensible with bananas and shredded wheat, however. I do not long to bore through the coral encrusted atop my lost youth. I don't dream of finding doubloons floating like krill, gold and silver at my fingertips. When Maugham's desire for life threatens to become feverish, I treat the symptoms by walking. The sight of a green heron motionless at the edge of a beaver pond, an oriole's nest hanging like a shoulder bag high in a white oak, a Philadelphia vireo singing himself into notice, pausing between announcements of "here I am" so that I can find him on a branch—such things soothe restlessness and make the present temperate and sunny, and very happy.

Through their middle years most men travel in packs, their barks choruses of the familial and the corporate. Time eventually winnows the kenneled, silencing their barks. The "et cetera" vanishes from the passions. Men's natures become less houndish, and they abandon the pursuit of money for the scent of Daphne or autumn olive. After wandering the stalls at a country fair and looking at countless trinkets, hobby-horses, gimcracks, and finnimbruns, Diogenes, Izaak Walton recounted, exclaimed to a friend, "Lord! How many things are there in this world of which Diogenes hath no need!" Material needs not only become fewer, but they also lose their appeal as a person ages. Paradoxically, however, as one lives more within the confines of a small room, his world expands. Artificial walls collapse, and a person becomes happier. He ceases to pay lip, pocket, and mental service to the conventional. As the cords binding his reason to the platitudinous loosen, his imagination beats its wings and sometimes takes flight. Gadflies no longer sting, and the swellings raised by their bites cease to embarrass. Order seems a restricting fiction depending on gewgaws and trick mirrors to keep people from realizing that life is a disorderly jumble—often a very happy jumble. If worker bees forsook their hives and spent sunny hours lolling atop pretty black-eyed Susan's ample petals, the class system would change as queen bees shrank then vanished. When Belvidera in Thomas Otway's *Venice Preserved* says "lutes, laurels, seas of milk and ships of amber," she does not seem mad to the aged. Every day is a mish-mash. Rather than trying to arrange such things in an artificial commonsensical order, better it is to rummage messily, pulling crackers off one shelf, peanut butter off another, heartache out of a drawer, and smiles from a greenhouse miscellany of scarlet chenille plants, violet King's Mantle, and lollipop plants, their winged, white flowers looking like paddles sticking out from all-day suckers of orange racemes. The sanity of the madness that packages oddities together without thought frequently stimulates and entrances while the madness of the sane disheartens and often terrifies, this last the specialty of government functionaries.

In "Tradition and the Individual Talent," T. S. Eliot wrote, "No poet, no artist of any art, has his complete meaning alone. His significance, his appreciation is the appreciation of his relation to the dead poets and artists. You cannot value him alone; you must set him, for contrast and comparison, among the dead." Age enables one to escape literary catacombs. Shaking off the skeletal fingers of the past frees a person to stretch and breathe. One realizes that Eliot's directive smacks of instructions for writing a freshman composition, a pedestrian academic exercise. Good living, as well as good writing, depends upon escaping the dominion of hard rules formulated by soft heads. "There are some men who will handle words and images in their talk," J. B. Priestley wrote, "as if they were making miniature watches instead of re-creating a world." To create happiness, if not an anchor hold, a person must jettison society's laborious emphasis on time. Even better, he should shake off the mind-cuffs of watch bands. If a person stopped wearing a watch, thought might come easier and clearer. Certainly he'd slip the confusion wrought by interstates of crowns, arms, dials, wheels, and mysterious displays that mark the interchanges swirling across the faces of watches. "To read the modern watch," my friend Josh said, "a person needs a GPS. To keep it running smoothly he should keep a mechanic on call."

Once a person shatters the boulder trapping him in a catacomb, thoughts roll in happy chaos. He ponders a myriad of things, if not Belvidera's laurels and ships of amber, then having a tooth and a Volvo serviced on the same day, a root canal for the first, new tires for the second. Randomness keeps me alert and often smiling. The mother of my friend Tim is one hundred and two years old. Six weeks ago she had a physical. After the physical the receptionist told her that the doctor wanted to schedule a follow-up. "That's fine; I should have a follow-up," Tim's mother replied; "schedule it on this day at the same time a year from now." Now that is a wondrous happy, optimistic response. Last month an old college classmate living in Florida sent me a clipping sliced from the "This Is Your Florida" page of the *Tallahassee Democrat*. "When I read this story, I immediately thought of you," my classmate explained. When Pillsby Belwhidder was seven or eight years old, his parents bought a goldfish at the Florida State Fair and gave it to him as a pet. Pillsby named the fish Shuster and fed it table scraps. The diet agreed with Shuster. When he outgrew his bowl in Pillsby's bedroom, Pillsby dumped him into the pond on the family farm west of the Apalachicola River.

In the pond Shuster shed his goldfish childhood and swelled into a giant and astonishingly long-lived carp. Pillsby never married, and sixty-five years later Shuster was "more than a pet." He was Pillsby's oldest and dearest friend. Pillsby summoned Shuster to dinner by whistling or singing "Dixie." The fish recognized the song and surfaced open-mouthed, eagerly expecting dough balls or drumsticks, and on special days, souse. This past spring Pillsby sold the farm. Accidents—among others, a tractor's rolling over and lumber's shifting on a flat bed and crashing into the cabin of a truck—led to Pillsby's suffering from debilitating arthritis, forcing him to stop farming. He decided to move into the Masonic Home of Florida in St. Petersburg. He did not want to leave before providing for Shuster, however. "If a fisherman came along and whistled 'Dixie,' Shuster would assume I was serving lunch and snap at the bait without looking. My goodness, he'd end up in a stranger's cooking pot. As a good Christian," Pillsby said, "I couldn't bear the thought of that happening to my buddy. Jesus would never let me forget it." Consequently, Pillsby installed a huge fish tank in the bed of his pickup. He then borrowed a neighbor's Bobcat, scooped Shuster out of the pond, and deposited him in the tank. Afterward he drove nonstop to Rosedale, Indiana, where a cousin owned a hobby farm and a small herd of Herefords. At the farm he dumped Shuster into the cow pond, "a mighty fine one, too, bigger than my pond in Florida, giving Shuster room to grow," Pillsby said. For the record Shuster already weighed a record-setting ninety-six pounds. "Won't nobody likely to whistle 'Dixie' in Indiana," Pillsby added, "and if somebody did sing 'John Brown's Body' or 'Marching Through Georgia,' Shuster wouldn't know what the hell they was talking about, and he'd stay safe and comfortable in the muck at the bottom of the pond."

Yesterday I received an e-mail from an expert on John Keats's poetry. The man saw David, my running companion, and me ambling along North Eagleville Road. "Good on you," the man wrote; "You are not joys forever but simply forevers." How nice to imagine that our stems could still shoot and if not bud, at least almost flex. How much better to imagine the fragrance of jasmine gardenia or the frothy pink clusters of Panama rose as one rolls the lawn mower out of the garage for the first time in early summer. How nice to be diverted from the garage's dank concrete floor splotched by stigmas of oil and anthers of grease. How astonishing to see fly bush, a South African carnivorous plant. Fly bush is scraggily and can grow six feet tall. Its leaves are luminously green, lance shaped, and elegant toothed. They erupt from a nodule in groups, twenty-four leaves in the group, I counted, and splay out in a dazzle like streams of water from a fountain. Droplets of resinous, sticky liquid dot the leaves. When I touched a leaf with my ballpoint pen, I had to peel the leaf away to free the pen. The liquid traps insects. Small assassin bugs then eat the insects. The bugs have padded feet and can walk across the plant without getting stuck. The excrement of the bugs is high in nitrogen, and when it falls and sticks to the leaves, the leaves absorb the nitrogen.

When a person is aware of wonders like fly bush, accuracy seems a small, imprisoning virtue. Nature is so wild with exaggeration that exaggeration becomes both truth and lie. A small spring puddle can contain thousands of tadpoles. Giraffes, tumblebugs, dragonflies, dandelions—what are they but wonders, exaggerations that startle then amaze? The actual so stirs the mind that a person happily absences himself from the actual and imagines the cockatrice, the king of serpents, the product of a cock's egg hatched in a nest of snakes. The breath of the cockatrice killed bushes, and its look so terrified that it caused instantaneous death. The person who imagines the cockatrice has in fact seen the serpent and survived. He has wandered from the stultifying familiar into myth and legend, the misty region from which creativity often rises and that is inaccessible to those who compare and contrast. How lively dreams would be if the "bugs" described by Reginald Scott in 1584 had not vanished from bedtime story: "bull beggers, spirits, witches, urchens, elves, hags, fairies, satyrs, pans, faunes, sylens, kit with the cansticke, tritons, centaurs, dwarfes, giants, imps, calcars," and "incubus." I'd rush to the mail box every morning if the front page of the newspaper described the antics of Tom Thumb, the Firedrake, Hob Goblin, the Man in the Oak, Boneless, the Witch of the Woodlands, and playful Bugaboo with claws long as butcher knives and a voice deep as that of a bear and who had the naughty habit of biting "Good Little Children." Instead, shutters slam down over my eyes when I see accounts describing the doings of hobidy-boobies and jobbernoules, that is, political blockheads and the merely athletic and partially educated.

Contrary to common belief, the first sunflower wasn't domesticated in Mexico five thousand years ago. Before the beginning of reductive time, a water nymph named Clytie fell in love with Apollo. Because Apollo did not return her affection, Clytie pined in sorrow, sitting on the ground, her hair unbound and falling around her. She did not eat or drink. In the morning when Apollo harnessed his chariot and drove the sun across the heavens, she followed the chariot until it disappeared into the sunset. The only part of Clytie's body that moved was her head, turning in order to keep Apollo and the sun always in sight. Eventually her arms and legs dug into the ground and became roots, and her head became a flower, the sunflower, which during daylight twists on its stem in order to gaze at the sun.

Once a person slips the gears of grinding mechanical accuracy, he is free to parody. Verses that cause headaches when a person struggles to remember them accurately become toys. The conclusion of Richard Le Gallienne's "When I Am Gone" is mawkish. The narrator noted that after he died birds would continue to fly and sing over the silent sky: "And the blue eye / Of some unborn and beautiful young thing / Will watch them fly, / And her young heart will break to hear them sing—/ When I am gone." Bert Leston Taylor's parody is more realistic. The narrator noted that when he was gone "The same old sky / Will meet the same old plain." Bye and bye "Some sweet young thing, with face against the pane, / Will scan the sky, / And say, 'I'll take m'umbrella; it may rain'—/ When I am gone." High seriousness strips oxygen from the air making thinking difficult. In the mental lowlands iambs are muddy, but breathing is easy, and smiles rather than grimaces accompany recitations. No one knows who wrote "The Modern Hiawatha," perhaps for "good" reason. For my lower part I wish I had written the poem.

> He slew the noble Mudjokivis
> With his skin he made him mittens;
> Made them with the fur side inside;
> Made them with the skin-side outside;
> He, to keep the warm side inside
> Put the cold side, skin-side outside;
> He, to keep the cold side outside,
> Put the warm side, fur-side, inside:—
> That's why he put the cold side outside,
> Why he put the warm side inside,
> Why he turned them inside outside.

"Every season of life has its proper virtues, as every season of the year has its own climate and temperature," Randolph Bourne wrote. Oddly, as a person ages and pays less attention to social virtues, the proprieties that the young are taught to observe but that strike them as silly become, for want of a better word, "proper" and appealing. For the old the salutation "how do you do" is a real question. No topic interests the young less and the old more than health. When a person over seventy greets a friend saying, "How do you do?" he expects a synopsis detailing the condition of his friend's eyes, teeth, heart, lungs, kidneys, and if the person is male, his prostate. Such descriptions are always jovial, no matter that the friend's teeth are false, his heart wobbly, and his prostate on the fritz. The young are acquisitive and ambitious. They are materialists; some are even capitalists. No person under forty really believes giving is better than receiving. In contrast, the dissociated know that giving makes them happier and keeps life smoother than receiving. "Givers," E. V. Lucas observed, "particularly careless ones—and most givers think too little—can survive to a great age and never have to practice any of the facial contortions and the tactful verbal insincerities which recipients of their generosity must be continually calling to their aid."

A person has to dig deep to reach the shallow. The till just under the top-soil of society is always petty with enthusiasts and propagandists discovering nuggets of greatness everywhere. People who aren't geniuses are rarities. Down amid the shallow, however, lies healthy, sleep-producing bedrock. J. B. Priestley once quipped, "A good author is his own worst book." Maybe, just maybe, in the shallows far from literary criticism, that worst book is the author's best book, his happiest book. Insofar as poets go, Anonymous is ubiquitous but not well known. He wrote this little ditty: "Susan poisoned her grandmother's tea; / Grandmamma died in agonee. / Susan's papa was greatly vexed, / And he said to Susan, 'My dear, what next?'" What next was a limerick also composed by Anonymous. "There was a young maid who said, 'Why / can't I look in my ear with my eye? / If I give my mind to it, / I am sure I can do it, / You never can tell till you try.'"

When I was a boy in Nashville, the Happiness Club met on Saturdays at the Belle Meade movie theater. Admission cost sixteen cents. A talent show featuring elementary school singers and magicians preceded the movie. At the end of the show and before cowboys galloped across the screen, the audience sang "Happy Days are Here Again." Yesterday I ran my fingers over a new beech leaf. The leaf was filmy with light green and softer than lawn. Beside a hobble of multi-flora rose a young rabbit crouched motionless as a doorstop. A Carolina wren rollicked into spondees from a perch in the woods. By the garage the lilacs I planted thirty years ago bent under bushels of blossoms. And, of course, the sky was blue—not blue "again" as in the song, but blue as it always has been, and especially since I began trying to look into my ear. Whenever I give a speech, I describe the attempts I've made to surf through the outer ear into the inner canal. I don't want the fellows who wear white sport coats and carry bug nets chasing me, so I attribute the attempts to Heavy, a boy I used to know in Hanover, Virginia. "Heavy's father," I explain, "worked on my grandfather's farm." "Heavy," I say, "was not a thing of beauty, but he has become very accomplished. His sporgled brandlings baa like bumblebees, and he is the president of the Hanover Chamber of Commerce. He has a dog named Gung, and every week he accompanies Pastor Johndrow to the Amy Phelps Floyd nursing home and plays the piano during prayer meetings. His wife's nose looks like Stilton cheese, but she is a very good librarian and for twelve years has been cookie manager for the local Girl Scout troop."

Heavy's son Snaix attended Harvard and runs a hedge fund in Crete, Nebraska. Minnie, his daughter, graduated from Abraham Baldwin Agricultural School in Georgia and made a fortune selling orange glow-in-the-dark-and-daylight turnips. She now breeds black Australorp chickens and markets them throughout the South. In most cemeteries in northern Virginia, gravediggers share caretaking duties with flocks of chickens. Worms thrive in cemeteries, and if the chickens did not crop the number of crawlers, "Southern body farms would become worm farms," Minnie told the owner of Hallelujah Funeral Supplies in Shelbyville, Tennessee. Whenever I mention Minnie's new business venture, I explain that the relationship between chickens and gravediggers is historic, dating from the end of the Revolutionary War when "Patriots" took terrible revenge on Loyalists, butchering families and stealing their land. Patriots killed so many people that sextons were forced to dig shallow mass graves, in the process creating potting soil hospitable to worms. The presence of extraordinary numbers of worms attracted chickens, thus forging a symbiotic relationship between parish and hatchery. Keeping the chickens was and is easy. In Hanover they roost in abandoned mausoleums. As a sales incentive, Minnie's advertisements stress that Australorp hens lay over two hundred brown eggs a year. Moreover, "their black feathers are mood and location appropriate."

"I'll be damned if I'll eat any egg dropped by a graveyard chicken. I'll never scramble another brown egg. That hen could have fed on worms that munched Aunt Eulalia or Uncle Rufus, and not on the choicest parts neither," a woman in Tennessee once said when I finished speaking. "That's right," a man chimed in, "and for that matter bumblebees don't baa." "Yes, they do," I answered. "They baa and bleat, and sometimes they neigh. And if your hearing is good and you listen carefully and are lucky, you might hear them buzz." I could have quoted Vicki and said, "What does it matter? We are all hurtling into nothingness." But I looked out the window. Golden chain trees were flush with yellow, and I was happy and wanted other people to feel happy, too.

Palm

Knowing the truth is good, a Syrian proverb states, but it is better to know the truth and instead of talking about it to talk about palm trees. The aim of writing, Dr. Johnson wrote, was "to enable readers better to enjoy life, or better to endure it." Enjoyment moderates spleen, procures gaiety, and helps people endure misfortune. Facts chop down palms and expose fictional heart woods to pitiless, shriveling analysis. "Let us scrap history on at least the first day of the year in so far as it binds us to the past with all its savagery and beastliness," Robert Lynd wrote. "History is not fit to be read unless by those who realize that it is a branch of indecent literature." Leaning against the trunk of a palm, shutting one's eyes, and hearing the trickle of water provide respite from slogging through the sands of an hourglass. Like a pallid harrier the imagination can take flight, not soaring outrageously but raising its wings into a cool *V* and gliding and swooping. In an apocryphal story, after studying a painting by J. M. W. Turner, a woman addressed the artist. "I never saw a sunset like that," she said. "No, I suspect not," Turner replied, "but don't you wish that you had?"

"How many more Arabs must we kill before they learn to love us?" my friend Josh asked recently. I didn't reply to Josh's question. I refused to think about our country's soft-spoken politicians whose savagery outdoes that of Tamburlaine. Better was it to lounge on a day bed smoking a hookah, imagination bubbling and helping me get things wrong. On a soft pillow Robert Herrick's famous "Gather ye rosebuds while ye may" becomes Oliver Hereford's "Gather Kittens while you may, / Time brings only Sorrow; / And the Kittens of To-day / Will be Old Cats To-morrow." How pleasant to drift amid the fumes, especially for someone like me whose behavior is often compulsive. Last Monday I drove to a doctor's office in Glastonbury forty-five minutes away from my house. My appointment was at eight o'clock; I arrived at 7:03. How nice to dip into hummus and baba ghanoush, munch falafel and fattoush salad while simultaneously recollecting the Hog Trees that grew throughout the south of my childhood—*Sus scrofa domesticus* trees. A shopper could buy almost as many cultivars at a grocery as a gardener could iris rhizomes at a nursery: Head Cheese, Black Pudding, Trotters, and Rind trees, Bacon and Egg bush, and, of course, Ham trees, these last generally salted or sugar cured.

A good hookah can transport its smoker east of the sun and west of the moon, back through decades to buttermilk biscuits, tomato aspic, greens, corn and butterbeans, iced tea, fried *Gallus gallus domesticus*, chess pie, and contentment. Sheltered places are oases. There dreaming blossoms into clusters of recollection and story. In the quiet a person realizes much can be said in favor of being dead. "Some say that old men fear death," Hilaire Belloc wrote. "It is the theme of the debased and the vulgar. It is not true." However, before the final darkness falls from the wing of night, "And the cares that infest the day / Shall fold their tents like the Arabs, / and as silently steal away," as Longfellow put it, escaping the halter of abrading social life and ignoring the din of event lower the systolic pressure of thought. "Mr. Pickering," a graduate student said to me, "think how much knowledge will be lost when you die." "Not much," I said, as I walked out of the classroom. Beyond the door to the building, roses radiated scarlet and pink around a sundial, their petals profuse and feathery and somehow sensible and calming. "I'm old," I said; "for years knowledge has been slipping from me. By the time I die no knowledge will remain to be lost."

In places apart from toil and endeavor, a person discovers the courage to be indolent. Indolence doesn't spring from lethargy but from a passion for life—the desire to live for one's self as one's self, not for others or as others demand one should live. When I am indolent, I read books that have no designs upon me. These books were once popular but are now neglected—rightly so. I never consider writing academic articles about them, and I forget them almost before I read the last paragraphs. Because acquaintances have rarely heard of the books, I don't have to trim my indulgence into acceptable conversation. Last weekend I read Charles Garvice's *A Heritage of Hate*, the hero of which was raised by his father on Vancouver Island. When his father died, Rath was seventeen. He could neither read nor write, had been taught to hate womankind, and was unaware of his aristocratic lineage. Of course "she" appears, and happily Rath learns about manners and love. Although I am a landlubber, I have read navy yards of sea stories. Next I read Captain Marryat's *Frank Mildmay; or The Naval Officer*. During a brisk action, Mildmay reported, with some glee, "A very curious incidence of muscular action occurred: a lad of eighteen years of age was on the forecastle, when a shot cut away the whole of his bowels, which were scattered over another midshipman and myself, and nearly blinded us. He fell—-and, after lying a few seconds, sprang suddenly on his feet, stared us horribly in the face, and fell down dead. The spine had not been divided; but with that exception, the lower was separated from the upper part of the body."

Often such books fall dead and fluttering from my hand, their spines broken. Then I nap under a tree or, less metaphorically, in bed. Last month I dreamed I was at an oasis surrounded by a menagerie. Perched atop a palm was the Queen of Sheba's parrot, famous for delivering love notes to and from Solomon. Beside the headboard, biting sandflies made Ezra's ass bray and kick his hind legs in the air. The ass did not foresee that he would die then return to life and be transported to paradise. If he'd had a premonition, he wouldn't have brayed so loudly and taken Pegasus's name in vain. Also present was Selah's giant camel calved from a boulder and who offered me a tot of arak. Despite being generous, good-natured, and a splendid cropper of dates, the camel was a nuisance. When thirsty, he drank for twenty-four straight hours and twice almost drained the well at the oasis dry. In waking hours I putter dozily about. Early in the morning I listen to a Carolina wren sing from the ornamental weathervane atop the garage. Some days I wander around the house and stand immobile beneath a rhododendron while a resident family of chickadees jumps around me, the birds chattering familiarly and perching eight or nine inches from my head. I move so slowly that the catbirds nesting in the forsythia ignore me and don't break into nervous scolding when I approach. Sleepy indolence awakens the senses, and on the air I can often smell sweet bay magnolias, the flowers small cups shaped from sugary paste and overflowing with lemon fragrance. Some days a breeze lifts perfume from the multi-flora roses that tangle abandoned pastures and like an atomizer sprays it across the neighborhood in lavender gusts.

Reading forgotten books isolates me from the conversational footnotes that acquaintances attach to bookish chat. Because almost everyone I know is over seventy, the footnotes are medical and invariably lead to the tomb. Of course graveyards are themselves oases, less suited for contemplation, however, than for the more active manifestations of courting. Still, the mattress of dirt covering a grave is usually soft; many headstones, especially older ones, tilt like recliners, and if a person searches carefully he'll discover a cool spot sheltered by boxwoods where he can stretch and lie down, eat an Eskimo Pie, and read, say, one of Jane West's novels, perhaps *The Infidel Father*.

Graveyards are on my mind. So many acquaintances have died recently that life seems a ball at which the only song played is The Dance of Death. I mention that particular dance because at Christmas a friend sent me a reproduction of Frans Francken's "Fiddling Death," painted in the 1640s. Because of famines, endless brutal wars, and disease, particularly the Black

Death of 1348, Death appeared in scores of medieval paintings and wood-cuts. In dances of death, skeletons played an orchestra of instruments: harps, mandolins, drums, and brass bands of horns. Often, Death danced, shaking grotesquely like a puppet. In Francken's painting Death played a violin, while leaning toward the right and staring mockingly at a wealthy merchant. Death's right, skeletal foot rested on an hourglass while the merchant's right foot lay on a stool covered with a thick cushion. The merchant was fat and wore slippers; he suffered from edema, and his leg was swollen. A gold chain hung around the merchant's neck, and he wore a scarlet hat and a heavy coat with a fur-lined collar. On the table beside him was a stack of gold coins. In his right hand he held other coins, showing them to Death in hopes of purchasing more life. Death himself was horrific. His head was a skull. On it patches of meat gleamed white looking pustular while his chest and arms were wormy strings of ligaments; yet, in his rictal scorn for the merchant, he appeared almost humorous—a nightmarish cartoon figure or a jokester enjoying the last laugh.

Actually he looked like he'd appreciate the pamphlets written by Barry Pain's neglected literary friend "First Authority on Everything," beginning with, say, "Bad Habits and How To Form Them" and "How to Avoid Originality: By One Who Has Done It." Regrettably indolence demands great concentration, and I don't have time to supervise Death's reading—not at least until he visits me in my study. In any case, what I really wondered about were the tunes the twiggy old scamp was playing, maybe, I told Vicki, some rollicking Bluegrass: "Billy in the Lowground," "Arkansas Traveler," or "Devil's Dream." "Not the last," Vicki said. "'Whiskey before Breakfast' would be much better."

For many people mustering the gumption to be indolent thrives in shadows apart from worldly fret. Out of the newfound passion for their own lives, however, spring exuberance and a willingness to respond to unheard but imagined calls echoing from the open road. Shortly after listening to Death stumble trying to play "Clinch Mountain Backstep" and thinking he ought to swap his fiddle for a banjo, I heeded the call of the road and back pedaled, ambling away in hopes of plucking a bouquet of early summer "Wildwood Flowers." Like an afterimage that appears in one's vision after exposure to the original image has vanished, grim doings appeared on the road. Asmodeus strode over the crest of a hill looking like a walking carnival. Asmodeus was one of the seven princes of hell and every year harvested fields of sinners wider than Nebraska. Happily he was associated with lust, a sin to which I am no longer susceptible.

Asmodeus's mother was a succubus, that is, an enchantress. His paternity remains mysterious though many biblical scholars believe Adam was his father. In any case, his mother distributed her favors democratically. According to gossip scribbled in the margins of the Dead Sea Scrolls, she enjoyed the companionship of an ark of Old Testament seers and kings, among others Solomon, King David, Samuel, Habakkuk, and Joseph, who, story has it, traded his Madras toga for the pleasures of a red hot evening. Another story says that she became a great friend of Abraham, a lie that, as locomotive engineers express it, "gained traction" during the Civil War. Many Christians do not read the Bible. Instead they cull theological knowledge from inspiration. During the War, a sect in Georgia merged the biblical Abraham with the presidential Abraham. For the record, neither Abraham Lincoln's mother nor his wife was a succubus. I realize that dens of Christians in the water moccasin belt will not believe that both Mrs. Lincolns were ordinary women. Still, a writer should tell the truth occasionally, even if people refuse to accept it and send him venomous poison pen letters.

Asmodeus patronized a more adventuresome haberdasher than did Fiddling Death. His right leg ended in three sharp spurs and resembled that of a fighting cock. He had a snake's tail, not thin and serpentine but fat like that of an adder, making him look well fed. He had three heads, one of a sheep, another of a bull, and the last that of a human. His ears looked like bat's ears, preternaturally alert, and fire drooled from his mouth. He sat astride a salivating lion that had been fitted with the neck and wings of a dragon. Although I am indolent, life's strange meetings rarely find me unprepared. The ammonia-like fragrance of fish discommoded Asmodeus. Once, to escape the aroma of fish entrails, he fled from the Levant to Egypt. The university world is hormonal if not lusty, and suspecting that I might meet Asmodeus, I armed myself with can of King Oscar sardines. When I drew the can out of my coat pocket and aimed it at him, Asmodeus immediately turned tail and heads, all his parts, and vanished. I regretted his sudden decamping. I'd hoped that he might have hung about and tidied his appearance. In many stories, he is a dapper chappie, known for a bawdy sense of humor and resembling a Brooks Brothers mannequin. I know a few Rabelaisian tales, and I hoped we'd chat then swap a joke or two. To blow away the smoke of Sheol and make Asmodeus feel comfortable, I'd start by asking, "Why didn't the Devil learn to skate?" I am certain that Amodeus's three heads could not figure out a good reply, even if they put their skulls together. "Okay, what's the response?" Vicki said when I asked her the question. "Where in hell would he get ice?" I answered. "That's so bad; it's obscene," Vicki said. "Nothing Asmodeus said could match that."

Once Asmodeus disappeared, I sauntered slowly, filling my bouquet with life. A Halloween Pennant perched on a cattail. The dragonfly's wings shined golden brown and were as flimsy as translucent tracing paper. A groundhog sat on its hind legs and studied me looking like a child's snuggly. In damp woods thrushes rang like doorbells. Bluegills schooled through Mirror Lake. A heavy snapping turtle breathed, pushing the tip of its head above the surface of the water. Water snakes curled atop broken reeds sunning themselves. Hundreds of white blossoms lay face up in a ruffle surrounding a Japanese stewartia. The flowers looked like silk boutonnières fallen from buttonholes after a night's dancing following a grand wedding party. Red-winged blackbirds scolded me as I circled the lake. Retreating from worldly fret does not change a person's nature. Even as I mulled indolence I behaved as I had done for thirty-five years. I collected trash: a bale of paper, newspapers, and the wrappings of picnic lunches, these last splotched with ketchup and mustard. Printed on a napkin from Moe's Southwest Grill was the statement, "You Can Make Art Out of Anything." 'No,' I thought, "making glib statements is easier." I picked up four plastic water bottles, all floating neck down, bottom plate up. Using a limb from a willow, I raked a can of Full Throttle "energy drink" out of the water. A one and a half liter bottle of Sauvignon Blanc shined florescent in the sunlight. I hooked it out of the lake, but in doing so I dropped my binoculars into the water. I also extracted a yellow tennis ball, an empty Pepsi can, cans of Bud and Busch Light beer, and a hand-sized three-ounce container of Axe Dry anti-perspirant.

I dumped the garbage in a bin and walked home. A ring-necked snake lay atop a clump of gravel. I picked the snake up, and for moment it dangled loosely in my hand like a shoelace. Then it tightened and pulled itself through the eyehole between my fingers, rolling over and suddenly becoming a soft gold necklace. A question mark butterfly lit on a log in the side yard. The butterfly's wings are natural jewels and always lift my spirits into glitter. The wings curve scalloped through brown and orange summer. Around their margins a whitish binding runs frosted and beaded like winter, cooling the appearance of the butterfly and soothing the eye. When I entered the kitchen, Vicki handed me a card. On it two dogs, one black and the other yellow, dozed in a hammock. "Happy Anniversary," the card stated. "A good thirty-five years," Vicki wrote. Vicki and I are not demonstrative, and all our celebrations are quiet, almost muted. No fiddler or three-headed demon appears. Rarely do we give any presents other than a squeeze or a smile to one another. At the grocery that morning Vicki bought a bottle of plonky champagne. I opened it, and we each drank a glass then walked over to Dog Lane Café for dinner. Vicki ate a crab cake sandwich while I had a cup of vegetarian chili and half an Italian Panino sandwich. We also drank an IPA beer with a name so exotic that we immediately forgot it. After dinner we walked back home and finished the champagne while we watched an episode of *Lilyhammer* on television. While washing the champagne glasses, Vicki discovered a waved sphinx in the corner of the kitchen window, the first such moth I'd ever seen. I plucked the moth off the screen and placed it on the trunk of a shagbark hickory in the back yard, on the dark side of the tree, not on the side brightened by lights from the house. "An anniversary gift," I said. "The years have surprised me," Vicki said. "Me, too," I said. "They galloped by when we weren't looking." By nine-thirty I was in bed. I had put on summer pajamas decorated with fans of coconut palms and planned to read a short biography of the eighteenth-century English writer Laurence Sterne. I did not get far. By the time Sterne's wife went mad and thought she was the Queen of Bohemia, I was asleep.

Afterword

Spring is timid this year. May is almost here, and only yesterday did the ground become spongy enough to bury paper-white bulbs. Signs of blooming weather are increasing, however. Landscapers are flocking through the neighborhood removing dead trees and sawing off rotten perches. Early every morning a fox pads through the dell stopping at the brush pile in the back yard. The state has stocked the Fenton River with trout. Above the riverbank in sinks leafy with last year's leaves, trout lilies are waking and nodding into yellow. Spring azures have begun to puddle the damp, their wings flicking and looking like shards of dry blue ice. Last week Vicki heard an olive-sided flycatcher calling from the edge of a pasture, and a robin has hung strips of plastic in the yew beside the front stoop and is building a nest. High overhead hawks are flying north almost in skeins. Buds on larches have swollen into turbans and look coiffed. Branches on weeping willows have turned green, drawing attention to the trees and making them look like partially woven baskets. Petals on the flowers of the Yulan magnolia hybrids planted behind the university library last year have begun to fledge, and from a distance the buds look like goldfinches hunching and fluttering before soaring into wheaty yellow. Late in the afternoon young groundhogs leave their burrows under houses and crop grass on the campus. The groundhogs are naive and do not trundle off when students approach. I wish I could warn them that only the wary will survive into summer.

Two days ago I stripped a garter snake off Davis Road. The snake had pasted itself to the warm asphalt, and I carried it down a slope away from the road and freed it in deep brush. Strangers leashed to dogs have sprouted on the university farm, walking the woods and fields and smiling unaccountably. On my desk sit two small pots holding purple hyacinths while on the tops of tables throughout the house, Easter lilies have burst into white trumpets. In the early evening, perfume flows from them in dozy notes. On the back stoop is a planter mottled yellow and violet with pansies. Along the driveway are three deep pots, each containing a dozen tulip bulbs. Since early winter the bulbs had lain in the pots at the back of the garage, hibernating in rich soil dug from the woods behind our house. On Saturday Vicki and I carried the pots out of the garage, and by Tuesday leaves had pushed up in trowels, at first olive and brownish like the earth itself but soon turning emerald.

In 1721 Nathan Bailey defined *spring* as a fountain. Spring is a time of beginnings as life erupts like pent-up water shining in the sun and raising rainbows from the muddy ground. Of course, life is more complex than dictionaries imply. Beginnings quickly trickle away, and beneath the rainbows lies black, its fabric decayed into compost and composed of colors once bright and glittering on a score of plants. Alas, often spring brings ending rather than beginning to mind. Even fresh new fountains can appear old and dry. Like stuffing ripped from pillows the fur of young rabbits clings to brush bordering woodland trails, and coyote scat is haggard with bones. The hundreds of daffodils I planted during past years have all died as have the Iris, columbine, Dutchmen's britches, grape hyacinths, Jacob's ladder, wild geranium, squill, asters, and clematis. Kerria has become too leggy to support blossoms. Hollyhock no longer seeds itself; migratory bloodroot has vanished from corners of the backyard, and weigela and mock orange have rotted and fallen. The rug of periwinkle is moth eaten, and day lilies have collapsed like tired lungs. Deer have gnawed the vitality out of azaleas and rhododendron, and a road crew chopped down the Carolina snowbell because it swayed out from the drive and hung over the telephone lines.

In describing the start of a new year, Filson Young wrote, "The first fortnight of January is the great Monday morning of the year, when, after the pause and disorganization of Christmas and the annual tidying-up of various temporal matters, we settle down into our normal routine, and Begin Again." The only people who loved "Beginning Again," Young wrote, were "the incorrigible failures." For my part the beginning proffered by spring brings too many losses to mind for me to enjoy it wholeheartedly. To a degree my attitude, or better maybe, mood, reflects my age. My almond tree, to paraphrase *Ecclesiastes*, no longer flourishes and has thinned. I lack the zest to grab a shovel and dig holes in the yard. Years have taught me that when the ground opens like the famous pie in the nursery rhyme and sprouts appear, not all the buds will fly into bloom and sing. Even worse, I can't bear to contemplate ending a book then Beginning Again. Completing a manuscript does not make me triumphant or sorrowful—only weary. I want to escape the intensity of Monday morning. Pondering turning over a new page or marking a clean tablet gives me mental diverticulitis.

Alas, I am an inebriate scribbler. Three times at the ends of previous books, I proclaimed that I was retiring from my desk and donating my pens to Special Collections at the university. Alas, no Writers' Anonymous knocked on the door and helped me. No Friends of William Sh. or of Jane A. rallied around and supported me like the Friends of Bill W. No Twelve-Step program mapped the way to abstinence. Even the muck of years that plugs my mind was useless. Words have worn ruts in my synapses, and while everything else gets stuck at a rest stop and forgotten, words trundle through. In the vernacular of the cerebral cortex, words keep on trucking. When this afterword began to loom, Vicki suggested I examine different topics, "if you can't stop writing." Habit shapes the present and determines the future. The mature can change the tenor of pages but not the subjects they have mulled for decades. Vicki urged me to write about politics, "all the institutional Molochs and Dagons that create misery." Maurice Egan said that "mental food" influenced his life as much as "physical food." "The mental system," he wrote, was "as capable of derangement through bad mental food as the physical system."

My digestive system works like a well-managed junkyard. It breaks down and recycles almost everything dumped into the premises. I can't stomach politics, however. A spoonful on the tongue and my gorge revolts and like a long-suffering proletariat jettisons the polite and the literary and rises sloganeering. In the seventeenth century Abraham Cowley stated that when a man dealt with other men, he often behaved like an animal, among others, like a fawning dog, a roaring lion, a thieving fox, a robbing wolf, a dissembling crocodile, and a rapacious vulture. The "civilest" nations, he wrote, "are those whom we account the most barbarous; there is some moderation and good nature in the Toupinambaltians who eat no men but their enemies, whilst we learned and polite and Christian Europeans, like so many pikes and sharks, prey upon everything that we can swallow." Change *European* to *American* or, indeed, to any nationality and substitute any sect for *Christian*, and Cowley's statement will be up to date. Such a thought heats sentences and like poison ivy twines through the pleasures of life irritating and narrowing thought and vision. When politics black-magically seeds itself, I try to uproot it. None of the solitaries I described in the essay on solitude are angry recluses festering at the ends of pitchforked roads. My solitaries live on country lanes. Some have boxwood gardens, and many plant coleus along brick walks. None of them drives a pickup truck, owns a pistol, or shoots an abandoned dog. They live temperate lives and are not addicted to whine. They don't believe the best way to defend freedom is to surround their houses with breastworks of corpses. They don't think that in order for a country to become wealthy, it must impoverish half its citizens. Not one of my solitaries, as folks in Connecticut often say of Republicans, was born bad and bound to grow worse.

One, I'm ashamed to admit, however, stole a quip from Oliver Herford and at a Christmas Eve egg nog party defined *lisp* as calling "a spade a thpade."

My domestic desk life suits me, and I have outgrown literary philandering. Vicki also suggested that I try my pencil at poetry. I am not like Tiresias, the blind prophet in Greek tale, who spent seven years of his life as a woman. I am clear sighted. Not only does changing literary identity not appeal to me, but such a change is also impossible. I am constitutionally indisposed to writing poetry. For the record, I must state that the more hormonal species of philandering has rarely asserted a rude presence in my books. The appearance of such doings usually makes me chuckle. Last week I received a one-line e-mail. "A gorgeous Russian bride could be yours. Why—wait?" the e-mail stated, all the letters of the message capitalized. I have never been a diner-outer. But even if I were tempted to attend a fleshly feast, I am old and practically a vegetarian. I'd totter into the dining room after the other guests had nibbled the choice bits leaving me to make do with hash. "Second-hand food does not attract me," I told Vicki, showing her the e-mail. "It damn well better not," she said. "What's for dinner?" I asked. "A Caesar salad swimming with anchovies—fit for a tsar," she said. "Good," I said.

Although I refuse to write poetry or rage about politics, I have reached the age of anecdotage. Because I have withdrawn all memories of my younger years from my brain-box and have, in fact, lost the key to the box, I fabricate. Old people are susceptible to many diseases. Some catch one thing, and some another, but all suffer from forgetfulness and spread virulent rumor-tism. A few blessed with noses that molt into dazzling, rubicund curiosity become specialists in imaginative lying. Fantasies are house- and yard-bound people's adventures. They breathe skip into halting steps and dull the biting discomforts of pharmaceutical hours. To imagine Medusa before Perseus gave her a respectable "perm" at the beauty parlor is to meet the real Medusa and to make her part of one's life. On my pages, unlike snakes, Medusas appear infrequently, and no reputations die. Recently I completed an article whitewashing the character of an extraordinarily prominent man whose name scandal-mongers have long sullied. "It is not true," I wrote, "that Mr. Sneath impregnated his half-sister or, to bring the accusation up to the twenty-first century, his half-brother. Neither did he transport his ninety-three year old mother across state lines for immoral purposes. It is true that his partner is named Bessie, but she sleeps in the house and not in the dairy." For my part, I enjoy rumors although most tales are scandalously understated. Because I won't spend much more time on this globe, I also value insincerity. I don't trust the sincere. The crafty and the dishonest feign the appearance of sincerity. Brokers and saints keep sincerity handy amid their burglar tools. In contrast, almost no one cultivates a reputation for insincerity. Generally the insincere are guileless. They act naturally and unlike the sincere behave honestly. As an almost-related footnote, let me add that the aged are wittier than the young. Distortion is the soul of wit. Only the deranged or people with poor memories are capable of wit.

Occasionally I have thought myself almost as distinguished a scholar as Professor Jack Horner. Rigorously and rightly educated readers will recall that Horner pursued his studies alone. He secreted himself in a neglected nook of the library apart from conventional academics. There he spent days digging into forgotten books. Many delighted him, and he fondly dubbed them "Christmas pies." His results were original. "Sweet as plums," he said in an interview, in the process congratulating himself for being "a good boy." I am, as I wrote earlier, a down and out bibliolater. Whenever I decide to go cold *Meleagris* and swear off writing, I find a drupe—piquant and rich. I bite into it, and before I notice, juices have spilled onto a page and miraculously run to sentences. Last week I discovered a red Bing of a quatrain. Supposedly a schoolgirl wrote the verse, but I think it smacks more of the trousered than of the frocked. "Miss Bess and Miss Beale / Cupid's darts do not feel. / How different from us / Miss Beale and Miss Buss." More like a clementine than a cherry niblet was the beginning of Eden Phillpotts's novel *Some Every-Day Folks*. "'I cared little for his sermon,' said Miss Watford, 'but I thought his teeth were singularly beautiful.' 'Which is easily explained,' replied Miss Minnifie, 'because the sermon was probably his own, whereas his teeth are not.'" Smacking of rindy grapefruit and nipping deeper than the tongue was Barry Pain's description of the qualifications necessary for membership in The Failure Club. "Proved failure in some art, science, or politics is an essential qualification. Friendliness and simplicity are also required. Swank is abhorred. A gentle melancholy, accompanied by a tendency to see the humor of one's misery, is a strong recommendation."

Resembling a crate of mixed fruit, the kind sent to wealthy bachelor uncles at Christmas, was an advertisement placed in the *Kentucky Agriculturalist* in 1890. "One-armed Child of God Clothed in the Sun seeks employment as a gardener and orthographer. Teeth and hair are original, and the arm is new. Very good with strawberries and understands the 'I before E except after C' rule. Has taught canaries to whistle 'Whispering Hope' and 'Sweet Hour of Prayer.' But has no objection to other faiths. Already circumcised and willing to be baptized Moslem or Italian. Comes from creative rootstock. Great-grandfather invented water-proof bathing trunks. 'No need to hang on the line after swimming. Just fold and put back in the chest of drawers.'"

"Why?" Vicki said after I read the advertisement to her. "I don't know," I said. "Now that you have finished this book, are you really going to stop writing?" Vicki asked. "Maybe," I said. "But did you know that the founder of the Failure Club believed that a neophyte who wished to enjoy artistic success had to do one of three things? 'He must go mad, or he must do a term of penal servitude, or he must become a policeman.'" "I guess I should not quote so much," I continued when Vicki shook her head. "H. G. Wells called writers who adorned their pages with quotations literary caddis worms." "Sam, no matter what you do," Vicki eventually said, "no matter how much you quote or purloin, no matter the absence of sales, nobody will confuse your writing with that of another essayist, and that's a good thing." Unaccountably, as Vicki spoke, a coin of recollection dropped from what I thought was the empty box of memory. The father of a childhood friend in Tennessee was great bird hunter. He bred and raised pointers, "better gun dogs than English setters," he once told me when showing me a litter of puppies. The man loved his dogs, and when a favorite dog died, he sent the body to a taxidermist. The taxidermist preserved the dog's tail and mounted it on a shield-shaped mahogany plaque. Beneath the tail, he fastened a brass plate to the plaque. Engraved on the plate was the name of the dog. I remember some of the names, Nancy, Old Bob, Young Bob, Tiny, and Lou. My friend's father hung the shields in the entrance hall to his house. The tails curved up slightly. Because the tails had been reinforced and were rigid, guests, especially sportsmen, were encouraged to hang their hats on them.

"Vicki," I started but stopped. Vicki has lived all her life in university towns. Like the father of my friend, she is a great dog lover, but of rescue not purebred, of indoor rather than outdoor dogs. I realized she'd think my account bizarre and probably perverse, too Southern and of a period long gone out of reality into fiction. "Vicki," I said, beginning again and laying the *Agriculturist* down on the kitchen table, "How about a glass or two or three of Champagne? Let's toast the end of my scribbling days." "A dandy idea," Vicki said. "I bought fresh shrimp today. I'll get them out of the refrigerator, and we'll have a celebration."

That night I dreamed about a two-headed monster that fed upon old people. At one end of the creature was a pale yellow head crusty with warts. The head was shaped like the front of a 1950 Studebaker sedan. At the opposite end of the creature was the green head of an alligator. Often both heads ate simultaneously. Because the monster lacked a colon, it retained everything it devoured. After breaking into a nursing home, the monster started swelling, eventually becoming so large that it filled the frame of my dream. When the creature pushed me to the edge of the bed, I awoke. I then shook Vicki and asked her what she thought the dream meant. "That's easy," she said. "You are the monster, and the people in your mouths are books. You don't have a colon because you have stopped writing and can neither digest nor rid yourself of pages. Eventually you will become monstrously obese and go mad. Ulcers will puncture your stomach, and literary gas will make your intestines bloat like fire hoses. Only writing can change you back to a human. If I were you, I'd get up before breakfast and sharpen my pencil. Pencils make splendid trocars. Every farm depot and bookstore sells them."